# DEMOCRACY IN TRANSLATION

## The Wilder House Series in Politics, History, and Culture

The Wilder House Series is published in association with the Wilder House Board of Editors and the University of Chicago.

A full list of titles in the series appears at the end of the book.

David D. Laitin and George Steinmetz, *Editors*

# DEMOCRACY IN TRANSLATION

*Understanding Politics
in an Unfamiliar Culture*

FREDERIC C. SCHAFFER

*Cornell University Press*

Ithaca and London

First published 1998 by Cornell University Press
First printing, Cornell Paperbacks, 2000

Printed in the United States of America

**Library of Congress Cataloging-in-Publication Data**

Schaffer, Frederic Charles.
   Democracy in translation : understanding politics in an unfamiliar
culture / Frederic C. Schaffer.
      p.  cm.
   Includes bibliographical references and index.
   ISBN 0-8014-3398-3 (cloth : alk. paper)
   ISBN 0-8014-8691-2 (pbk. : alk. paper)
   1. Democracy—Senegal.  2. Democracy—Cross-cultural studies.
I. Title.
JQ3396.A91S34   1998
320.9663—dc21                        97-49950

Cornell University Press strives to use environmentally responsible
suppliers and materials to the fullest extent possible in the publishing
of its books. Such materials include vegetable-based, low-VOC inks and
acid-free papers that are recycled, totally chlorine-free, or partly composed
of nonwood fibers. Books that bear the logo of the FSC (Forest Stewardship Council) use paper taken from forests that have been inspected and
certified as meeting the highest standards for environmental and social
responsibility. For further information, visit our website
at www.cornellpress.cornell.edu.

Cloth printing   10  9  8  7  6  5  4  3  2  1
Paperback printing   10  9  8  7  6  5  4  3  2  1

**FSC** FSC Trademark © 1996 Forest Stewardship Council A.C.
SW-COC-098

*"To speak is to reveal oneself"*
(Ku wax feeñ)
*Wolof proverb*

# Contents

## Maps

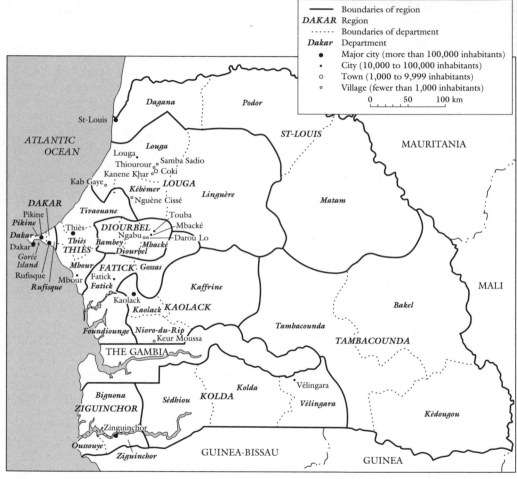

**Map 1**. Senegal

# Preface

One morning in February 1991 I traveled to Thiès, one of the largest cities in the West African country of Senegal, to attend and tape-record a political rally. When I arrived, I learned that the rally would not get under way for another hour or so. With the prospect of some free time, I approached a nearby group of young men who happened to be playing cards. They invited me to join the game.

As I sat down, the oldest of the players began to deal the cards, and told me we would be playing a game called "Senegalese belote." After a few hands, and even with some coaching, I realized that the game did not proceed according to the conventions of any card game with which I was familiar. I threw down a king and it was taken by a jack. I played a ten, and it was taken by a nine. When I put down an eight, someone took it with a ten. The relative strengths of cards seemed all askew. Jacks were stronger than kings, and tens were stronger than eights, but not as strong as nines. The game was soon interrupted, and before long the rally began.

That night, back home, I couldn't stop thinking about that card game. The cards, the shuffling, the dealing, and the order of play seemed familiar, but the rules and strategies, even the values of the cards, seemed very strange. My thoughts darted back and forth between the card game and what I had been hearing from my informants about what speakers of Wolof—the most widely spoken language in Senegal—called *demokaraasi*. Both, I realized, evidenced a peculiar mixture of familiarity and strangeness. *Demokaraasi* was both similar to and significantly different from notions of democracy to which I was accustomed, just as Senegalese belote was similar to and significantly different from the card games I knew.

Learning the rules of a card game and comparing them to the rules of other card games, I have since learned, is a far easier task than learning and comparing the rules of complex "games" such as democracy and *demokaraasi*. All the same, this is the task at hand in this book.

If the subject matter here seems narrow, the goals are nevertheless broadly comparative. I ask how this curious but recognizable Senegalese understanding of *demokaraasi* relates to American understandings of democracy to inquire more generally about how social scientists should investigate and describe the functioning of democratic institutions in societies dissimilar to their own. This question, in turn, raises larger issues about the nature and meaning of democracy, about the universality of democratic ideals and practices, and about the advantages and limits of using the concept of democracy for cross-cultural research.

These concerns may appear abstract, but they are of great practical importance. The World Bank and the U.S. government routinely adopt policies to promote competitive elections in developing countries, with hopes of improving accountability and economic performance in these poorer nations. Yet the social science research on which these policies rest tends to ignore local people's understanding and use of electoral institutions. Without examining these topics, no one can easily foresee the political and economic consequences of the transitions to a multiparty system that such policies encourage.

To explore these issues concretely, I examine how institutions that Americans normally consider democratic function and how the rough equivalent of democracy is conceived in a society culturally divergent from that of the United States. Senegal provides a useful case study for this purpose. It has a history of electoral politics that dates back 150 years, so its people are by now well acquainted with some of the main institutions of democracy. At the same time, the Islamic and agrarian traditions of these people set the country apart.

In terms of theory, this book draws heavily on insights provided by ordinary language philosophy and related fields, for many of the most unyielding complexities associated with both the study of democracy and cross-cultural research are conceptual in origin. An analysis of concepts and language is thus uniquely positioned to aid thinking about the most difficult issues that loom ahead.

These difficulties stem in part from the fact that language is a medium of both political action and political inquiry. The student of politics often perceives this dual role as a problem to be overcome. The source of the problem lies in the fact that the meanings of words often vary with their context. Thus the term "democracy" may not mean the same thing in the context of, say, basketball as it does when one speaks about town hall meetings or electoral politics. These multiple meanings are troubling for those who wish to categorize and compare a wide range of phenomena, for they complicate efforts to figure out what counts as an instance of democracy. Researchers often respond by reformulating concepts so that they have distinct boundaries and can, in the words of Giovanni Sartori (1970, 1043), act as "fact-storing containers." Consequently, these views of Felix Oppenheim (1981, 1) are widely shared: "To make political concepts suitable for political inquiry, it seems to me necessary to reconstruct them, i.e., provide them with explicative definitions; these must in certain cases deviate from ordinary language to avoid ambiguities and valuational overtones." In the case of the concept of democracy, as we shall see, in the course of reconstruction the boundaries of the concept are often redrawn, so that its meaning applies to only a particular set of institutions.

Despite its apparent advantages, this strategy is problematic to the extent that it presumes as a predicament what might better be viewed as an opportunity to augment the researcher's analytic possibilities. Everyday political language need not always be viewed as something to be reconstructed. Social scientists can, alternatively, take political language—ambiguities, valuational overtones, and all—as an object of inquiry, and use this inquiry to gain insight into shared understandings about the political world. Language provides, after all, "the intersubjective meanings which are the background to social action . . . a certain set of common terms of reference" (Taylor 1977, 119–20).

This kind of linguistic inquiry, of course, requires researchers to reflect on the everyday meanings of their own concepts. To understand better the state of democracy throughout the world, in other words, it is essential to ask what "democracy" (or its rough equivalent) means—both to ourselves as outside observers and to local practitioners. We are, in the end, likely to miss something when we make generalizations about the political practices of a society without reflecting on both our own distinctions and theirs.

For this reason, at the most fundamental, conceptual level I ask what *demokaraasi* means, where these meanings come from, and how they differ from the meanings of the English-language concept of democracy used by American social scientists. I also ask what is and is not universal about both *demokaraasi* and democracy. These issues are taken up in Chapters 2, 3, and 6.

At the substantive level, I explore how a study of Wolof political concepts helps outside observers understand political reality in Senegal. I seek to shed light, in particular, on the question of why voters (and nonvoters) act as they do, and how these actions affect the accountability of public officials and the exercise of power in the country. I also inquire, more generally, about the likelihood that policies designed by the United States and the World Bank to promote democracy in developing countries will succeed. These are the topics of Chapters 4 and 5.

At the methodological level, I ask to what degree a social science concept—in this case, democracy—derived from one group's political experience provides a meaningful framework for understanding the political practices and institutions of a population with divergent cultural traditions. A consideration of this question requires us to assess the strengths and weaknesses of existing social science strategies for studying democracy. It is to this assessment that we turn first, in Chapter 1.

This investigation of Wolof concepts, in sum, not only is intended to teach us something about Senegalese political culture and the functioning of one of Africa's oldest multiparty systems; it also can help us think about larger issues: the interaction of culture and institutions, the formation and use of social science concepts, and the relation of American practices to those of populations with divergent traditions. It is intended, in short, to enrich not only the study of Senegal and democracy but also the practice of cross-cultural inquiry more generally.

It would have been impossible for me to write this book without the help of many people. I am most indebted to Hanna Pitkin, George Lakoff, and Robert Price for providing the time, interest, and intellectual inspiration that launched this study. Special mention should also be made of David Laitin, David Collier, Donal Cruise O'Brien, and Babacar Kanté. Each contributed thoughtful advice and kind encouragement. In addition, many colleagues offered insightful critiques of the manuscript, specific chapters, or earlier incarnations of this work. I thank in particular Suzanne Berger, Catherine Boone, Bob Bullock, Warren Finch, Sheldon Gellar, Richard Joseph, Mouhamed Moustapha Kane, Mikael Karlström, Douglas Lummis, James Martel, Amy Patterson, Rob Pirro, Lucian Pye, Nate Teske, Myron Weiner, Harold Wilensky, and an anonymous reader. I am also grateful to my Wolof tutors at Berkeley, Mamadou Mbaye and Libasse Niang, for their dedicated work. I am indebted in addition to Peter Kubaska, Eva Nagy, Cory Welt, and Frank Tipton for their help in preparing the manuscript; and to Roger Haydon of Cornell University Press for his judicious editorial advice.

The bulk of the fieldwork for this study was completed in fourteen months, during two extended stays in Senegal in 1991 and 1993. Many people there provided guidance, assistance, access, and hospitality. I must single out for thanks Amadou Dialo, chairman of the Department of Linguistics at the Université Cheikh Anta Diop; Abdoul Aziz Diaw and Jean-Léopold Diouf at the Centre de Linguistique Appliquée de Dakar; Arame Fal and Mamadou Ibra Sall at the Institut Fondamental d'Afrique Noire; Benoît Ngom of the African Jurists Association; Mame Less Camara of Radiodiffusion Télévision Sénégalaise; Serigne Diop of the Faculté des Sciences Juridiques et Economiques at the Université Cheikh Anta Diop; Jérôme Faye, El Hadj Sarr, and Rebecca Winchester at the American Cultural Center; and Saliou Mbaye, director of the Archives du Sénégal. Others who helped in significant ways include Oumar Watt, Commissaire, Babacar Ndiaye, Babacar Sène, Allé Galaye Mbaye, Jana Oxenrider, and Gabin Faye. For tireless and dedicated research assistance I owe a great deal to Saliou Diallo. Special thanks are also due to my longtime friends at the Baobab Center: Gary Engelberg, Lillian Baer, Doyen Sow, and Daniel Badji. And of course this project would not have been possible without the goodwill of the many informants who so patiently fielded my questions.

For supporting this research financially, I am most grateful to the Fulbright-Hays Doctoral Dissertation Abroad Program, the West Africa Research Association, the Institute of International Studies at the University of California at

Berkeley, the National Endowment for the Humanities, and the School of Humanities and Social Science at MIT.

Finally, I owe to my wife, Jeanne, more than she knows. Her critical eye improved the book immensely, and her loving support gave me the stamina to see it through to the end.

FREDERIC C. SCHAFFER

*Cambridge, Massachusetts*

# Abbreviations

| | |
|---|---|
| ADP | Agence de Distribution de Presse (Press Distribution Agency) |
| AJ/MRDN | And-Jëf/Mouvement Révolutionnaire pour la Démocratie Nouvelle (Act Together/Revolutionary Movement for the New Democracy) |
| AJ/PADS | And-Jëf/Parti Africain pour la Démocratie et le Socialisme (Act Together/African Party for Democracy and Socialism) |
| CAMCUD | Coordination des Associations et Mouvements (des Jeunes) de la Communauté Urbaine de Dakar (Alliance of Dakar Youth Associations and Movements) |
| CCP | Chinese Communist Party |
| CDP | Convention des Démocrates et Patriotes (Convention of Democrats and Patriots) |
| CFA | Communauté Financière Africaine (African Financial Community) |
| CNRV | Commission Nationale de Recensement des Votes (National Commission for Vote Tabulation) |
| FONGS | Fédération des Organisations Non-gouvernementales du Sénégal (Federation of Senegalese Nongovernmental Organizations) |
| LD/MPT | Ligue Démocratique/Mouvement pour le Parti du Travail (Democratic League/Labor Party Movement) |
| MDP | Mouvement Démocratique Populaire (People's Democratic Movement) |
| NDI | National Democratic Institute for International Affairs |
| ONCAD | Office Nationale de Coopération et d'Assistance au Développement (National Office of Cooperation and Assistance for Development) |
| ORTS | L'Office de Radiodiffusion et Télévision du Sénégal (Radio and Television Office of Senegal) |
| PDS | Parti Démocratique Sénégalais (Senegalese Democratic Party) |
| PIT | Parti de l'Indépendance et du Travail (Independence and Labor Party) |
| PLP | Parti pour la Libération du Peuple (Party for the Liberation of the People) |

| | |
|---|---|
| PS | Parti Socialiste (Socialist Party) |
| RND | Rassemblement National Démocratique (National Democratic Rally) |
| RTS | Radiodiffusion Télévision Sénégalaise (Senegalese Radio and Television Service) |
| UPS | Union Progressiste Sénégalaise (Senegalese Progressive Union) |
| USAID | U.S. Agency for International Development |

# A Note on Wolof Orthography

In this book the spelling of Wolof words follows the orthographic conventions established by linguists at the Centre de Linguistique Appliquée de Dakar and the Institut Fondamental d'Afrique Noire. Consonants that are written differently than in English include:

| | |
|---|---|
| *c* | *ch* as in *chin* |
| *x* | *ch* as in German *Buch* |
| *ñ* | *ny* as in *canyon* |

Vowels are pronounced roughly as follows:

| | |
|---|---|
| *a* | *a* as in *about* |
| *à* | *a* as in *car* |
| *e* | *e* as in *bet* |
| *é* | *é* as in *élite* |
| *ë* | *i* as in *girl* |
| *i* | *i* as in *trip* |
| *o* | *o* as in French *pomme* |
| *ó* | *o* as in *no* |
| *u* | *oo* as in *book* |

Vowels may be short, as in the above examples, or long, in which case the letter is doubled (*aa, ee, éé,* etc.). Further details can be found in Fal (1990) and Fal, Santos, and Doneux (1990).

I do not follow these orthographic conventions in writing the names of people, places, languages, and groups for which other spellings are commonly accepted. Thus I render the name of the president of Senegal as Abdou Diouf rather than Abdu Juuf. Except where I have noted otherwise, all translations from Wolof and French are my own.

# DEMOCRACY IN TRANSLATION

# I

# The Definition and Study
# of Democracy

T. S. Eliot once wrote that "when a term has become so universally sanctified as 'democracy' now is, I begin to wonder whether it means anything, in meaning too many things" (1940, 11–12). The question whether democracy means anything is obviously important to social scientists. To compare democracies, to identify factors that promote their consolidation, to examine the effects of democracy on economic development, or to ask any number of questions about the causes and consequences of democracy requires us to determine what makes a regime, state, or society count as democratic.

Yet, as Eliot understood, there is no simple criterion for doing so. Scores of books have been written attempting to define democracy. Past decades have produced heated debates about whether one-party or communist states can be rightfully deemed democratic. Serious questions have even been raised about the extent to which the political system of the United States can be properly called a democracy.

The word "democracy" derives from the Greek *demokratia*, or "rule by the people," a notion famous for its multiple meanings. Giovanni Sartori (1987, 22), for instance, identifies six ways "the people" might be understood, ranging from literally everybody, to a great many, to only the lower class, to a bare majority. As for what type of "rule" is entailed by democracy, Jack Lively (1975, 30) suggests seven popular variants that range from everyone participating actively in the business of governance to rulers merely acting in the interest of the ruled. The concept of democracy itself can be stretched so wide that it rarely appears without a modifier—pluralist, direct, liberal, participatory, representative, or the like.

Not even a core notion of "rule by the people" sets outer limits on how the term may be used. Consider some of the surprising but everyday ways in which Americans speak of "democracy in action." Gourmet ice cream provides one example. A columnist described the invention of this "affordable luxury" as "street-corner democracy in action: for five gooey mouthfuls, a secretary could eat as well as Donald Trump" (*Washington Post,* March 26, 1989). Then there is the restaurant critic who described diner menus as "testaments to democracy in action" because they result from "decades of customers voting 'yes' on the choices that remain and 'Are You Kidding?' to all attempts to sway their tastes" (*Chicago Tribune,* March 7, 1985). Or take the sportswriter who characterized the essence of "democracy in action" on the basketball court as "one man, one shot. There are no designated shooters; every citizen on the court is welcome to exercise his aim at the rim" (*Los Angeles Times,* December 21, 1985). It is difficult to imagine a secretary who indulges in gourmet ice cream as "ruling" in any meaningful sense of the term. And while the basketball players may be involved actively in the collective endeavor of playing a game, in what sense can they be said to rule? Finally, there is the democracy experienced in picking from menu items. Unlike the choice made by voters, the selection of entrées in a restaurant is not intended to legislate or select leaders for the whole community. The notion of ruling does not appear in these extended uses.

## The Schumpeterian Solution

To deal with democracy's many meanings, a significant number of empirical social scientists choose to consider this concept only in its institutional aspects, and define it in terms of some set of procedures or mechanisms. The most important thinker in this project has been Joseph Schumpeter.[1]

In his 1942 book *Capitalism, Socialism, and Democracy,* Schumpeter defined democracy as a particular "method" for making decisions. In specific terms, this method involves the selection of leaders through competitive elections (1962, 242, 269). Defining democracy in this way, he believed, would provide "a reasonably efficient criterion by which to distinguish democratic governments from others" (269). Consideration of democracy in its institutional aspects would thus make possible rigorous comparative analysis.

---

[1] One could also discuss Max Weber's view of democracy here. No doubt Schumpeter's intellectual debt to Weber was great. All the same, those interested in the empirical study of democracy today are far more likely to draw on Schumpeter's work than on Weber's.

To appreciate the power of this argument, consider a concrete example. Harold Lasswell, an influential political scientist and a contemporary of Schumpeter's, advanced a purposive understanding of democracy as part of his comparative study of the democratic character. A democratic community, according to Lasswell, is "characterized by wide rather than narrow participation in the shaping and sharing of values" (1951, 473). There are eight of these values ranging from power to affection to rectitude.

One problem with this conception of democracy is that it is likely to embroil one in endless debates about which values need to be widely shared for democracy to exist. Must there really be widespread sharing of affection? Another disadvantage, one especially acute for those who wish to categorize and compare a number of cases, is that this definition of democracy is unwieldy. It includes a large number of indicators, many of which are attitudinal and thus hard to observe or measure. Daunting problems are posed to any researcher who attempts to measure and compare, cross-nationally, degrees of rectitude. By comparison, Schumpeter's institutional understanding of democracy is straightforward and simple to operationalize.

It is for this reason that Schumpeter's approach has had such an enduring influence on how social scientists conceive of and study democracy. Many scholars agree with Samuel Huntington when he makes the Schumpeterian argument that "fuzzy norms do not yield useful analysis" (1991, 9). For these scholars, institutional definitions alone provide the "empirical referents" necessary to make them analytically "useful" (7). As a result, the number of scholars who today draw explicitly on Schumpeter's formulation is impressive.[2]

Such election-focused approaches offer, to repeat, an important benefit to scholars engaged in comparative research. As Schumpeter argues, they make measuring democracy easier by designating observable referents such as the presence or absence of competing candidates and parties, universal suffrage, electoral fraud or intimidation, and adequate levels of voter turnout. They thereby simplify the task of classifying and comparing large numbers of regimes. To give one example, Huntington, using an electoral definition of democracy, was able to classify the political systems of all independent countries (with a population of one million or more) as democratic or nondemocratic at twenty-year intervals from 1922 to 1990, a task that required the coding of 488 cases. These longitudinal data revealed a surprising fact: the proportion of democratic regimes to nondemocratic ones at the peak of the "third wave" in 1990 was virtually the same as it had been sixty years earlier (1991, 26). Democracy, in one important sense, has not been on the rise after all.

---

[2] To cite a few: Lipset 1983, 27; Weiner 1987, 5; Di Palma 1990, 15–16. Other scholars make fewer explicit references to Schumpeter, but work in a "Schumpeterian mode" nonetheless. Like Schumpeter, they focus on the most important institution available to citizens for choosing leaders: elections. See Eckstein 1966, 229; Powell 1982, 3; Przeworski 1991, 10.

Another benefit of election-focused approaches is that they encourage scholars to focus on how particular electoral arrangements shape political outcomes, an area of inquiry that has produced a number of successes, only one of which will be mentioned here. In an elegant study, Arend Lijphart demonstrated that proportional representation (PR) systems are much less likely than non-PR systems to produce "manufactured majorities"—which occur when parties fail to win a majority of votes but win a majority of seats. He found that majorities were manufactured in an average of 45 percent of elections held in the majority and plurality systems of Canada, New Zealand, the United Kingdom, the United States, France (Fifth Republic), and Australia; but in only 7 percent of elections held in countries that use PR systems (1984, 167).

## The Limits of "Electoralism"

These successes notwithstanding, election-focused studies of democracy have occasioned their share of controversy. Return, for a moment, to Lijphart's seemingly cut-and-dried finding regarding manufactured majorities. While the finding itself may not be open to dispute, one reason for the widespread interest in it is that recurring manufactured majorities provide a potential indicator of how democratic a political system may or may not be. Thus Lijphart and others who study electoral laws do not simply chart varying outcomes of different electoral systems; they go on to ask which systems are the most fair, inclusive, representative, or democratic. Yet these questions admit no categorical answer, and debate among scholars about how to interpret the significance of divergent outcomes is intense.

This emphasis on electoral laws and arrangements has, in addition, troubled careful students of politics in Asia, Africa, and Latin America. These scholars have come to recognize that many countries adopt formal electoral institutions without becoming democratic in more significant ways. Marina Ottaway thus finds it useful to distinguish between "the ritual of democracy" and its "substance," given that "many African leaders are learning to play the election game—giving aid donors an election barely clean enough to receive a low passing grade, but dirty enough to make it difficult for the opposition to win" (1993, 3, 4). Terry Lynn Karl argues that the Salvadorian elections of 1982, 1984, and 1985 were held before any agreement was reached by major political actors on the basic rules of political competition, or on the proper role of the military. Consequently, she maintains that these contests produced only "the most common surface manifestations of a democratic polity—parties, electoral laws, contested campaigns, and the like" (1986, 34). Such scholars as Ottaway and Karl rightly see that a too narrow focus on elections—what both call "electoralism"—provides inadequate criteria for categorizing regimes as democratic.

Furthermore, for those who see social or economic equality as an important element of democracy, election-focused understandings of democracy are tainted with ideological conservatism. Georgina Waylen, for instance, argues that "the narrow concentration . . . on democracy as simply an institutional arrangement means that wider definitions of democracy couched in terms of the real distribution of power in society are considered illegitimate" (1994, 332).

Advocates of a Schumpeterian approach have thus not been able to provide refuge from controversy. Comparativists still find themselves forced to ask what democracy really means, which electoral systems approximate it best, and what institutions, in addition to elections, might be necessary to achieve it. These questions, in turn, have occasioned a heightened attentiveness to the normative meaning of democracy in the field.

Underlying this attentiveness is a tacit recognition that one cannot meaningfully discuss electoral institutions without reference to the ideals toward which they are oriented. Democracy, after all, is a concept that encompasses both purpose and institution. It is used to refer to both political ideals and a set of institutions designed to realize these ideals. As a set of institutions, democracy is often associated in the United States today with elections, multiparty competition, and laws that guarantee political equality.[3] As an ideal, democracy has something to do with the goal of people participating meaningfully in their own governance, a goal that democratic theorists have associated closely with a variety of other ideals, including autonomy (Held 1987, 267–77), equality (Macpherson 1966, 33), civic-mindedness (Barber 1993, 69), and moral and intellectual development (Mill 1975, 274). In the attempt to do away with ambiguity and fuzziness, strict institutionalists risk emptying democracy of the very ideals that provide electoral institutions with sense and purpose. The resulting definition, in the words of one critic (Kim 1993, 15), "may wind up being devoid of what all ordinary usage takes to be the concept's very essence."

Some proponents of a strict election-focused institutional approach recognize this difficulty, even if their solutions are not wholly satisfying. For instance, Jeane Kirkpatrick, in defending "descriptive" or institutional approaches to studying democracy, acknowledges that "because people are value maximizers and political institutions are stabilized (structured) patterns of value-oriented interactions, the descriptive approach involves one in a consideration of values" (1981, 343). Kirkpatrick proposes that we consider such values from a particular perspective. "The point of departure," she states, "is the identification of values

---

[3] Included in this understanding of institutions are formal, standardized practices (such as elections) and the rules or laws that generate and maintain them. Of course, some of the institutions that political actors and analysts today associate with democracy, such as parliaments and certain kinds of interest groups, were originally set up to achieve different goals and only later were used to realize distinctively democratic ideals.

and value processes in functioning institutions" (344). Kirkpatrick then offers a list of "values" maximized through electoral systems, such as consensus, stability, and strong government. For Kirkpatrick, the "values" of democracy are simply those outcomes that are or might be maximized by electoral systems.

The problem with this formulation is that less desirable consequences might also be realized. To Kirkpatrick's list we might add the "values" of violence and deception—for elections can also exacerbate ethnic, class, or religious tensions, or stimulate politicians to lie. Institutions, in their day-to-day working, may well operate imperfectly. We are thus not surprised that electoral institutions sometimes produce outcomes that most Americans would not normally consider democratic. Few would want to include violence or deception as ideals of democracy. But Kirkpatrick provides no grounds for discounting these outcomes, no way to identify them as consequences that fall outside a range of *democratic* values. Missing from her account are standards by which to judge whether particular outcomes maximized by electoral institutions are in fact democratic.

Indeed, we might ask how Kirkpatrick knows that electoral systems are a fundamental feature of democracy in the first place. To say that they are seems to presuppose some standard by which to judge the presence of democracy. How does she know that these institutions do not operate instead in the service of justice or punishment or disease control or, more to the point, plutocracy or some form of aristocracy? Kirkpatrick can identify the institutional features of democracy only if she first recognizes a certain set of institutions as somehow involved in the project of democracy rather than, say, punishment. She cannot identify electoral institutions as democratic without first discerning the ideals they serve. As Giovanni Sartori puts it, "all the outcomes that have entered the fabric of democracy have indeed been *preceded* and *promoted* by consonant ideas and ideals" (1987, 16; emphasis added). There is, then, more to considering the ideal aspect of democracy than simply identifying outcomes maximized in existing institutions.

To sum up, taking into account the ideal aspects of democracy, however difficult and contestable a task this might be, is essential to the empirical study of democracy. Without consideration of such ideals and the standards they imply, it would be impossible to identify democracy's institutional side, or judge whether a given set of institutions does in fact fit ordinary understandings of what it means to be democratic.


## Dahl's Circle-Closing Solution

Among social scientists, it is perhaps Robert Dahl who has integrated the study of democratic ideals and institutions most successfully. One of his central concerns throughout his long career has been to "close the circle" between understandings of democracy that begin with values and goals and understandings that start with actual institutions (1956, 75). He has done so by positing ideals of democracy and then determining whether, and which, electoral and nonelectoral arrangements have been successful in approximating or securing these democratic ideals (see, for instance, Dahl 1971).[4] The advantage of this strategy is to allow researchers to ask which institutional arrangements are democratic and why. It thus sensitizes those who use it to the diverse institutional forms that democracy might take.[5]

But taking democratic ideals as a starting point, it is important to note, also introduces a problem distinct from concerns about fuzziness and ambiguity raised by Schumpeter and Huntington. Simply stated, those who rely on ideals of democracy as standards against which to measure and define political practices around the world risk ignoring how local populations understand their own actions.

Take an example from the work of Dahl. Using democratic ideals as a starting point, he asks what kind of citizen would be necessary to make democracy work. His conclusion is that "it would seem to require a certain level of political competence" (1992, 45). "Competence," for Dahl, seems to be the capacity of citizens to make reasoned judgments about public affairs, judgments that may spring either from concern for the public good or from a calculation of self-interest (46, 51).

Dahl's choice of competence as a measure is telling. People who do not make reasoned judgments about public affairs are, by implication, incompetent. And Dahl finds a worrisome number of citizens in both new and established democracies to be incompetent (1992, 45, 48). The problem for political analysts is that incompetence is a residual category into which all kinds of behavior might fall. It may be that citizens who appear to be incompetent players of the democratic game are playing a game whose objectives are somewhat different. What looks like incompetence may actually be virtuosity of a different sort.

Perhaps the point can be made clearer by a look at a real-world example. William Miles, an American political scientist, conducted a careful ethnographic study of multiparty elections held in 1983 in the northern Nigerian town of Yardaji. Miles described what happened there on election day: "Fulanis traveled substantial distances, on foot and in the powerful daytime heat, to get to the

---

[4] For Dahl, the primary goal or ideal of democracy is the responsiveness of a political system to its citizens (1971, 2). Elsewhere, he disaggregates this ideal of responsiveness into five criteria that any "ideal democratic process" would have to satisfy: equality in voting, effective participation in collective decision making, the enlightened understanding of each citizen in making such decisions, final control over the agenda by citizens, and inclusiveness (Dahl 1984, 6; see also Dahl 1979).

[5] For another example of this kind of circle closing see, most notably, Schmitter and Karl 1991.

Yardaji polls. Very old people participated. Crippled and deformed villagers limped over. The half-blind and the totally blind voted" (1988, 100). This behavior puzzled Miles, for he found that "elections, politics, [and] 'democracy'" were "processes" that ordinary Yardaji-ites "had never quite mastered or controlled" (117). He wondered therefore whether "a good proportion of voters simply might not have known what they were doing" (104). Upon further reflection, Miles concluded that "even with minimal understanding of politics, candidates, parties, or platforms, and in the absence of any coercion to do so, people from even the most peripheral areas elected to vote—because in some sense they felt it was *right* to do so" (100–101).

These statements indicate a tension between the voting behaviors Miles observed and the lack of understanding he attributed to voters. On the one hand, voters had little grasp of how the democratic process ought to work. On the other hand, voting carried important meaning. Voters thus exhibited both democratic incompetence and some other kind of virtuosity, something that propelled them to do what they felt was right.

Given voters' unfamiliarity with candidates, parties, and platforms, it seems unlikely that a desire to do the right thing was connected with a wish to voice preferences, impose accountability, make leaders responsive, or the like. Were their actions then motivated by different ideals and aimed at different goals? We want to know why voting was the right thing to do without assuming a priori that it was part of a game that Yardaji-ites perceived as democratic.

## An Alternative Circle-Closing Strategy

Such considerations have led me to pursue an alternative circle-closing strategy, one that takes institutions as a starting point; for it seems important to ask whether voters might use electoral arrangements to achieve ideals that diverge from, or only partially overlap with, ideals generally considered democratic by Americans. This strategy starts with functioning electoral institutions and investigates comparatively the *variety* of ideals toward which they might be oriented. This type of investigation is highly relevant to the study of many countries that have recently (or not so recently) adopted institutions normally associated with democracy, but in which people use these institutions in ways that do not seem democratic at all. Perhaps the people in question are simply engaged in different (though possibly related) kinds of activities.

Acknowledging and studying the variety of ideals that attend electoral institutions around the world provides essential information about electoral actors—their values and concerns, their repertoires of actions, their motives for voting, and their criteria for distinguishing what is just from what is unjust. The virtue of this approach is that it avoids presuming that these constructs are too problematic for study (as a Schumpeterian might argue) or that they simply manifest democratic incompetence (as a Dahlian might contend). By comparing ideals cross-culturally, we will be better able to investigate how the meaning of electoral institutions varies from place to place, and better able to describe the intentions of people who make use of them. This information is both intrinsically interesting and potentially useful.

## Conceptual Analysis

Although there are good reasons for wanting to study ideals cross-culturally, it is less clear how this should be done. Within the empirical subfields of social science, this task has been addressed most commonly through investigations of "political culture." The usual goal of such investigations, as far as the study of democracy is concerned, has been to identify the values that lend stability to democratic institutions (see, for example, Almond and Verba 1963). My aim, in contrast, is to identify the range of ideals toward which electoral institutions in different societies might be oriented.

To examine ideals empirically I use a language-centered approach, what we might call conceptual analysis. By "conceptual analysis" I refer loosely to a diverse set of methods and sensibilities derived from cognitive science, ordinary language philosophy, political theory, and Bible translation that includes looking at (1) the structure of concepts, (2) how concepts get used in ordinary contexts, (3) how specific concepts fit into a semantic field of related concepts, (4) how the meanings of concepts evolve over time, and (5) issues that arise in translating. Though ordinary language philosophers, linguists, cognitive scientists, and language-oriented political theorists often disagree about matters of method, meaning, and the nature of language, I have found important contributions in each field and draw freely from them all.

By studying the concept of democracy—or roughly equivalent concepts in other languages—we gain access to the frames of reference they provide. The value of this type of approach is perhaps best illustrated by an example from J. L. Austin's (1979) analysis of acceptable and unacceptable excuses. David Laitin does an excellent job of showing how this study provides a clearer sense of English speakers' shared standards of responsibility:

Although [Austin] is not explicit on this, one could derive from his discussion a guide to an anthropologist or ethnolinguist who came to study the English tribe. The anthropologist should notice that it is acceptable to tread on a snail "inadvertently," tip over the salt shaker "inadvertently," but *not* to tread on the baby "inadvertently." "Inadvertent" means, according to Austin, "a class of incidental happenings which must occur in the doing of any physical act," and is used when that incidental happening causes some (usually small) distress. Our foreign anthropologist, in learning English, might capture the sense of "inadvertence" as meaning merely "unintentional" (which, incidentally, is the definition in my dictionary). Suppose he does tread on a baby in one of the native's houses, and offers, "I did it inadvertently." And suppose the native returns with "That wasn't inadvertence! That was pure callousness." What is our anthropologist to think? Is he getting a lesson in the English language (he used "inadvertent" when he should have used "callous"), or was it a lesson in morality (treading on a baby is far more egregious than treading on a snail; and for the former, a simple excuse is not sufficient)? In fact, what the anthropologist is learning is both the English language *and* the standards of misdeeds among English speakers. (1977, 154)

In a similar fashion, for a non-English speaker to learn what the word "democracy" means is to learn not only a piece of the English language but also standards for calling something a "democracy."

Identifying the full range of such standards is complicated, however, by how meaning works in language. Words are not labels that tag particular classes of things in the world. As Wittgenstein (1972, par. 43, 77, 139, 532) argued, the meanings of words consist in the actual ways in which they are used in various contexts. To study how people understand "democracy" requires investigating how they use this word in *all* its ordinary contexts, both political and nonpolitical. The meaning of the word "democracy" and the concept of democracy amount to no more than, and no less than, these usages.

Consequently, to say that we can identify the standards implicit in a concept is not to claim that a language houses a single set of standards. A plurality of standards may circulate in a language, even within the discourse of a single speaker and within a single concept. Speaking of *the* concept of democracy may thus be misleading; it would suggest that a consensus exists about the way membership or rule should be understood. There is, of course, no such consensus.

When I speak of the meaning of democracy, then, I mean to include not only points of agreement, but also areas of ambiguity, ambivalence, and contestedness. A complex concept such as democracy encompasses a range of standards, some of which are in tension or matter more to certain people than to others.[6] Furthermore, linguists, sociologists, and psychologists remind us that language use, meaning, and standards can also vary with the speaker's class, gender, age, or race.[7] It remains an open question whether particular standards of de-

[6] For one attempt to show how different "contested" meanings of democracy relate to one another, see Gallie 1955–56.

[7] The literature on these subjects is large. On gender differences see especially Lakoff 1976 and Gilligan 1982. On class variations see Labov 1966. On racial differences see Labov 1969.

mocracy are shared equally among different groups of English speakers. Such an investigation is, unfortunately, outside the scope of this book.

## Everyday English and Ideals of Democracy

Nonetheless, a look at how the word "democracy" gets used in everyday American English talk reveals at least some of these standards, even if we cannot ascribe particular ones to specific groups of people. Examining how people use the term in *non*political contexts is especially helpful for our purposes, for such contexts reveal most starkly the standards people ordinarily associate with the concept, and they show how social scientific uses of "democracy" are anchored in ordinary language. To examine these nonpolitical uses, I conducted a broad search of the Nexis and Lexis electronic databases. These databases, with their vast stores of newspaper and magazine texts, revealed a wide range of meanings.

"Democracy" may, for instance, simply mean a state of social equality, often brought about by an agent that eliminates, or at least dampens or makes irrelevant, privilege and distinction. One such democratic leveler is the New York subway. In the words of one columnist, "Perhaps more than any other institution in the city, the trains are the great democratizer, where the maid and stockbroker sit side by side, sharing in the same advertisements for relief of hemorrhoids and the tales of woe spun by bedraggled panhandlers" (*New York Times,* August 31, 1991).

In a related usage, democracy can mean a state of distributive equality, in which an advantage or privilege previously enjoyed by or reserved for a small number of people gets extended to a wider population. Gourmet ice cream is one such benefit. Sometimes it is not an advantage, but an affliction that spreads to the broader public. Thus a journalist, explaining how AIDS may strike anyone regardless of sexual preference, wrote of the "democracy of the plague" (*New Republic,* November 2, 1992).

Another cluster of meanings revolves around notions of inclusive participation in a cooperative or collective activity, where the emphasis is placed less on an equal status than on widespread involvement. The director of a New York arts center said of a multiethnic dance festival he was organizing: "It's very participatory. . . . Like any form of community dancing, it's democracy in action — everybody can have a good time" (*New York Times,* December 2, 1983). Earlier in the chapter we saw how this participatory sense gets extended to basketball, a variant popularly known as "hardwood democracy."

Democracy in its participative sense may also denote the opportunity to take one's turn in the limelight. Used in this way, the term appears frequently in connection with the performing arts. A theater critic, for instance, reviewing a play staged by the Potomac Theater Project, wrote: "There are a lot of small parts . . . but there really isn't a bad one. Everybody gets a punchline, a bit of business, a moment front and center. What we have here . . . is an endearing illustration of democracy in action" (*Washington Post,* July 27, 1990). This idea is even more common in the world of music, where sharing the limelight, rotating principal players, or dividing up solos has been called variously "rock," "musical," or "orchestral" democracy.

Finally, "democracy" may be used to refer to a range of consumer choices. Consider the reviewer who describes the current market for electronic mail systems as "democracy in action" because "each user can choose the mail service of his liking and still be able to communicate with everyone electronically" (*PC Week,* May 15, 1989). Sometimes "democracy" refers not simply to the existence of consumer choice but to the unintended effects of many such choices made over and over again—what we described earlier as diner patrons "voting with their pocketbook."

What is interesting about these ordinary uses is that they are not random or arbitrary. They appear, on the contrary, to be extensions of familiar understandings of democracy. A plausible case can be made that the idea of democracy as social and distributive equality derives from notions that emphasize the sharing of power by the poor and the rich and that define "the people" as including the lower classes. Both understandings encompass a concern with diminishing class distinctions.

Similarly, the use of "democracy" to mean inclusive participation might derive from notions of democracy that understand "rule" to entail active involvement in decision making, a form of democracy often called "participatory." And notions of democracy as consumer choice, with their emphasis on buyers choosing from a selection of products, appear related to the way voters choose among candidates. Democracy as consumer choice, seen from this perspective, may well be an extension of the way Americans understand the institutional side of representative democracy, not unlike the way it was conceptualized by Schumpeter and made even more explicit by Anthony Downs (1957).

Even so, it would seem strange to claim that shooting baskets is an instance of democracy in the same sense that meeting with fellow citizens to decide some matter in town hall is. In fact, the basketball example seems not to be intended literally at all. To call basketball players "citizens" is to speak metaphorically, just as when I say "She was so mad her blood was boiling," I do not mean literally that her blood boiled; I am simply using a metaphor to conceptualize anger as heat.

It is not, however, always so easy to classify particular uses, for a significant number of cases are hard to figure out. Take the restaurant patrons who vote with their pocketbooks. We could well imagine, under certain circumstances, instances of purchasing or spending as acts of participation in collective decision making (if menu selections seem too frivolous to be the objects of democratic choice, then consider political campaigns, which, of course, accept financial contributions). In such cases, consumer choice is arguably not merely *conceived* in terms of democracy; it is also a *form* of democratic action, and therein lies the difficulty in classifying particular uses of the term.

This difficulty notwithstanding, recognizing and distinguishing (when possible) literal meanings and metaphorical extensions of democracy enable us to identify standards that American English speakers commonly use in judging the presence or absence of democracy. When they call a situation, institution, or practice a "democracy" or "democratic" in the more literal senses of these words, they do so because they find present one or more of these attributes: inclusive participation in collective decision making, the leveling or discounting of differences that infringe on this inclusive participation, and the availability of meaningful options in the decision-making process. And when they call a situation, institution, or practice a "democracy" or "democratic" in the more metaphorical senses of these words, they also ordinarily find either participation, equality, or choice present—but in ways that do not relate directly to the collective making of decisions.

To prevent misunderstanding, let me repeat two points. First, the list of examples on which these conclusions are based is not exhaustive. There may be other meanings of democracy I have not identified. Second, neither identifying a limited number of meanings nor distinguishing between literal and metaphoric uses diminishes the contestedness of the concept. People may well disagree about what counts as "participation" or "meaningful options," or what kinds of social or economic inequalities matter. People may also disagree about which of the three dimensions (participation, equality, and choice) is most essential to democracy. What makes a situation democratic along one dimension may undermine it in another.

## The Comparative Study of Concepts

We have identified some important standards that American English speakers use for judging the presence or absence of democracy. Whether roughly equivalent words in other languages share similar standards is an important question, albeit one not often posed.[8] Conceptual analysis provides a method for identifying the meanings of these concepts across languages. It enables us to compare the meanings that underlie "democracy" and its rough equivalents around the world, and to see the extent to which different societies endow electoral institutions

---

[8] Interesting comparative work has, however, been done on other types of concepts. Rodney Needham (1972), for instance, examines what it would mean to call "belief" a universal human experience.

with different meanings. There is, after all, little reason simply to assume that non-Anglophones will engage in political behavior whose meaning is occasioned by the English word "democracy." Xhosa speakers do not discuss the merits of the new South African "democracy." There are no popular cries for "democracy" in China; no intellectuals in the Czech Republic called for a quickened pace of "democratic" change. Xhosa speakers today talk of *idemokrasi,* Chinese students demonstrated for *minzhu,* and Vaclav Havel attempted to institute *demokracie.* These examples are hardly trivial. Translating *minzhu, demokracie,* or *idemokrasi* by "democracy," as journalists and scholars regularly do, is potentially problematic because the cultural premises that infuse American practices and institutions may not be universal.

## Senegal: Situating the Case Study

The West African country of Senegal presents an unusual opportunity to explore the extent to which the meaning of electoral institutions varies across cultures. On the one hand, Senegalese society is marked by a distinctive set of cultural traditions, social organizations, and political practices that reflect the life conditions of its predominantly Muslim, agrarian, and poor population. In this regard, Senegalese society provides a stark contrast to the predominantly Christian, industrial, affluent society of the United States.

On the other hand, Senegal, with the exception of a fourteen-year period from 1960 to 1974, has a tradition of competitive politics that stretches back 150 years, so much of its population is by now well accustomed to voting and participating in the electoral process. This tradition dates, more precisely, to 1848, when France granted voting rights to the male African inhabitants of the "Four Communes"—the colony's major settlements of Dakar, Rufisque, St-Louis, and the island of Gorée. Though this enfranchised population voted often (for municipal councilors, councilors to the General Council of the colony, and deputies to the National Assembly in Paris), their numbers were small. In 1922, for instance, only about 18,000 townsmen, 1.5 percent of the indigenous population, enjoyed the rights of citizenship (Johnson 1971, 38–62; Coulon 1995, 494). This small number of voters does not, however, reflect the impact of the franchise on the rest of the population. Women in the Four Communes joined political associations, wrote political pamphlets, and sang songs praising their preferred candidates and ridiculing any opponents (Lacroix and Mbaye 1976, 35–36; Siga 1990, 133–35). The urban franchise also helped politicize the rural residents of the colony. A leading historian has noted that "by 1920 it was apparent that political action in Senegal, though technically limited to the Four Communes, was slowly spreading to encompass the entire geographic heartland of Senegal" (Johnson 1971, 218).

Townswomen won the right to vote in 1945, as did various categories of rural dwellers in 1946. By 1956, suffrage was universal (Morgenthau 1964, 55–56; Lacroix and Mbaye 1976). Voters had ample opportunity to exercise their electoral rights. Between 1945 and 1958 they were called to vote nine times on various referenda and for delegates to the Constituent and National Assemblies. As one scholar remarked, "frequent elections maintained an almost continuous climate of electioneering" (Morgenthau 1964, 55).

Senegal achieved independence in 1960. Between 1960 and 1966, the ruling Union Progressiste Sénégalaise (UPS), led by Léopold Sédar Senghor, gradually absorbed or repressed all rival political parties. In 1974 President Senghor reversed this process, and allowed several independent parties to form legally and compete for power. Since then, multiparty presidential and legislative elections have been held in 1978, 1983, 1988, and 1993.

The ruling party has won the presidency and a legislative majority in each of these contests. Still, opposition parties have garnered significant and increasing electoral support. Their presence in the legislature almost doubled from 1978 to 1993 (Opposition parties won 18 percent of all legislative seats in 1978, 30 percent in 1993). Turnout for the most popular opposition candidate for the presidency, Abdoulaye Wade, similarly rose from 16 percent in 1978 to 32 percent in 1993. Indeed, in 1993 Wade received more votes in the capital city of Dakar than the incumbent candidate, President Abdou Diouf.[9]

Senegal's long history of electoral politics makes it unique in Africa and rare among France's former colonies. Its citizens, in comparison with many African, Asian, and Middle Eastern peoples, are well acquainted with electoral institutions. We might gainfully ask, then, whether the citizenry of Senegal holds democratic ideals roughly similar to those espoused by Americans.

## Methods

To investigate the extent to which the two populations do or do not hold similar ideals, I examine how the people of Senegal understand the concept that corresponds most closely to the institutional aspect of the American concept of democracy. That is, we will look for the concept that the Senegalese use to refer to electoral institutions and then ask whether this concept and its American counterpart encompass similar ideals.

---

[9] It should be noted that the success of the ruling party in 1978, 1983, and 1988 was due in part to ballot rigging, legally sanctioned public voting, and unequal access of parties to the broadcast media. A greater degree of fairness and openness marked the 1993 elections, a result of a new electoral code that put an end to public voting, increased opposition parties' access to the media, and gave them the right to participate in the administration of the elections.

Identifying a "Senegalese" concept, however, is complicated by the plurality of languages spoken within the country. The French presence in Senegal dates to the 1500s. By the early 1800s the territory had formally become a colony, and it remained one until 1960. French, spoken widely by the political and economic elite, is still the official language of government and the medium of public education. Although this language is the mother tongue of few Senegalese, 1988 census data indicate that about one quarter of the population is literate in it (République du Sénégal, Ministère de l'Economie et des Finances 1990, table 4.06).[10] In addition, more than a dozen indigenous languages are spoken, the most widespread being Wolof. This is the native tongue of almost half of Senegal's 6.8 million residents. Most native Wolof speakers are of Wolof ethnicity, but close to 400,000 belong to other ethnic groups.[11] Wolof is also the second language of another 1.5 million Senegalese. In all, it is spoken by at least seven of every ten people in the country. Other major languages include Pulaar (the native language of 22 percent of the population),[12] Serer (13 percent), Diola (5 percent), Manding (4 percent), and Soninké (1 percent) (ibid., tables 3.15, 3.16).

A project that has at its core the study of language use must necessarily take language groups as a basic unit of analysis. Different language groups, however, may have different political vocabularies and conceptions, and it would be impractical to study all the languages spoken in Senegal. This book focuses primarily on Wolof, the country's dominant indigenous language, and secondarily on French, the country's official language of government.

A conceptual approach is well suited to exploring the relationship between French and Wolof. Many political concepts that developed in France and are used today in the halls of Senegalese government have no direct equivalents in Wolof. Nevertheless, modern forms of governance have required that the non-French-speaking majority adopt a new political vocabulary, a vocabulary they create by either projecting Wolof words into the new political context or borrowing vocabulary from French and, to a lesser degree, Arabic.[13] These projections and loans carry with them meanings embedded in local cultures (or in the case of French and Arabic loan words, meanings derived from the way local people experience these cultures) that reveal how the Wolof-speaking Senegalese understand their political institutions. An analysis of both French and

---

[10] Still more Senegalese can speak some French, although census takers do not know exactly how many.

[11] Wolof is both a language and an ethnic group. Forty-four percent of the population is of Wolof ethnicity; the Wolof language is the native tongue of 49% of the population. Not all native Wolof speakers are of Wolof ethnicity, and not all who are of Wolof ethnicity speak Wolof as a first language (République du Sénégal, Ministère de l'Economie et des Finances 1990, table 3.15).

[12] Pulaar includes both the Peul and Toucouleur dialects.

[13] Arabic words were brought to the Senegal River basin with trans-Saharan trade and the propagation of Islam during the early centuries of the second millennium. Lexicons prepared by European explorers and missionaries indicate that many Arabic loan words—such as *dunyaa* (the world), *àjjana* (heaven), *Yalla* (God), and *asamaan* (sky)—were already well integrated into local lan-

Wolof languages, and of both indigenous and borrowed concepts in Wolof, will thus provide essential information about how the country's elite and its Wolof-speaking majority understand such concepts as democracy—or, more precisely, how they understand the French and Wolof terms that correspond most closely to democracy's conventionalized meaning of electoral institutions.

Using the methods of ordinary language philosophy in a language other than one's own is, however, a daunting task. While I am nearly fluent in French and an advanced Wolof speaker, I am not a native speaker of either language. I therefore rely heavily on the language use of native French and Wolof speakers and the insights of native Wolof- and French-speaking informants.

To identify the Wolof and French concepts that correspond most closely to the institutional aspects of the American concept "democracy," it was first necessary to determine the relevant lexicon, or "semantic field." The task in French was made relatively easy by the existence in Senegal of a flourishing and plural press. A variety of newspapers, tracts, pamphlets, and party organs offer extensive discussions of politics by different factions of the country's political elite. Analysis of these texts revealed that the French term *démocratie* was used widely in ways that closely paralleled the American English usage of "democracy."

Since Wolof is by and large a spoken language, not a written one, analysis in that language was somewhat more complicated and required the collection and study of oral texts. The goal was to identify the universe of relevant terms and expressions. Recognizing that language use may vary with speakers and contexts, I collected twenty-five samples that represented the speech of different segments of the population[14] and reflected the types of language used in a range of situations.[15] After transcribing these texts into standardized written Wolof

---

guages, in this case Wolof, by the eighteenth century. See "Vocabulaires guiolof" 1845 and "Petit vocabulaire" n.d. Several more recent studies identify French and Arabic loan words in Wolof, but none of them discusses the vocabulary of politics in any detail. Most notable are Mouradian 1963 and Dumont 1983.

[14] The twenty-five informants were chosen through a quota sampling strategy to ensure that speakers of different age, sex, class, education, religion, dialect, ethnicity, party affiliation, and area of residence were included. While this method produced a relatively small sample of Wolof language use, it should be recalled that large samples are not as necessary for linguistic surveys as for other surveys since, as many linguists note, linguistic behavior is more homogeneous than other types of behavior. Furthermore, the goal was not a statistically representative sample but one that yielded a high number of terms and phrases. On quota sampling see Bernard 1988, 96–97. On sample size in linguistic research see Samarin 1967 and Sankoff 1980.

[15] On the importance of sampling both people and contexts see Honigmann 1970; Hammersley and Atkinson 1983, 45–53; and Milroy 1987, 18–38. To collect samples of different language situations, I conducted some interviews in one-on-one settings, others in groups. To reduce the problem of informants' changing their linguistic behavior in formal interview situations, I also recorded casual conversations on political topics. And to collect samples of public discourse as it is naturally spoken, unaffected by my personal priorities or biases, I monitored political discussions broadcast on the radio, obtained recordings or transcripts of speeches broadcast on radio and television during the 1983, 1988, and 1993 electoral campaigns, and recorded dozens of speeches made at political rallies.

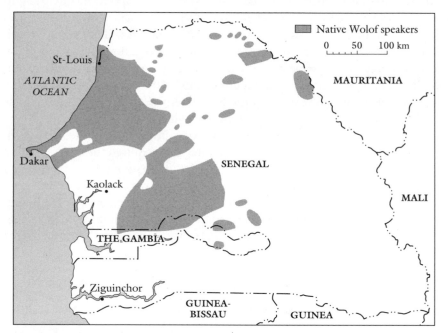

**Map 2**. Distribution of native Wolof speakers. (Based on Christopher Moseley and R.E. Asher, *Atlas of the World's Languages* [New York: Routledge, 1994] map 113.)

with the aid of a native Wolofone, I selected key words, phrases, metaphors, and proverbs that seemed relevant to what Americans would call democracy.

In addition, I studied the historical origins of these key words (in both French and Wolof) to uncover other connotations and shared meanings. For this task I used a variety of sources, including ethnographies, grammars, dictionaries, and lexicons dating back to the early eighteenth century, colonial reports and letters, songs, newspapers and party organs, and campaign literature. In this endeavor, I took advantage of the rich collections of several research institutions in Senegal, most notably the Archives du Sénégal, the Centre de Linguistique Appliquée de Dakar, and the Institut Fondamental d'Afrique Noire, and, in Paris, the holdings of the Bibliothèque Nationale and the Bibliothèque Interuniversitaire des Langues Orientales.

As it happens, there is a Wolof word—*demokaraasi*—that is etymologically linked to the English word "democracy." It derives from the French *démocratie,* a word that gained common currency in Senegal, at least among Francophones, during the early twentieth century. It was at this time that French colonizers were building the foundations of the modern Senegalese state, establishing its bureaucratic institutions and, most important in this context, expanding the use of elections. Like its rough equivalents in English and French, the Wolof term today can be used to refer to electoral institutions and multipartyism. All three concepts, in short, have similar institutional referents. The main question, however, is whether they also share ideals or standards.

To determine how the French-speaking elite understand *démocratie* and the Wolof-speaking majority understand *demokaraasi,* I examined how these and other relevant words and phrases were used by ordinary speakers in concrete contexts. For the French concept, I analyzed the written source materials and also conducted twenty open-ended interviews with government and opposition-party leaders. For the Wolof concept, I conducted another one hundred interviews, again using a quota sampling strategy[16] and asking open-ended questions (Agar 1980, 138–49), such as "Is there *demokaraasi* in Senegal today?"; "Is *demokaraasi* good or bad?"; and "Is there a place or a country in the world that does not have *demokaraasi?*"

This reliance on interview data posed special problems, for the interview setting itself may have affected how respondents understood my questions—the questions of a nonnative Wolof speaker and a non-Senegalese. Their answers may thus have reflected what they assumed I wanted to know or what they thought it was in their interest for me to know (for a more theoretical discussion of this problem see Gumperz 1982; Rieder 1994).

---

[16] Almost all of these interviews were conducted in four geographic areas: (1) the capital city, Dakar, and its satellite city of Pikine; (2) the departments of Kébémer and Louga, in northern Senegal; (3) the department of Mbacké, in the central part of the country; and (4) the department of Nioro-du-Rip, the southernmost zone in which Wolof speakers are concentrated.

For this reason, it was important to corroborate that interviewees were using words such as *demokaraasi* in natural, ordinary ways. Once I arrived at understandings of what particular terms meant, therefore, I verified my findings by generating sentences that highlighted regularities in the French and Wolof languages and thus indicated ordinary contexts in which a word or expression might occur naturally. Since correct interpretation depends ultimately on the production of examples that native speakers find convincing, I asked another set of thirty informants (twenty-five for Wolof, five for French) who showed a particular sensitivity to distinctions in their own language to judge whether these sentences sounded right.[17] Austin (1979, 185) produces a good example of the kind of questions this method might yield:

> You have a donkey, so have I, and they graze in the same field. The day comes when I conceive a dislike for mine. I go to shoot it, draw a bead on it, fire: the brute falls in its tracks. I inspect the victim, and find to my horror that it is *your* donkey. I appear on the doorstep with the remains and say—what? "I say, old sport, I'm awfully sorry, &c., I've shot your donkey *by accident*"? Or "*by mistake*"? Then again, I go to shoot my donkey as before, draw a bead on it, fire—but as I do so, the beasts move, and to my horror yours falls. Again the scene on the doorstep—what do I say? "By mistake"? Or "by accident"?

By asking questions of a similar form, I was able to delineate, with a reasonable assurance of validity, the contours of the meanings of *demokaraasi, démocratie,* and related concepts.

To summarize, this book makes use of techniques derived from linguistic philosophy and related fields to address issues of critical importance to the comparative study of democracy. It investigates the extent to which a singular focus on electoral arrangements or the use of democratic ideals as sole standards of evaluation provide adequate frameworks for understanding electoral practices in societies that are culturally divergent. To this end, it examines the degree to which concepts and the ideals they contain are contextually mutable. It takes as a case study how Wolof and French speakers in Senegal, the country in Africa with the most sustained tradition of multiparty rule, have adopted and transformed European political concepts such as *démocratie.* It uses the resulting understanding of these concepts and the ideals they contain to shed light on the functioning of electoral institutions in that country. Investigating these issues should help social scientists reflect more deeply on political realities in many Asian, African, Latin American, and East European countries and develop methods and concepts that permit more meaningful cross-cultural comparison.

[17] On this standard of proof see Searle 1969, 12–15; Pitkin 1972, 15; and Cavell 1976, 33–37.

# 2

# From *Démocratie* to *Demokaraasi*

The linguistic landscape of Senegal, like that of many postcolonial countries, is tiered. French is the language of officialdom and the acculturated elite. Wolof is the native tongue of almost half of Senegal's population and the country's lingua franca. Five other major languages are spoken. This multiplicity of languages complicates an analysis of political concepts in Senegal. Different language groups have different political vocabularies. Political ideas garnered through the medium of French may differ in important ways from those uncovered in Wolof, Serer, Diola, or Pulaar.

To complicate matters more, language choice for the country's bilingual and multilingual population varies with social and linguistic context. Take the case of one typical Serer family living in Dakar. Linguists found that while the parents speak Serer to one another and to their preschool children, the father addresses the older children in French. Among themselves, the children use Wolof (Heredia-Deprez 1987). Other researchers have noted that schoolchildren speak French in the classroom, but Wolof in the school yard (Dreyfus 1987). Young men in Dakar often switch back and forth between Wolof and French in the same conversation, even in the same sentence.[1] Legislators who speak French on the floor of the National

[1] Indeed, in the largest urban areas of Senegal many people today speak a Wolof deeply penetrated by French, a form known locally as Dakar Wolof. As one linguist (Swigart 1994, 176) explained, "it usually takes the form of a Wolof 'matrix' 'embedded' with a number of French lexical items, . . . phonologically assimilated to Wolof or not, which create subtle stylistic or connotational effects. Sometimes a French verb will be inflected with Wolof tense or aspect morphemes. . . . Sometimes a French phrase like *il paraît que,* 'it seems that', or *tant que,* 'as long as', will play an

Assembly or in meetings with fellow deputies may well switch to Wolof when talking with their peers in less formal settings or when addressing their constituents. Doctors working with bilingual psychiatric patients at Dakar's Fann Hospital observed that language use varied with emotional state. A patient who normally spoke Wolof with his family, for instance, switched to French after each psychotic break (Dorès and Mbodj 1972). Language choice, in short, varies with the formality of the social setting, relations of power, and even state of mind.[2]

A study of Wolof political concepts thus faces numerous difficulties, not least of which is the fact that a large number of Wolof terms are of French origin. Unfortunately, we do not know the particular conditions under which many French terms entered the Wolof language. Wolof is primarily a spoken language, and apart from a few dozen lexicons and dictionaries written by explorers, traders, Catholic missionaries, and colonial administrators in the eighteenth, nineteenth, and early twentieth centuries, there is scant written record of how the language was adapted to the arrival of the French.[3]

One of the few attempts to study these early written sources was carried out by Pierre Dumont (1973, 87–94), who analyzed the French loan words contained in a 1902 Wolof-French dictionary. He identified 142 loan words, many of which belonged to specialized domains such as seafaring and Christianity. None, however, related directly to politics.

Yet by the early twentieth century, many Africans had become participants in French-style politics. As part of a broader policy of assimilation, the French had extended citizenship rights to a substantial number of Africans living in the Four Communes. By the early 1900s these new voters were sufficiently numerous that politicians courted their votes aggressively.

One advantage enjoyed by African candidates over their French competitors was that they could address African audiences in Wolof. During the 1914 elections, many rallies for the African candidate Blaise Diagne were held at least partially in Wolof. Diagne himself spoke both Wolof and French, while his lieutenant, Galandou Diouf, pleased the crowd with his eloquent Wolof oratory (*L'AOF*, March 21 and May 9, 1914). Yet Diouf's Wolof was not pure. An observer at one rally in April 1914, for example, noted that a number of French words peppered his speeches, among them: *vote, droits, liberté, commandant,* and

---

important connecting role between two otherwise pure Wolof clauses. An entire phrase in French may also be followed by several sentences in Wolof, creating a back-and-forth pattern that proceeds without pauses or other hesitation phenomena. It is not uncommon for 'loan translations' to be used, where a Wolof expression is translated word-for-word into French or a French expression is rendered literally into Wolof." For a more detailed description of Dakar Wolof see Swigart (1992).

[2] Carol Myers Scotton (1983, 1988, 1990, 1993), among others, has explored in detail the various social and psychological motivations that enter into such choices in African bilingual and multilingual communities.

[3] As Judith Irvine (1993) argues, drawing conclusions from these early sources is further complicated by their ideological content. Positions on linguistic matters often mirrored (and sometimes promoted) positions taken in larger debates about colonial policy in France.

*commis* (*L'AOF,* April 21, 1914). Whether Diouf's non-French-speaking audiences understood these terms is uncertain. We do know, however, that at least one word of French origin was widely understood by Wolof speakers at this time— *politig* (from the French *politique*). Interestingly, Wolof speakers identified an understanding of *politig* that was uniquely Wolof: it meant simply to lie or deceive. As one Wolof-speaking candidate in the 1914 elections wrote at the time, "the word *'politique'* taken from French means in Wolof: circumlocution, lies, false-hoods" (Pellegrin 1914). There was, however, no conclusive proof that the term *démocratie* had entered Wolof discourse by the early twentieth century, even if this French word was used widely in debates on colonial policy at that time.

The French origins of the Wolof term *demokaraasi*—whatever the historical details—present a set of puzzling questions: Where, exactly, should we draw the line between the Wolof concept *demokaraasi* and the French concept *démocratie*? Does the word *demokaraasi,* uttered in a Wolof sentence, mean the same as *démocratie* in French? Or does meaning change when the word is transferred from French to Wolof, as seems to have happened with *politig*?

The notion that there is a uniquely Wolof concept of *demokaraasi* would today be questioned by many Senegalese intellectuals. In conversation, several academicians expressed their open skepticism that the uneducated majority of Senegalese had any coherent understanding of the concept at all. This concern is hardly frivolous, given the high rates of illiteracy and the almost total absence of broad-based civic education. Indeed, while most Wolof speakers I interviewed, even those in the remotest villages, were at least vaguely familiar with the term *demokaraasi,* a few had no clear notion of what the word might actually mean. One old woman said with some exasperation, "*Demokaraasi*—I don't know what it is exactly, it's just some word I hear a lot on the radio." Other intellectuals doubted whether there was anything unique in the way Wolof speakers understand *demokaraasi* and even took issue with calling this a Wolof concept at all. For them, there is no Wolof word *demokaraasi,* only the French term *démocratie* spoken with a Wolof accent. That is, the words differ in pronunciation, not in meaning.

The cumulative weight of these considerations—the existence of different language groups, variance of language use by context, and fuzzy boundaries between French and Wolof—make it necessary to isolate and explore political discourse in well-defined settings. In this chapter I look at how one segment of Senegalese society—the political elite[4]—makes use of the terms *démocratie* and

[4] Because the term "political elite" is used widely yet inconsistently in social science literature, a few words of explanation are in order to clarify what this term means in this book. Here it refers to those people who either exercise important governmental functions (top civil servants, government ministers, members of the national assembly) or contribute actively to national political debate and policy formation (journalists, high-level educators, and leaders of opposition parties, civic associations, and labor unions). For a more detailed sociological description of Senegal's political elite see Blanchet 1983. Excluded from this definition are leaders of Senegal's Muslim brotherhoods, who, although they exert strong pressures on government officials and party leaders, rarely engage openly in public political debates beyond making vague calls for national unity and peace. For a different view see Coulon 1970.

*demokaraasi* in the public discussions and debates that take place in newspapers, conferences, party organs, radio broadcasts, and political meetings. I ask how the members of the French-speaking political elite in Senegal speak of *démocratie,* what channels they use to disseminate their views to the wider population, and how the meanings of this concept shift when political leaders are compelled to develop a new Wolof vocabulary and set of metaphors to convey messages to the non-francophone population. The aim is to see how and where French discourse on *démocratie* shades into Wolof discourse on *demokaraasi.*

## *Démocratie*: French Language Debates

The return to multiparty politics in Senegal after 1974 ushered in a new era of political debate. Previously illegal and semiclandestine political groups engaged in open political activity. They challenged the political status quo and sought to alter the very rules of political competition, which they perceived as skewed in favor of the ruling party. These challenges persist to this day. The constitution has been revised seven times since 1974, and the electoral code more than fifteen, most recently in 1992. For this reason, the various factions of Senegal's political elite today see the country's *démocratie* as open-ended and still emerging.

Some members of the political elite conceive of this emergence in biological or developmental terms. A recurrent theme in speeches of President Abdou Diouf over the years, for instance, is that Senegalese *démocratie* is either youthful or mature, depending on his political needs of the moment. Thus when Diouf assumed power in 1981 and lifted restrictions placed by the former president Léopold Senghor on the number of parties that could legally be created, he declared that "having achieved the age of adulthood, with the 21st anniversary of our independence, our democratic system has to refine, reform, and improve itself" (Nzouankeu n.d., 82–86). Yet when Diouf wished, four years later, to justify the slowness of democratic reform, he portrayed Senegalese *démocratie* — and African *démocratie* in general — as having reached only its adolescence and displaying the limitations and promises of youth: "African *démocratie* is a young *démocratie*. It thus has the weaknesses of its youth. But it also has energy, enthusiasm, faith, without which nothing durable or grand could be built" (*Le Soleil,* July 2, 1985). While opposition leaders do not usually speak in such biological terms, certain parties have, nonetheless, implicitly adopted this metaphor. The Convention des Démocrates et Patriotes (CDP), founded by the historian Iba Der Thiam in June 1992, adopted the nickname *Garab gi,* Wolof for "medicine," to indicate its determination to cure Senegalese *démocratie* of its ills. *Démocratie,* in this metaphoric scheme, is a natural body that not only ages and matures but also succumbs to sickness or recovers good health.

Other Senegalese intellectuals see *démocratie* in engineering terms, as something to be erected or constructed. Ousmane Tanor Dieng, the president's *di-*

*recteur de cabinet,* wrote an article in homage to the "architects of our *démocratie*" who laid "the cornerstones of the democratic model that we want to build and to perpetuate" (*L'Unité pour le Socialisme,* August 1991). Some independent observers believe the opposition, in particular the strong Parti Démocratique Sénégalais (PDS), wants simply to tear down the *démocratie* built by the ruling Parti Socialiste (PS) (see, for instance, the cartoon in *Le Cafard Libéré,* March 10, 1993). Members of the PDS, in contrast, view their role in a more positive light: "The kind of *démocratie* that we have and want to build has never, anywhere in the world, issued from an 'experiment' conducted by one man for the benefit of the people. Everywhere it has been a laborious undertaking—constraining, often bitter and sad—but always exalting the different components of an active nation. . . . But this *démocratie* will work because it rests on solid institutions" (*Sopi,* April 5, 1991). Certain opposition figures place less stress on the construction of a new edifice than on maintaining the one already built. Madior Diouf, the secretary-general of the Rassemblement National Démocratique (RND), campaigned in 1993 as the presidential candidate who would clean up the sullied building of *démocratie,* a promise that did not go unnoticed by cartoonists, who unfailingly portrayed him with broom in hand during the campaign period.

Engineering and maintenance metaphors of *démocratie* are in tension with those that depict an aging natural body. Envisioning the political actor as an architect, engineer, or custodian implies that society is created and sustained by human artifice, while the image of an aging organic body underscores the naturalness of the Senegalese political community. Furthermore, whereas the image of the architect or engineer implies that Senegalese *démocratie* needs to be redrawn or rebuilt, the image of biological development or building maintenance underscores the need to ensure continuity. Thus images of biology, engineering, and housekeeping contain tensions—tensions inherent in politics and attempts to change the political world: political society is both natural and artificial; it is subject to both continuity and change. Yet despite these tensions, these metaphors share the sense that Senegalese *démocratie* is unfolding, in progress, in the process of becoming. The debate is over the future, about how to move Senegalese *démocratie* forward on its developmental path, how to cure its ills, how to strengthen and build on its foundations, how to clean up the refuse that sullies it.

In more concrete terms, debates about Senegalese *démocratie* stem from disagreements over whether political competition has been fair and whether elections have been free of manipulation. Virtually every election since the return to multiparty rule in 1974 has taken place amid opposition accusations of fraud and unfairness. Nonetheless, the opposition appears committed to what we might call the democratic game. Indeed, the recent defeats of ruling parties in other African countries have provided strong proof to the Senegalese opposition that a more robust multiparty *démocratie* is possible in Senegal, but that it requires a legal framework that can guarantee fair competition.

Because the very rules of the political game are in contention, debates about Senegalese *démocratie* have been heated. Leaders of each party have their own ideas about the steps needed to secure its foundations, restore it to health, or scrub it clean. The specifics of the debate have, moreover, shifted with time. From 1974—the year that President Senghor initiated the return to multiparty politics—to his resignation in 1981, debate over Senegalese *démocratie* centered around Senghor's controlled liberalization of the political system. At the heart of this scheme was a revised constitution that provided for three political parties representing three constitutionally defined ideological positions. The governing UPS, the forerunner of the PS, specified itself as "socialist and democratic," leaving a position open to its right for a "liberal and democratic" party and one to its left for a "Marxist-Leninist" or "communist" party. In 1978 a constitutional amendment created a "conservative" slot, bringing the total of recognized parties in this system of limited multiparty rule to four. These openings were filled by well-established Senegalese politicians heading parties they had already (somewhat clandestinely) organized.

During this period, the debate about *démocratie* was dominated by opposition figures who led parties denied legal recognition by the new constitution. They argued that restricting electoral competition to parties that reflect only a narrow range of political opinions, defined by the president, no less, placed artificial and arbitrary limits on Senegalese *démocratie*. Babacar Niang, at the time a leader of the RND, called the new constitution "quasi-monarchical" (*Taxaw,* April 1977); while Mamadou Dia—a former prime minister imprisoned by Senghor in 1962 and future founder of the Mouvement Démocratique Populaire (MDP)—wrote:

> The constitutional reforms of 1976–1979 claim to open an era of *démocratie*: in reality they have the effect of confining and walling in *démocratie*. . . . The law on the ideological traditions and the organization of parties has instituted a limited pluralism (3 then 4 parties) permitting the government to choose *its opposition,* to remove from public life those associations that are most representative of public opinion. It arbitrarily freezes in place the political structures of Senegalese society without prior public consultation. (*Andë Sopi,* September 1979)

Unrecognized political organizations thus saw the reforms as despotic measures manufactured to divide the opposition, marginalize the most significant forces for political change, and arrest the development of *démocratie*.

President Senghor (1980, 226) defended himself vigorously against these accusations. To him, there was no contradiction between selective legalization and *démocratie*. In fact, he believed some restriction on political activity was essential to assure its balanced growth. As one of his defenders explained a few years after the president left office, "The very principle of limiting the number of political parties is compatible with the exigencies of *démocratie*, because the proliferation of parties could, under certain circumstances, engender anarchy and lead to dictatorship" (Nzouankeu 1984, 33). Unlimited pluralism, then, risked chaos. The steady progress of *démocratie* required the channeling and restriction of political activity.

The PDS, seeking to preserve its privileged position as the leading legalized opposition party, approved of the limitations placed by Senghor on the number of officially recognized political parties. As an editorialist for the PDS journal *Le Démocrate* wrote:

> It is entirely normal that political life be regulated because, as we have always maintained, multipartyism should not be a savage pluralism where each citizen hears voices like Joan of Arc or de Gaulle, and creates his own party. Even in competitive sports, not everyone who wishes to be a participant can become one, otherwise this would result in anarchy and there would be no game. That is to say that certain restrictions are desirable, even if we can argue about the acceptable number of political parties. (April 1976; quoted in Desouches 1983, 63; translation in Fatton 1987, 9)

While the PDS supported limited pluralism, it disputed the high-handed manner in which Senghor designated the parties to be legalized. The PDS believed that such a decision should be made not by the whim of the president but by public referendum (Desouches 1983, 63; Fatton 1987, 9).

The debate of the late 1970s, then, was dominated by the question of whether the exclusion of various political organizations from electoral competition expanded *démocratie* by staving off dictatorship and forcing the legalized political parties to represent a wider general interest, or constricted *démocratie* by arbitrarily denying recognition of parties that represented views of large segments of society. In 1981 the terms of the debate shifted dramatically. Senghor resigned, passing the presidency to his groomed successor, Abdou Diouf. Diouf, upon assuming office, opened up political competition by amending the constitution to provide for the legal recognition of all political groups regardless of ideology. By January 1982, Senegal counted fourteen opposition parties. Elections were held in 1983; Diouf and his party won by a landslide, albeit under the opposition's charges of fraud and irregularity.

After the 1983 elections, any doubts whether the PDS was the dominant opposition party were put to rest. The PDS presidential candidate, Abdoulaye Wade, received eight times the vote of the other three opposition candidates combined. It was clear that the PDS was singular in its organizational vigor and ability to challenge the ruling party. Because of this strength, the PDS played a leading role in defining the debate on the future of Senegalese *démocratie* through the 1980s. It persuasively disputed the legality of an arguably biased and flawed electoral system and requested reforms that appeared quite reasonable.

Among the more important reforms sought by the PDS were a series of measures intended to make electoral fraud more difficult: an independent electoral commission to replace the Ministry of the Interior in handling the administration of elections, publication of returns for each polling station (rather than for the whole department) to make verification of the results possible, the right of parties to name representatives to each polling station, and a requirement that all electors show identification before being allowed to vote. In addition, the PDS pushed to extend voting rights to citizens between the ages of eighteen and twenty-one and to those living abroad. The PDS believed it had strong support among both groups and that these citizens had been excluded in order to guarantee an electoral advantage for the ruling party. Another reform called for by the PDS was equal access to the state media. In the 1983 elections, PS legislative candidates received as much airtime as all the opposition candidates combined. The PDS also pressed for the right to form coalitions between parties that wish to present a common list of candidates. Laws prohibiting such coalitions, it argued, prevented the opposition from presenting a serious, unified challenge on election day. The PDS called, finally, for a return to secret voting. (After 1976 the use of private voting booths had become optional, allowing the PS to apply coercive pressure on voters) (Parti Démocratique Sénégalais 1986a).

By presenting a seemingly fair and reasonable reform project, the PDS compelled the leaders of the PS to articulate a defense of the electoral system put in place by Senghor and Diouf. This defense addressed the PDS's claims point by point. PS leaders argued, for instance, that the prohibition of coalitions served to prevent any "instability" and "insecurity" that might result from a shaky governing coalition. As for the optional use of voting booths, this practice ensured each voter's liberty of free expression and, moreover, conformed to traditional practices of public voting. They also contended that requiring voters to produce identification would lower voter turnout, and waste time at the polling stations. To the ruling party, in short, the electoral code was eminently fair and democratic (Parti Socialiste du Sénégal, Ecole du Parti 1987).

The dispute between the PS and opposition reached a climax in 1988. In presidential elections held in February, Abdou Diouf was declared a winner despite widespread allegations of fraud and irregularity. Opposition parties banded together to contest the results, and urban rioting broke out. The government responded by jailing several opposition leaders and declaring a state of emergency that lasted for months.

These events forced the president to reappraise the electoral code. He eventually concluded that future social peace hinged upon consensually achieved reform. Thus in 1991 he announced the creation of a commission to draft a new code. The commission, composed of representatives of each party and a magistrate, negotiated and approved the new code within a year. This code integrated many of the reforms put forward by the PDS and other opposition parties, including restoration of the obligatory use of voting booths, mandatory voter identification, reduction of the voting age to eighteen, and legalization of party coalitions. Most important, the new code gave each political party the right to supervise, monitor, and participate at various stages of the electoral process.

The presidential election of February 21, 1993, was the first to take place after the promulgation of the new code. Almost 1.3 million voters went to the polls to choose among eight presidential candidates. The leading contenders were the incumbent, Abdou Diouf and Diouf's longtime adversary Abdoulaye Wade. Except for a few violent incidents in the region of Ziguinchor, election day was calm. Announcement of the results, however, was delayed by sharp disagreements among members of the Commission Nationale de Recensement des Votes (CNRV), a body composed of representatives of all candidates and a magistrate from the Court of Appeals. Representatives of opposition party candidates called for the annulment of results issuing from several of Senegal's thirty-one departments,[5] alleging fraudulent use of special voting "ordinances" by PS supporters. After two weeks of deadlock, the CNRV passed its responsibilities on to the Constitutional Council, the final arbiter of electoral disputes. On March 13 the council declared Abdou Diouf the winner with 58 percent of the vote; Abdoulaye Wade came in second with 32 percent. Many supporters of Wade and other opposition candidates, concentrated in Senegal's largest urban areas of Dakar and Pikine, contested the validity of these figures and in the days that followed expressed their frustration in acts of violent protest and vandalism. To the dismay of Abdou Diouf, the new code failed to restore the confidence of many disaffected urban dwellers in the integrity of the electoral process.

Another major initiative undertaken by Diouf in response to the 1988 crisis was the inclusion of various opposition parties in a series of government coalitions, starting in 1991. Participating parties praised these coalitions as a breakthrough for Senegalese *démocratie*. Among excluded parties and independent-minded intellectuals, however, this development caused apprehension. They feared that it would diminish the role of the electorate in public life by transforming elections into simple gauges of party strength to be used by leaders in backroom negotiations over power and privilege.

Through the 1980s and into the early 1990s, then, the major debates concerning *démocratie* centered on the scale of electoral fraud, reform of electoral rules, and the impact of governance by coalition. To the opposition, the overarching issue has been the unfairness of an electoral system created and operated

---

[5] Senegal is divided administratively into ten regions, each of which is composed of three departments. For the purposes of these elections, the city of St-Louis was separated from the department of Dagana and designated a "fictive department," bringing the total number of departments to thirty-one.

by the ruling party. To them, the only real proof of electoral fairness would be the removal of the ruling party through the ballot box. The definitive prerequisite of movement towards true *démocratie* would thus be party turnover or, as it has come to be called in Senegal, *alternance*. In speaking about the "defects of Senegalese *démocratie*," Abdoulaye Bathily, the secretary-general of the Ligue Démocratique/Mouvement pour le Parti du Travail (LD/MPT), said in 1992 that "the institutions, as they are now, exclude all possibility of political *alternance*. The same party has been in power since independence. As long as we don't have free and transparent elections . . . Senegalese *démocratie* will remain an illusion" (*Jeune Afrique,* July 30–August 5, 1992). One leader of the PDS, Fara Ndiaye, put it more succinctly in a radio and television broadcast during the electoral campaign of February 1983: "Without democratic *alternance* there is no *démocratie*" ("Campagne électorale 1983" 1991, 125). For the opposition, then, *démocratie* requires not only free elections but party turnover as well.

It follows that members of the opposition and other critics of the government view Senegal as a laggard in *démocratie,* surpassed in 1991 by Cape Verde, Benin, and Zambia, each of which saw electoral victories by the opposition. The experience of these other countries is, as one journalist put it, "the most explosive proof that *alternance* is not a utopian dream in Africa" (*Le Cafard Libéré,* January 16, 1991). If *alternance* is the measure of *démocratie,* then Senegal is clearly not a front-runner. As one Senegalese commentator remarked, "African countries until now reputed to be backward are providing superb lessons, threatening to relegate Senegal to the last rank of idlers" (*Wal Fadjri,* March 29, 1991). To certain critics, Senegal not only lags behind its African neighbors, it has also regressed vis-à-vis its own past democratic achievements. Abdoulaye Wade, for instance, wrote in 1986 that "contrary to other African countries, Senegal has practiced multiparty rule and liberty of press for over a century and a half. . . . That is why the present situation, for the Senegalese people, constitutes a movement backwards in relation to its own democratic traditions" (Parti Démocratique Sénégalais 1986b; see also Wade 1987, 14). Whether the reference point is its own historical performance or the accomplishments of other African countries, to would-be reformers, Senegalese *démocratie* is in a dark state of stagnation or regression.

The ruling party, not surprisingly, sees the situation in rosier hues. For the PS, Senegalese *démocratie* is a path-breaking achievement, a model to be emulated by other African countries. One PS journalist, for instance, wrote that the introduction of multiparty rule in 1974 "is today an uncircumventable historical reference point on the continental atlas" (*L'Unité pour le Socialisme,* March 1991). Other PS leaders have called Senegalese *démocratie* a "beacon" and a "unique experiment" (*Ndab Li,* April 1991) that has allowed the country "to have played, from the point of view of *démocratie,* a pioneering role" (*L'Unité pour le Socialisme,* March 1991). One PS cadre went so far as to write that Senegal today serves as the shining example of *démocratie,* "a role formerly filled by Athens and Greece, where *démocratie* was born" (*L'Unité pour le Socialisme,* April 1991).

To make such claims, of course, leaders of the PS have had to be somewhat vague about what they mean by *démocratie.* One thing it seems not to entail is routine *alternance.* Or, in the opaque wording of one PS leader: "*alternance* must not come to signify automaticity" (Famara Ibrihima Sagna quoted in *Le Démocrate,* July 1985). Yet in a country that has never seen party turnover, the distinction between periodic *alternance* and the principle of *alternance* has no practical significance. By attacking "automaticity" the PS is maligning *alternance* as a criterion of democratic governance. The idea of *démocratie* propagated by PS intellectuals has thus come to represent a form of truncated multipartyism in which party leaders are allowed to trumpet their programs and agendas but not to displace the ruling party. This understanding is not, it should be noted, static. PS leaders have deftly adjusted it to meet changing needs. When the PS brought opposition parties into "governments of national unity" in 1991, 1993, and 1995, these same leaders argued that there are means other than *alternance* to provide political parties access to political power, namely by integrating them into government coalitions. It is above all for this achievement that they feel justified in calling Senegalese *démocratie* an exemplary, albeit unfinished, model.

Current debates about the meaning of *démocratie,* then, are grounded in political struggles between a hegemonic party seeking to legitimize its long rule and an opposition striving to discredit it. Various factions of the political elite can agree that Senegalese *démocratie* is "under construction" yet disagree sharply about how to proceed. Whereas opposition leaders see a pressing necessity for fairer electoral competition and consider *alternance* a means to renovate a shaky edifice, PS officials have proposed governance by coalition as one way to build on the already solid foundations of *démocratie.*

## Channels of Dissemination

Debates over *alternance,* multipartyism, and governance by coalition are shaped primarily by party leaders, who are for the most part university educated. These leaders have much at stake in how the broader population comes to understand *démocratie.* It would be hard for the incumbent party to justify its continued rule should the electorate come to embrace *alternance* as a central component of *démocratie.* Opposition parties, alternatively, have a compelling interest in broadening the people's understanding of *démocratie* beyond notions of truncated multipartyism. For this reason, political parties expend great amounts of energy disseminating their particular views. To gauge how effective these efforts are, it is important to examine exactly how ideas of *démocratie* are disseminated to the wider population. What are the channels of diffusion and whom do they reach? Four important ones are the education system, print media, the airwaves, and political meetings.[6]

### The Education System

The formal public education system affords the ruling party an opportunity to propagate ideas advantageous to its continued power. Political education in the Senegalese school system takes place principally in civic education classes at both the primary and secondary levels. Not many children, however, are exposed to this education. Although primary school education is compulsory, most children do not attend classes: fewer than half of all seven-year-olds have enrolled annually in educational institutions in recent years (UNESCO 1991, 23). The children that do enroll come overwhelmingly from urban areas (République du Sénégal, Ministère de l'Education Nationale 1990, 3).

Enrollment rates in secondary schools are even lower. Only about 30 percent of thirteen-year-olds are enrolled in any given year; for fifteen-year-olds it is a mere 2 percent (UNESCO 1991, 23). These depressed rates explain the overall low number of Senegalese who have a post–primary school education—fewer than 500,000 in 1988, more than half of whom lived in the region of Dakar, and 85 percent of whom lived in urban areas (République du Sénégal, Ministère de l'Economie et des Finances 1990, table 4.04). As a percentage of the total adult population, a best estimate is that only about 9 percent of the country's 2.9 million people aged twenty or older have more than a primary school education (ibid., tables 1.03, 4.04; République du Sénégal, Ministère de l'Education Nationale 1990, 3, 5). These figures suggest that those citizens who received political education in civics classes are few and concentrated in Dakar and other urban centers.

### The Print Media

The vying factions of the political elite have at their disposal today other channels to disseminate their particular views of *démocratie*. The French-language print media afford one of them. Both the ruling and opposition parties publish an array of organs and journals. Also important are several privately owned newspapers without formal ties to any political party.

The impact of these publications is, nevertheless, constrained by a weak distribution system. The Agence de Distribution de Presse (ADP) maintains a virtual monopoly over the distribution of most publications, and it does not distribute papers widely outside of Dakar and its satellite city, Pikine (Diouf 1987, 529; Pagès 1991, 79). These two cities together account for over one hundred

---

[6] A more detailed discussion of these channels can be found in Schaffer 1994, 96–118.

distribution points, while the next largest city in Senegal, Thiès, has only three. As a result, most papers are sold in the Dakar region. The state-owned daily *Le Soleil,* for example, sells 75 percent of its papers in the capital city, despite the fact that fewer than 20 percent of the country's population live there. For independent newspapers and party organs, the percentage sold in Dakar is even larger (interview with Diarra Cissé, ADP sales manager, March 1993).

One reason for this restricted distribution is weak demand. Few people outside the Dakar region possess the French-language skills necessary to read the papers. It makes little economic sense for ADP to maintain a far-reaching distribution network to cover the almost 200,000 square kilometers of the country when most people capable of reading a French-language paper are clustered in an area of 550 square kilometers.

Even in this small area, sales are concentrated in places where bureaucrats, business people, and managers work and live (Gontier 1981, 65–70). It is this segment of the population that possesses not only the linguistic skills needed to read the papers but also the money to buy them. Indeed, demand is quite price-sensitive in Senegal: when the selling price of *Le Soleil* increased a few years ago from 100 to 150 CFA francs (from about 33 cents to 55 cents), circulation dropped by about 30 percent. Cost as well as literacy limits demand.[7]

While the problem of cost cannot be eliminated easily, political parties, government agencies, and independent publishers have made sporadic attempts to overcome the barriers posed by high rates of French language illiteracy by publishing journals, pamphlets, and newspapers in Wolof, a language understood by at least 70 percent of the population. Most of these publications are written in Wolof transcribed with the Roman alphabet. Yet only an infinitesimal percentage of the population possesses the literacy skills necessary to read them. Of the 3.9 million people who are unschooled in French, fewer than 5 percent can read and write any of the six national languages (République du Sénégal, Ministère de l'Economie et des Finances 1990, table 4.07). The literacy rate in Wolof is lower still.

If knowledge of the French alphabet is rare among non-French speakers, such is not the case with the Arabic script. Since it is common practice for Muslim parents to send their children to Koranic schools for religious instruction, many children learn to read and write Arabic characters, and some even learn the Arabic language itself. About a quarter million people unschooled in French are today literate in Arabic (ibid., table 4.07). The number of people who can read Arabic characters is probably much higher. Two political parties, the PDS and the RND, have attempted to capitalize on this situation by printing all or

---

[7] The CFA franc (franc of the Communauté Financière Africaine) is the currency of fourteen African states, most of them francophone. It is tied to the French franc. Before 1994, 1 French franc equaled 50 CFA francs. After the 1994 devaluation, 1 French franc equaled 100 CFA francs. The U.S. dollar amounts provided here reflect the exchange rate before devaluation.

part of their organs in Wolofal—Wolof written with Arabic characters. The publication of such materials has, however, been sparse and intermittent.

To sum up, the print media generally reach only people who can read French, who have the money to buy the relatively expensive publications, and who live or work close to where the journals are sold. Those who lack the money or literacy skills, or who live far from a distribution center, are shut out. Attempts to reach a wider audience through publication in Wolof and Wolofal have been largely unsuccessful, since such publications appear infrequently and reach only a small fraction of the uneducated population.

### The Airwaves

Radio and television have the potential to reach a far wider audience than the print media. Census takers in 1988 found that more than one of every ten Senegalese households owns a television set and seven of every ten a radio (ibid., table 7.06).

Until 1991 the state-run agency L'Office de Radiodiffusion et Télévision du Sénégal (ORTS) maintained a near monopoly over the domestic airwaves. It operates several regional radio stations and two channels at the national level: the "international" channel, which broadcasts exclusively in French, and the "national" channel, which broadcasts in local languages, mostly Wolof. ORTS also operates a television channel—until recently it was the only one. Its programming is mostly in French, with some shows in Wolof and other indigenous languages.

The state-run media have not, it should be noted, treated political parties evenhandedly. Opposition parties have open access only during the official two- or three-week period of the electoral campaign that precedes presidential and legislative elections, as mandated by the electoral code. Yet even during this period, legislative candidates of the ruling party received as much airtime as all the opposition party candidates combined. However limited, this airtime has been essential to parties otherwise denied full access to the state media. The few weeks of nightly broadcasts that precede every election have provided the best way for small, organizationally weak parties to reach a wide audience.

In 1991 the government instituted a series of reforms aimed at liberalizing the state media, reforms that were themselves part of the ruling party's larger goal of strengthening its legitimacy in the wake of its bitterly contested victory in 1988. First, the president created a commission empowered to watch over the electronic state media; the commission's task was to safeguard impartiality and pluralism in news reporting and to ensure equal access of political parties to radio and television. Second, the government transformed ORTS from a state-owned public enterprise into a financially autonomous "national company," renamed Radiodiffusion Télévision Sénégalaise (RTS). Finally, the government exposed the newly reorganized RTS to competition.

For a variety of reasons these three governmental actions had limited effect, at least through 1993. Political parties remained shut out of the state media, with the notable exception of airtime during the official electoral campaign periods. Furthermore, the source and content of political information accessible to the non-francophone majority remained restricted to the Wolof and other national-language programming of the PS-dominated national channel and RTS television.[8]

## Political Rallies and Party Congresses

Politicians campaign aggressively for several weeks before elections. Much of the campaigning takes place at political rallies—formal public meetings that mix the drumming, dancing, and praise singing of griots with the speechmaking of candidates, party leaders, religious dignitaries, and local officials. These speakers usually combine in their speeches French, Wolof, and the mixture of French and Wolof known as Dakar Wolof.[9]

Rallies in regional centers attract anywhere from a few hundred to a few hundred thousand people. To reach a wider audience, political parties often record speeches given at these gatherings and disseminate cassette copies to party activists and supporters. Political parties also hold regional and national congresses attended by party notables, cadres, and activists. Many parties conduct these meetings in French, although some parties, such as the Parti pour la Libération du Peuple (PLP), which advocates the use of Wolof as the language of public discourse, conduct many congresses in this native language.

## French Speakers, *Démocratie,* and *Demokaraasi*

This survey of communication channels shows that the population of Senegal is bifurcated in terms of access to the messages disseminated by the political elite. The francophone, mostly urban minority has access to rich and varied sources of information on politics and *démocratie.* For those Senegalese who do

[8] In a potentially significant development, several domestic private radio stations—such as Sud FM, Dunya FM, and Radio Nostalgie—went on the air in 1994 and 1995. I cannot assess the effects of this new competition since I conducted my last interviews in 1993.

[9] Such language alternation allows political leaders to be understood by an audience of varied linguistic competence. It also sends messages about the speaker's identity and social distance from the people assembled (Scotton 1988, 1990). Nevertheless, political leaders do not always realize the extent of their language mixing and switching. Abdoulaye Wade, who more frequently than any other political leader of national stature delivers his speeches in Dakar Wolof, told a researcher (Swigart 1994, 185): "I don't like to mix Wolof and French. . . . I think it is a bad practice. That is why, in my campaign speeches, I used either one language or the other. It is preferable to speak either pure French or pure Wolof. Only in that way will young people be encouraged to keep Wolof and other Senegalese languages free of outside influences."

not understand French well, the flow of information follows considerably narrower channels.

Does this bifurcation affect the way different segments of the population understand *démocratie* and *demokaraasi*? To get a sense for how members of the francophone bilingual and multilingual fraction of the population use and understand these terms, I interviewed twenty-two Senegalese who had attained at least nine years of schooling.[10] The interviews were open-ended and conducted in both Wolof and French.

Several people spoke of *démocratie* and *demokaraasi* as the freedom to form political associations and express opinions and grievances, views that echoed arguments advanced by the governing party. A thirty-seven-year-old woman who owned and operated a preschool in Dakar, had never voted, and did not belong to a political party remarked in French that she believed there was *démocratie* in Senegal because "Abdou Diouf has allowed many political parties to be formed—there are now seventeen." She later added in Wolof that to her, *demokaraasi* meant "to be free to say whatever you want, according to your conviction." An unemployed thirty-year-old who professed attachment to the PLP but had never voted stated in Wolof that "*demokaraasi* is liberty of expression, to say your opinion without denigrating others." A fifty-one-year-old library archivist employed by the PS explained in French that "*démocratie* means letting people express themselves in speech and in writing, letting them say what they want and what is bothering them." Other people spoke of *démocratie* and *demokaraasi* in terms that paralleled the views of the opposition, emphasizing the centrality of *alternance*. Typical was the statement of a sixty-five-year-old retired industrial worker who had supported the PDS for over ten years. He explained in French that "*démocratie* is coming slowly, but it is not quite here yet. It doesn't work the way it should yet because those who rule today haven't allowed other parties to take their place. If they did, then there would be *démocratie*."

It thus appears that members of this educated segment of the population use both the French and Wolof terms in roughly similar ways. Furthermore, it seems that their views of *démocratie* and *demokaraasi* reflect loosely elite ideas reported in the French-language media. Of the twenty-two people interviewed, only four discussed *demokaraasi* or *démocratie* in ways that did not reflect elite understandings (their responses will be discussed in the next chapter).

Most Senegalese, however, are cut off from the views of *démocratie* presented in the French language. Their understanding of this concept is conditioned by

---

[10] Nine years of education corresponds to the fourth level of the first cycle of secondary education. It is at this level that students in public schools learn about *démocratie,* the operation of Senegal's electoral system, and the vocabulary of politics (Thiam, Pflieger, and Faye 1980). Most Senegalese students, it should be recalled, must learn not only how to write but a new language and lexicon as well.

the Wolof-language speeches given at meetings and rallies, heard on cassettes, or broadcast on radio and television. What picture of *demokaraasi* do political leaders paint in these Wolof speeches, and does it differ from views presented in French?

## From *Démocratie* to *Demokaraasi*

The messages that get disseminated most widely and most frequently are those propagated by leaders of the PS, who enjoy easy and wide access to the broadcast media. We will examine these messages and then attend to the opposition's.

### Images from the PS: Muezzin and Imam

In Wolof broadcasts, representatives of the PS usually associate *demokaraasi* with the liberty of political parties to organize freely and to express their grievances openly. As one PS candidate for the National Assembly phrased it during a Wolof speech broadcast on radio and television during the 1988 legislative electoral campaign: "There is *demokaraasi* here thanks to Abdou Diouf; he is the one who brought us seventeen political parties. Thanks to Abdou Diouf *demokaraasi* has flourished to the point that everyone can do what they want or say what they want without fear" (Abdoulaye Niane, February 25, 1988).

Daouda Sow, a member of the PS Bureau Politique in 1988 and a deputy to the National Assembly, made a similar point during a rally also broadcast across the country. He excoriated opposition leaders for failing to understand what *demokaraasi* is all about:

> There are those who say that there is no *demokaraasi* in Senegal. But if there weren't, we wouldn't have seventeen political parties. You know, as Abdou Diouf said, "the mosque is there; whoever chooses to do so may call his faithful to pray." Today there may be many calls, but only one is compelling. If they tell us that *demokaraasi* doesn't exist, I think it's because they don't know what *demokaraasi* is. If there were no *demokaraasi,* Abdou Diouf wouldn't have agreed to compete against three or four other candidates. I believe that even by European standards, there could not be more *demokaraasi* than we have now. So anyone who says there is no *demokaraasi* in Senegal is just speaking blather. You know there is *demokaraasi* here. (Radio and television broadcast, legislative electoral campaign, February 9, 1988)

The reference to Diouf's statement is worth examining, for the connection it makes between *demokaraasi* and mosque not only is evocative but reflects a theme to which the president, his lieutenants, and regional PS leaders returned repeatedly during both the 1988 and 1993 electoral campaigns. One local candidate from the city of Kaolack, for instance, told a crowd: "Abdu Juuf [Abdou Diouf] is the one who opened up the mosque. Now, whoever wants to give the call to prayer can do so. Diouf's the one who gave us democracy [*demokaraasi*]. Now, take a good look and choose the person who pleases you" (quoted in Heath 1990, 217).

The mosque, according to this metaphor, is the locus of electoral competition. Political leaders are muezzins; their programs are calls to prayer; and voters are the faithful. The competition between muezzins is *demokaraasi*.

The function of the muezzin in Islam is to announce the hours of the five daily prayers and to call the congregation to the special Friday-afternoon prayer. In Senegalese Islam, a muezzin need have no special qualifications beyond the ability to learn the calls, and there are no standard procedures for choosing or appointing him. Rarely is there open competition for the position; anyone who wishes to call may do so, as long as he has adequately learned the calls. Any given mosque may have several muezzins who rotate their responsibilities. As it happens, the muezzin often belongs to the mildly disdained caste of praise singers, the *géwél*. In the organization of Islam, the muezzin does not enjoy a particularly weighty moral authority. In the mosque it is the imam who leads the prayer, and outside the mosque spiritual leadership is provided by the leaders of Senegal's religious brotherhoods.

Why did Diouf choose this metaphor for explaining *demokaraasi* to the country's Wolof speakers? One reason is that it draws on an image rooted in Senegalese culture. By saying that *demokaraasi* is analogous to what goes on in a mosque, Diouf is attempting to ground this French import in meanings generated out of everyday life. The metaphor thus inaugurates a fresh way of looking at politics by inviting people to reflect on the familiar.

On another level, Diouf is engaging in a battle to define the concept in a way beneficial to his party; he seeks to convey the idea that *demokaraasi* involves only the freedom to express oneself and to organize political parties. The muezzin stands atop the minaret to summon the faithful to prayer in the same way that the political leader beckons to potential voters. Both call out their message and wait for believers to appear. The equation is simple and powerful.

The image of the mosque also grounds *demokaraasi* in the legitimacy of Islam. By appropriating the language of Islam, it wraps the profane realm of politics in the sacred mantle of religion. That political leaders seek to borrow religious symbols to bolster their own claim to legitimacy is hardly new in Senegal. For centuries Wolof *buur* (roughly, kings) presented themselves as sacred beings. It should be added, however, that political and religious symbols of authority are rarely isolable in Senegal, since the two have influenced each other. The ways devout religious disciples today show obedience to religious authority—by kneeling, showering themselves with dust, and remaining stooped over in submission—are borrowed from the manner in which subjects showed deference to Wolof *buur* in years gone by (Cruise O'Brien 1971, 15, 17, 105, 136). Religious leaders also borrowed from French colonial rulers, patterning their own title *khalife-général* after the title of the French *gouverneur-général* (122). The appropriation of the image of the mosque might best be seen, then, as a novel attempt to tap old sources of legitimacy.

The mosque metaphor is all the more attractive to Diouf because it pushes the issue of *alternance* to the background. Absent from this metaphor is any reference to power or authority. The job of the muezzin is simply to call. It is the imam who leads the prayer, and it is the leaders of the Islamic brotherhoods who are the true moral leaders of the religious community. By equating political leaders with muezzins, Sow sidesteps—as does Diouf—the fact that presidential candidates do not merely woo supporters but aspire to rule the country. The metaphor of the muezzin thus hides the issue of governance. The mosque has many muezzins. The powerful voice of one does not preclude the calls of others. *Demokaraasi,* according to this metaphor, is limited to efforts to attract supporters. The metaphor breaks down when one tries to imagine one of the muezzins as a president who not only calls but governs.

The mosque metaphor thus obscures the issue of *alternance.* If a mosque can have several muezzins at a time, why cannot Senegalese *demokaraasi* accommodate several presidents at a time? Why must voters choose only one? Why cannot three or four presidents govern at the same time? The logic may seem stretched, but it is not an altogether inconceivable extension of the metaphor. In fact, one Senegalese cartoonist, known as an acute social observer, poked fun at people who think in just this way. His cartoon strip follows the travails of a character named Goorgoorlu, or Try-to-do-well, a usually unemployed *dakarois* who flounders comically and tragically in his day-to-day efforts to provide for his wife and children. In one strip, after Goorgoorlu and his friend Tapha watch the four candidates in the 1988 presidential elections make their campaign promises on television, Tapha asks Goorgoorlu if he knows who he is going to vote for. Goorgoorlu declares: "Of course! For Savané, who promises me work; for Mbaye Niang for education in national languages for my children; for Diouf, who guarantees me *demokaraasi*; and for Ablaye, who promises me rice and fish every day. I'm no longer undecided. I'll vote for all four."[11] When Tapha tries to explain that he cannot vote for all four, Goorgoorlu rebuts with both defiance and earnestness: "Why not? We have a *demokaraasi,* no?" (*Le Cafard Libéré,* February 13 and 20, 1988). Although the mosque metaphor does not appear in the cartoon, by muting the issue of *alternance* it may be giving rise to understandings of *demokaraasi* not altogether intended.

[11] Goorgoorlu is calling the candidates by their familiar names. Savané is Landing Savané, secretary general of And-Jëf/Mouvement Révolutionnaire pour la Démocratie Nouvelle (AJ/MRDN). Mbaye Niang is Babacar Niang, secretary general of the PLP. Diouf is President Abdou Diouf. Ablaye is Abdoulaye Wade of the PDS.

Perhaps aware of these difficulties, Diouf rearranged the metaphor when he returned to it in the 1993 electoral campaign. The new formulation moves the issue of leadership squarely to the center. He explained in Wolof: "I want the country to have *demokaraasi*. . . . Here is the mosque; anyone who wants to call people to prayer may do so. But if there are many muezzins, there can be only one imam" (radio and television broadcast, presidential electoral campaign, February 6, 1993). In this revised version, the muezzins are presidential candidates and the president is the imam, the member of the religious community who *leads* the prayer. Both an imam and a president are classified by Wolof speakers as belonging to a category of leaders known as *njiit*. A brief examination of this category will illuminate the nuances Diouf conveyed to Wolof speakers by equating president and imam.

The term *njiit* shares with the verbs *jiite* (to lead or govern), *jiital* (to put first, to choose a leader), and *jiitu* (to go in front) the sense of being in front or leading. The prototypical example of *njiit* is the imam who stands in front of the faithful assembled at a mosque to lead them in prayer. The Arabic term *imām,* not coincidentally, derives from a root that means "in front of" (Lewis 1988, 31–32). *Njiit* are people whose duty it is to lead or to guide. Additionally, *njiit* should be people who are *put* in front by the community. *Njiit* refers to leaders who are chosen by those they lead, and claim a moral right to lead because they have been chosen. Thus the president, who is chosen by the electorate, is also a *njiit*.

*Njiit* can be counterposed to another class of leaders known as *kilifa*. *Kilifa* comes from the Arabic word *khalīfa*. Deriving from a root signifying "to come after" or "instead of," the Arabic term dates to at least the sixth century A.D. At that time it combined ideas of succeeding or replacing; and it meant something like "deputy" or "viceroy" in pre-Islamic Arabia. Upon the death of Muhammad in 632, Abu Bakr, the prophet's companion, assumed leadership of the community. He became known as *khalīfat rasūl Allah* (deputy of the prophet of God), thus beginning a long tradition of bestowing the title *khalīfa* on the leader of the Muslim community and establishing the institution of the caliphate. With the decline of the caliphate in the thirteenth century, various Muslim princes appropriated the title for themselves and the term came to mean little more than "Muslim king" or "sovereign" (Margoliouth 1922; Sourdel et al. 1978; Lewis 1988, 43–50).

By this time, Islamic beliefs and practices had begun to spread south of the Sahara Desert, carried by Berber merchants plying trans-Saharan trade routes (Trimingham 1962, 20–33, 40–47). Islam had already reached the Wolof by the mid-fifteenth century, when the Venetian navigator Alvise de Ca da Mosto, sailing under the Portuguese flag, reported that Wolof *buur,* and to a lesser extent the common people, professed attachment to the faith. Despite the long presence of Islam among the Wolof, the term *kilifa* did not appear in any written description of the Wolof language until the early nineteenth century, although it probably entered the language much earlier.[12]

In Wolof usage, *kilifa* has come to refer to any hereditary or customary leader who holds his position through ascriptive criteria. Typical *kilifa* are the leaders of the charismatic Islamic brotherhoods (*kilifa diine*), leaders who are direct descendants of the brotherhood founders or their most loyal followers. By extension Wolofones also use *kilifa* as an honorific term for older men, heads of households, husbands, and fathers. A *kilifa* is a leader who has moral authority by virtue of age, heredity, custom, and gender; whereas *njiit* refers to any leader who is chosen or placed in front. Thus *njiitu diine* refers to those lower-level religious leaders (such as the imams) who are usually chosen by the community, whereas *kilifa diine* refers to the highest order of religious leaders who descend from the brotherhood founders. For many Wolof speakers, there is no question that *kilifa* enjoy a higher moral authority. As one proverb puts it, "Running up front does not measure up to being a *kilifa*."[13] Because *kilifa* enjoy a more weighty moral authority, they are able to command (*yilif*), whereas *njiit* can only guide (*jiite*).

In this context, it is worth noting two derivatives of *kilifa*: *muskallàf mi* denotes a serious, responsible person, and *kàllafe* means to give the impression of being such a person. Linguists included in a recent Wolof-French dictionary the following phrase to illustrate the meaning of *kàllafe*, an example that highlights the heavier moral weight associated with *kilifa* and its derivatives: "*Seen njiit li kàllafewul dara*"—which means "your *njiit* is not at all *kàllafe*," or "your guide does not seem at all responsible" (Fal, Santos, and Doneux 1990, 106). It would not, in contrast, make sense to say "your *kilifa* is not at all *kàllafe*." A *kilifa* is, by virtue of his ascriptive position, considered a serious personage; a *njiit* must demonstrate seriousness by his or her actions.

Now we can see the implications of Diouf's equation of the president with an imam. By making this connection, Diouf is reinforcing the idea that both are *njiit,* a category situated between muezzin and *kilifa*. Unlike the muezzin, the *njiit* assumes important leadership responsibilities in the community. Practically anyone can become a muezzin; one must meet higher standards to become an imam, for a mosque has only one. By drawing a parallel between imam and president, then, President Diouf is attempting to put himself in a class above the other presidential candidates qua muezzins. And unlike a *kilifa*, the *njiit* is chosen by the community on the basis of actions and character. The

---

[12] The term had already penetrated the Niger River basin by the mid–thirteenth century. According to the medieval Arab historian Ibn Khaldun, Soundiata, the founder of the Mali empire, named his fourth son Khalifa. Khalifa himself ruled the empire from 1274 to 1275 (Trimingham 1962, 235–36).

[13] In Wolof: "Daw jiitu du mate kilifa" (Dard 1826, 136; Kobès 1869, 276).

president qua *njiit* is placed in front of the nation by the electorate and does not enjoy the automatic allegiance, respect, and affection of the *kilifa*. The introduction of the imam into the mosque metaphor thus injects into *demokaraasi* notions of character, singular leadership, and community choice.

The insertion of the imam into the mosque metaphor clears up some of the complexities that would lead a voter (such as Goorgoorlu) to want to vote for three or four candidates. In the mosque there can be only one imam; in *demokaraasi* there can be only one president. The introduction of the imam, however, cloaks the idea of *alternance* in another way. Simply stated, muezzins do not in practice become imams. Their powerful voices may bring new worshipers to the mosque, but their caste status generally precludes them from becoming *njiit*. Thus electoral competition may pit candidate against candidate; but the position of the president remains unaffected. *Demokaraasi,* in this formulation, licenses Diouf to remain president for an indeterminate period.

The overlapping of religious and political themes takes on added significance in this context. Already within Senegalese Islamic culture there is widespread belief that it is God who ultimately chooses the world's mortal leaders. This idea is expressed in an oft-cited Wolof proverb: "It is better to throw more wood on a fire lit by God than to put it out."[14] The implied message is that since it is God who put the leader in power (lit the fire), humans should not attempt to remove him (put out the fire).

The PS has attempted to tailor this notion to its own uses. During the 1988 electoral campaign, calendars appeared with a picture of Abdou Diouf and a Wolof caption: "President Abdou Diouf: The President That God Gave Us." The tactic appears to have worked on at least some voters. One old woman explained that "I had to vote for Abdou Diouf because God placed him here."

Bassirou Diagne, the *grand serigne* of Dakar,[15] directly linked *demokaraasi* to the idea of divine sanction for Diouf's presidency in a Wolof speech during the 1988 electoral campaign:

The *demokaraasi* we have here does not exist in many other countries; everywhere people are grasping for it. Yet in our own country there are those in the opposition who do not want it because they did not help build it. If *demokaraasi* could break out of its shackles, it would save Africa because in many African countries they do not accept multipartyism; they have only one party. Thus if Abdou Diouf accepts other parties, you should help him by acting with respect and restraint so that *demokaraasi* can bring peace here. Even in France, to be a candidate for the presi-

[14] In Wolof: "Taal bu yalla taal, sanni ci matt moo gënn fey ko."

[15] The *grand serigne* (great marabout) of Dakar is the leader of the Lebou community. The Lebou are a Wolof-speaking ethnic group that migrated in the eighteenth century to the Cap Vert peninsula, an area that corresponds to today's region of Dakar. Abdou Diouf played an important role in having Bassirou Diagne named to the position in 1986. Diagne, in return, has been a staunch supporter of the president.

dency you need five hundred signatures, and the people who sign the petition must be notables in their communities. There, you must have credibility to become a candidate. But here in Senegal Abdou Diouf said: "Here is the mosque. Anyone who can call the faithful to prayer—let him call." So we all need to play the game democratically. Every person has the right to vote for the candidate he pleases. On election day, we will support Abdou Diouf. I ask you all to vote for him. If it were in our hands to elect [*fal*] Abdou Diouf, we would do it without even voting. But since it is God who chooses our leaders, all we can do is to cast our ballots for Abdou Diouf. . . . Let's be fair and realize that the seat of the presidency is made for only one person. And the person who should sit there will be chosen by God; let's help him. (Radio and television broadcast, presidential electoral campaign, February 25, 1988)

It is God's choice that Diouf be president. To vote for him is to act out God's will. *Demokaraasi* may entail the acceptance of opposition parties, but it also appears to involve doing God's bidding. Diagne's rendition of the mosque metaphor thus implicitly reinforces the idea that God has sanctioned Diouf's leadership and rule, and that this is an integral part of *demokaraasi*.

One final motif embedded in the mosque metaphor needs to be discussed: the image of political society as a religious community. The metaphor transforms the tangle of competing and contradictory interests that mark political society into a community of believers joined by prayer and the adoration of one God. Unlike politicians (and their supporters) who believe in differing programs and visions of how society should be organized, imams, muezzins, and the faithful are engaged in a communal experience of worship. Conflict recedes into the background. *Demokaraasi,* viewed in this light, involves communality, harmony, and reconciliation.

The mosque metaphor, then, grafts onto *demokaraasi* connotations not stressed in the view of *démocratie* presented by the PS in its French-language discourse. Onto the idea of multipartyism and freedom of expression and association get heaped layers of meaning: undertones of communality and harmony, a pastiche of religious motifs, and the diffusion of *alternance* as an issue through the promotion of an image of the president as *njiit*.

### Images from the Opposition: *Buur* and *Nguur*

The image of the mosque is not the only picture of *demokaraasi* that gets disseminated to Wolof speakers. Opposition parties try to convey a different message, one that emphasizes the centrality of rules for fair electoral competition and *alternance*. Abdoulaye Wade, for instance, emphasized the need for a strong legal framework to make *demokaraasi* work in this 1988 speech at a PDS convention:

*Demokaraasi* requires that people who live together in a country or the same household, or work together in the same office or company, have laws that each individual must respect. If each person did whatever he pleased, nobody would have his own space and nobody would stay. What we want for Senegal is this: a constitution that will be respected by whoever comes to power. We can have peace in this country. We say that the president, deputies to the National Assembly, and the prime minister should be chosen according to the laws of the country. . . . Not all laws are just laws. Which are just? The constitution of Senegal is just. It says that whoever wins a majority becomes president. Simply because Abdou Diouf writes a law doesn't mean it's just. You made me secretary general of the PDS, right? You know I can do a lot of things, but you also know there are things I don't have the right to do. Can I, right here, jump on someone and hit him, do to him what I please? If I did that, you would resist me. So if you elect me, there is a point at which I must stop. I cannot go beyond that point. The same holds true for Abdou Diouf. He has limits beyond which he should not go. He has, however, already gone beyond those limits. That is why I invoke the constitution: "He who has the majority wins." Abdou Diouf wants to bring in some of his people, his brothers, to count the ballots.[16] It would be like me taking my brother Moustapha Wade to count the ballots. Is that *demokaraasi?* He said his brother would be in charge of counting the ballots. That will not happen here in Senegal! (Speech at the Third Ordinary Congress of the PDS, Dakar, January 2–3, 1988)

*Demokaraasi* entails a respect for laws, especially those concerning the transfer of power.

The message of the opposition is, nonetheless, prone to mutation as it moves from French to Wolof. One fascinating glimpse at how meanings can be transformed is provided by a speech delivered by Landing Savané, the secretary general of AJ/MRDN. This speech was broadcast on radio and television three days before election day in February 1988. Savané delivered the first part of the speech in French, then provided a Wolof summary. Both parts are reproduced here in full:

[In French:] Dear fellow citizens, the struggle for *démocratie* is a permanent requirement of political combat. In our country it is a vital necessity. *Démocratie* is not measured simply by how many political parties exist—the fascist Chile of Pinochet has many. It is not measured simply by the presence of opposition journals—Haiti and the Philippines have many; they even have independent radio stations. *Démocratie* is most importantly the existence of state institutions above the grasp of any party. It is the acceptance of the principle of *alternance* as the manifestation of the natural evolution of societies. It is also the free expression of all the

---

[16] Several cabinet ministers at the time, including the minister of the interior (the official charged with overseeing elections), were indeed relatives or close personal friends of the president, a situation that continues to this day. See *Wal Fadjri,* April 12–18, 1991.

organized interests of society via the state-run media, which should no longer have a monopoly on communications. It is above all the existence of a dynamic counter-power. It is also the respect for the right to hold different opinions regarding ideology and policy. It is the acceptance of a critical, even radical, opposition. It is tolerance. It is the respect for the right of citizens to have access to all information concerning the normal functioning of state institutions. It is also the possibility for every citizen to elect his representative freely and to demand accountability from him. It is naturally the strict separation of temporal and religious power, and an education that helps citizens to understand better the problems of the nation.

The present electoral campaign proves that the budding fascists of the PS are far from understanding and further still from accepting these elementary principles, since some among them dare to declare that even the decrepit *démocratie* in place today is too much for our people to handle. Mr. Diouf himself made thinly veiled threats against the opposition and *démocratie* itself. Confronted with the totalitarian impulses of Diouf and his partisans, And-Jëf [AJ/MRDN] is ready to assume its responsibilities. I call on all the opposition parties, all the democrats of this country, organized or not, to rise up and block the way of this advancing fascism. If Diouf and his partisans attempt on election day to follow through with their electoral coup d'etat, then the people will have to strengthen their resistance by engaging in a massive civil disobedience campaign. The young people, the women, the men of this country can block the path of these apprentice fascists, and impose the will of the people against massive fraud, rising prices, huge cutbacks, and the unauthorized disengagement of the state.

Thousands and thousands of people have come out during the electoral campaign to voice their rejection of Diouf's regime; a regime of lies, embezzlement, mediocrity, and misery. We have to organize this general discontent. We have to organize a vast political, economic, social, and cultural resistance movement to open the way for an alternative. In the final analysis, the future of our country in these critical days is in the hands of the people. Thank you.

[In Wolof:] Fellow Senegalese, I just spoke about *demokaraasi* in Senegal. I explained how the *demokaraasi* that is in place today is an emptied *demokaraasi* because it does not give the people of Senegal any authority—something the people in the government [*waa nguur*] reserve for themselves. Anything that the people need or want to do, the government [*nguur*] prohibits if it is not in its own interest. That is why we say that this *demokaraasi* is not enough for us, and we will fight it. Those who argue that this *demokaraasi* is excessive are partisans of the PS. Their declarations show the true mentality of the party: they think they don't need to consider any opinions but their own. They want others to do what they say—something we can never accept. We are here to strengthen the authority of the people. We want to consolidate *demokaraasi*. The elections will soon be here. Abdou Diouf and his supporters are planning to fix the elections so that he can falsely declare himself the winner. We should not have to see that kind of thing. They want the farmer to pay his taxes, but they haven't done anything for him. The farmer should refuse to pay, along with everyone else, to weaken the government [*nguur*] or to make it fall.

The Wolof portion is in some ways a stripped-down version of the French speech. Retained is the central idea that the *demokaraasi* practiced by Diouf and his partisans is inadequate because it denies people a real say in government affairs. Also retained is Savané's attack on those who claim that there is too much *demokaraasi,* and his closing call for resistance. Absent are the references to Chile, Haiti, and the Philippines, totalitarianism and fascism, and the specific aspects of *démocratie* mentioned in French: media, education, and opposition parties.

Without these references, the discussion of *demokaraasi* in Wolof is in one respect uprooted from its original context. Gone are the ready-made benchmarks provided by countries and movements around the world against which the performance of Senegal's *demokaraasi* can be measured. Also gone are references to the specific institutional arrangements that make a call for *demokaraasi* concrete and imaginable. In the Wolof portion, Savané calls vaguely for increasing the authority of the people, but he does not explain what such an arrangement would require or how it would operate. Perhaps he omitted these allusions to fascism and Haiti because he reasoned they would have little meaning for the non-francophone majority of the population. (Indeed, in interviews I conducted weeks after the precedent-setting elections in the West African country of Cape Verde, few non-French-speaking Senegalese could say what took place there, despite wide coverage in the French-language media and moderate coverage in Wolof-language broadcasts).

Connotations not present in the French part of the speech ground the Wolof portion in Senegalese culture, however. Savané's choice of words here is revealing. When referring to the government, he consistently used the Wolof word *nguur,* as opposed to the universally understood French loan word *góornëmaa* (from *gouvernement*). Perhaps he made a deliberate attempt to speak a Wolof unadulterated by French loan words; this explanation is supported by the fact that Savané is not a native Wolof speaker. Having publicly acknowledged this fact on radio and television several days earlier, he may have felt compelled to express himself in relatively "pure" Wolof. The particular word choice, though, may have served other purposes. *Nguur,* unlike *góornëmaa,* carries a web of connotations that implicitly reinforce the image of a Senegalese government inimical to *demokaraasi.*

*Nguur* is a complex term that covers a semantic field significantly wider than *góornëmaa,* a term first introduced into Wolof during the colonial era to describe the machinery of modern bureaucratic government introduced by the French. Today *góornëmaa* refers rather narrowly to the institutions of government, the body of persons who occupy offices of government, or the president's cabinet.

The word *nguur* finds its origins in precolonial political institutions. It appears to derive from, and remains closely associated with, the term *buur.* Since the time of the French Revolution, European travelers, traders, and missionaries have translated *buur* as, roughly, "king" or "sovereign." In Wolof society, the *buur* were members of royal lineages who, once ascended to power, had the right to collect tribute from landowners in a given territorial unit (Diop 1981, 115–52).

The term *buur* has taken on strong evaluative connotations. Many proverbs paint a picture of the *buur* as arbitrary, cruel, and egotistic. One proverb cautions that "the *buur* is not a relative."[17] That is, the egoism of the *buur* can push him to sacrifice his closest relatives to further his self-interest (Sylla 1978, 217). Another proverb declares that "it is not bad to love a *buur,* but a *buur* that loves you is better."[18] Wolof folktales also reflect popular perceptions of the *buur.* One recounts the deeds of two brothers, Samba Satan and Amary Muslim. The pious Amary Muslim treats all he encounters with respect and courtesy, and ends up a blind beggar. Samba Satan violates every interdiction—he kills his father's horse, his mother, his newborn brother, and an old man whom he then eats—and becomes a *buur* who rules over many subjects (Kesteloot and Mbodj 1983, 88–101). To be a *buur* requires not godliness and civility but impudence and brutality.

The egoism of the *buur* pushes him to lead a life of indulgence. In popular culture, the *buur* is someone whose desires are satisfied, whose wants are fulfilled. It is perhaps for this reason that *buur* has also come to mean "to be complete or full." *Gémmiñam buur na,* for example, can be translated as "He has a full set of teeth." Literally, his mouth is complete (Fal, Santos, and Doneux 1990, 49).[19]

*Nguur* appears to derive from *buur* because in Wolof an initial consonant *b* may mark singularity while an initial consonant *g* or *ng* marks plurality, as in *bët* (eye) and *gët* (eyes). An original meaning of *nguur* may thus have been "royalty." These consonants may, however, also mark a relation of product to producer, as in *buy* (fruit of the baobab tree) and *guy* (baobab tree). In this case, *nguur* may have originally meant something like the reign established by the *buur.* Whatever the original sense or senses may have been, today *nguur* has several meanings. It can mean "reign," as in *nguurug Yalla* (the reign of God). It can also be used to mean "power"—something that can be assumed (*yor nguur*), renounced (*gedd nguur*), competed for (*xëcco nguur*), or taken by force (*foqati nguur*). And like *góornëmaa,* it can refer to the administrative machinery of government or the people who run it.

The connotations of egoism and fulfillment contained in *buur* have also colored *nguur.* In Wolof, someone who enjoys leading a comfortable lifestyle is

---

[17] In Wolof: "buur du mbokk."

[18] In Wolof: "Sopp buur aayul, wante buur bu la sopp a ko gënn" (Dard 1826, 135).

[19] Note that in this respect, *buur* is similar to the English term "king," which has been extended to imply wealth (a king's ransom), luxuriousness (king-sized bed), a lavish lifestyle (to live like a king), or pampering (to treat like a king).

said to "like *nguur*" (*bëgg nguur*). If someone is said to "like *nguur* too much," it is implied that the person is greedy.

An important cognate of *nguur* is the verb *nguuru*, which is formed by the root *nguur* and the reflexive suffix *-u*. Translators sometimes render *nguuru* with the English "to govern" or "to rule," translations that are not wholly adequate. The reflexive suffix turns the governing inward; it connotes holding power for oneself or in one's own interest. It involves not only the exercise of power but the gaining of pleasure or enjoyment from it (Diagne 1981, 42). The meaning of *nguuru* has evolved to the point where enjoyment and satisfaction have become more central to its meaning than ruling. To many Wolofones, *nguuru* means simply to be comfortable, to enjoy something, to feel good. Sitting in a nice cushy chair is *nguuru*. The sense of governing has been diluted.

Given these connections between *nguur* and pleasure or satisfaction, to say that *nguur* simply means power, government, or reign is not quite right. *Nguur* in its various uses is closely associated with egoism, contentment, and completeness. This term implies that the one who holds power benefits materially from his position. Ideas of governance flow into connotations of enjoyment and gratification. It is said that when Abdou Diouf came to power, he avoided using the term *nguur* precisely because it conjured images of contented, privileged government officials, images at odds with his public emphasis on the state as an instrument of development. It was perhaps for this reason that he told the nation repeatedly during the 1983 campaign that he was *jammu seeni soxla*, literally the "slave of their needs"; in other words, their servant.

Savané, by repeatedly referring to the Senegalese government as *nguur* in his Wolof explanation of *demokaraasi*, played on these blended notions of governance, egoism, and self-gratification. The officials of the *nguur* are portrayed as people who exercise power for their own benefit. In the words of Savané, they "reserve" power for themselves; they do not "consider any opinions but their own," and they "prohibit" what is not in their "own interest." Real, consolidated *demokaraasi*, according to Savané, implies giving people a voice in the way they are ruled, to force the *nguur* to govern in the general interest.

Yet the webs of meaning surrounding *nguur* make a different interpretation of *demokaraasi* possible, one Savané did not intend. It is possible to understand calls for *demokaraasi* in this context to mean that those in power should share the privileges that only they enjoy. *Demokaraasi* gets transformed from a redistribution of power to a redistribution of pleasure and benefit. That is, *demokaraasi* shifts from meaning that everyone should *nguuru* (rule) to meaning that everyone should experience *nguuru* (gratification). This interpretive shift is not farfetched. Consider the following statement by an elderly woman living in the poor Médina neighborhood of Dakar. When asked whether there was *demokaraasi* in Senegal, she answered: "Yes, there is *demokaraasi* here. The Socialist Party chose a local elder to be the delegate for this neighborhood. Everything he gets from the party, whether it's rice or sugar, he shares with us.

Whenever I have a family occasion, he gives me money." The essence of *demokaraasi* for this woman appears to lie not in choosing her representative to the government or in having a say in who rules the country but in enjoying the benefits this delegate brings home. *Demokaraasi* for this woman means receiving material goods.

Now consider a few lines from the 1991 hit song by Khar Mbaye Madiaga titled *Démocratie*. She sings in Wolof: "Senegal is the place to imitate when it comes to *demokaraasi*. . . . Hey, my friend Abdou [Diouf], what you swore to do not so long ago at the Palace of Justice, you haven't gone back on your word. You said, 'Whatever benefits come my way from this office that I don't share with Senegal—those are benefits I prefer not to have.'" Senegal is an exemplary *demokaraasi* because the president vowed to share the advantages of his office. *Demokaraasi* as used in this song implies that those who *nguuru* (rule) should make an effort for all to be *nguuru* (comfortable).

In the Wolof portion of his speech, then, Savané left out references to other countries and to specific institutional arrangements that would not resonate with his audience, opting instead to put the discussion of *demokaraasi* into a context that people would understand. This context was provided by *nguur*, a term grounded in popular culture. The problem inherent in this shift is that these connotations drag *démocratie* away from its originally intended meaning. That is, the attempt to link the Wolof concept *nguur* with the French concept of *démocratie* seems to have contributed unintentionally to the creation of a Wolof hybrid—*demokaraasi*.

### Images from the Opposition: *Fal* and *Folli*

Two additional terms are of particular importance to the opposition in its attempts to associate *demokaraasi* with *alternance*. These terms—*fal* and *folli*—mean roughly "to elect" and "to vote out of office," respectively.[20] For instance, Abdoulaye Bathily, the secretary general of the LD/MPT, explained during the 1988 presidential electoral campaign (radio and television broadcast, February 7) that *demokaraasi* means: "Fal naa la; defuloo lu baax, folli naa la; loolu mooy demokaraasi." One way to translate this statement is "I elected you; you didn't do anything good, so I voted you out of office; that is *demokaraasi*." At least, this is the message that Bathily intended to get across, a message that conveys the centrality of *alternance* to *demokaraasi*. The words *fal* and *folli*, however, carry connotations that render such a translation problematic and make it unlikely that many Wolof speakers comprehended his words in this way.

---

[20] *Folli* derives from the root *fal* plus the inversive suffix *-i*. Other examples include *ub/ubbi* (to close/open); *takk/tekki* (to attach/detach); and *boot/botti* (to carry on one's back/remove from one's back) (Ka 1981, 16–17).

To understand why this is so requires a brief overview of the traditional practices with which *fal* and *folli* have long been associated, practices of choosing rulers from among several pretenders, common in the precolonial Wolof states of Bawol, Jolof, Kajoor, and Waalo over long periods of their history.

In each state, eligibility for rulership was restricted by birth. Pretenders to the throne, called *lawax* in Wolof, had to descend through the paternal line from the original founder of the state and also belong to particular noble lines on the maternal side.[21] The power to select (*fal*) or depose (*folli*) rulers resided primarily in a council of men of the most important lineages. The councils— known as *waa réew mi* in Kajoor, *seb ak baawar* in Waalo, and *njenki* in Jolof— sometimes included leading members of the freeman and slave orders, although their influence does not appear to have been great.[22] Later, as the influence of Islam grew, leaders of the Muslim community were sporadically included (Diouf 1990, 61). There is some ambiguity in the historical record about the size of these councils. Several European and Wolof sources suggest that each council consisted of fewer than ten men, while others imply that the councils were larger bodies of nobles and freemen, and that the named dignitaries were simply the leading members.[23]

Deliberation by each council usually required a series of meetings. In Waalo, for instance, the selection of a ruler normally required three gatherings of the *seb ak baawar*. The first meeting was a conference of the dignitaries of the three leading noble families. A second meeting included the leading members of two other noble families. At the third and last meeting, during which the *seb ak baawar* announced its selection, the participants of the first two meetings were joined by notables from the order of royal slaves (*jaami buur*) and two tributary territories, who assumed a consultative role (Gaden 1912, 21).

The historical record suggests that these councils placed little emphasis on the formal procedures of choosing. What was important was achieving a consensus, not the protocols (raising hands, counting voices, casting ballots) that are central to Western notions of voting and electing. The historian Joseph Ki-

[21] An exception was Jolof, where there were no matrilineal requirements; it sufficed to descend from the founder of the state on the paternal side (Gaden 1912, 27). In the states of Kajoor, Jolof, and Bawol the rulers were always men. In Waalo, as Boilat noted, women sometimes ruled (1853, 284).

[22] *Waa réew mi* means "people of the country." The meaning of *njenki* is unknown. According to legend, the term *seb ak baawar* recalls the rivalrous relationship of the two sisters who founded the two principal noble families of Waalo. The first sister, Waalil, had only one daughter. Jealous of her sister Fajeng, who had many children, she called them *baawal*—"to spread all over." Believing that saying such things would bring misfortune on Fajeng, their mother called Waalil *sib*—"to scorn." *Seb ak baawar*, then, may be a deformation of *sib ak baawal*—"to spread all over and to scorn" (Gaden 1912, 20, 27; Diouf 1990, 61).

[23] Compare the descriptions of Bawol (Martin and Becker 1976, 499) and Kajoor (Bérenger-Féraud 1879, 45) with the descriptions of Kajoor (Sylla 1978, 130–31) and Waalo (Azan 1864, 335; Gaden 1912, 20).

Zerbo had this difference in mind when he remarked that in many traditional African states, including those of the Wolof, "There was not an arithmetic, formalist *démocratie* that posted the yes's and the no's in a numerical balance sheet; but a *démocratie* that lived by unending dialogue that lasted until exhaustion" (quoted in *Le Soleil*, July 2, 1985; see also Diagne 1976, 18–42; Ayittey 1990, 39–75). Whether the deliberation of the councils counts as *démocratie* is open to question; Ki-Zerbo is, nonetheless, correct to emphasize the consultative as opposed to computative nature of the process.

We must be careful, however, not to romanticize these traditional practices.[24] Conflict in the councils was often sharp, as one chronicler noted of the *seb ak baawar* in Waalo: "Circumstances often rendered discussion very stormy, because the council could not always find an heir who met the desired conditions; or it could be presented with several candidates that filled the requirements equally" (Azan 1864, 335). Moreover, when the councils failed to reach a consensus, the ultimate arbiter was force. Another observer made these remarks about the selection of rulers in Kajoor and Waalo: "It is not rare that various competitors employ violent or occult means to conquer the coveted position. And among the Wolof, as among all others, blood is often spilled in the name of this or that ambition" (Bérenger-Féraud 1879, 44). The existence of deliberative processes, then, did not always ensure the cheerful achievement of consensus.

The practical limitations of *fal* and *folli* in the councils notwithstanding, Wolof speakers to this day closely identify these concepts with consultation and agreement. One woman explained that *fal* meant "people joining together to agree on someone they all trust."

Because *fal* and *folli* were linked to the selection and deposition of rulers, these terms have become common in talk about the modern electoral process in Senegal. The terms do not, however, correspond neatly to Western democratic concepts of "electing" and "voting out of office," since *fal* and *folli* carry different connotations: deliberation and consensus especially. *Fal* and *folli*, in short, require the airing and harmonization of opinions, not the counting of votes. As one high-level government administrator observed, "our system of values has not, up to this point, integrated the vote. In traditional Africa it was consensus that prevailed" (*Le Soleil*, August 13, 1982).

This connotation of consensus undermines the very notion of *alternance* that is central to Bathily's intended meaning. Undertones of harmony have leeched from the concepts *fal* and *folli* to color the concept of *demokaraasi*, reinforcing images of consensus that are already present in the mosque metaphor.

Fractions of the francophone political elite are today vying to define *démocratie* in ways that advance their own political interests. While the ruling party argues

---

[24] For a more general discussion of this tendency see Simuyu 1988, 49–70

that true *démocratie* is simply the right of political parties to organize freely and advocate their agendas openly, the opposition insists that the term also entails fair rules of electoral competition and *alternance*. In competing to lend exclusive legitimacy to its positions, each faction uses a variety of channels to disseminate its views to the wider population, trying to win new adherents and supporters.

Yet the people of Senegal are segmented in their access to political knowledge. The literate, mostly urban minority that attends French-language schools, reads French-language books and journals, and understands French-language radio and television broadcasts has access to diverse sources of information on politics and *démocratie*. Views of *démocratie* held by this educated segment of society tend to reflect broadly the ideas and positions held by the various factions of the political elite. For non-Francophones, in contrast, the key channels are political rallies, cassette recordings, and Wolof-language electronic media programming, especially electoral campaign broadcasts.

Because concepts such as *démocratie* have no direct equivalents in Wolof, members of the political elite have attempted to convey their views of *démocratie* by projecting traditional Wolof words into new political contexts or by using metaphors to bridge the gap between the familiar and unfamiliar. These projections and metaphors, however, carry with them meanings embedded in popular culture that pull *démocratie* from its semantic foundations. The mosque metaphor and the use of the words *fal* and *folli* stretch *demokaraasi* with connotations of communality and harmony, while the use of *nguur* extends *demokaraasi* to signify a wide distribution of material benefits.

To what extent are such shifts in meaning intentional? Certainly Diouf's choice of the mosque metaphor was carefully considered, as may have been Savané's repetition of *nguur*. Nonetheless, political leaders are not always adept speakers of Wolof, as their frequent blunders suggest. Abdou Diouf once referred to himself as *càmmiñ*—a term that means "brother" but whose usage is restricted to women. In the most recent presidential campaign, the twisted and sometimes incomprehensible Wolof of Madior Diouf was the target of much reproach by Wolof speakers throughout the country. In the harsh appreciation of one taxi driver, "He doesn't have anything going for him; he doesn't even understand Wolof" (reported in *Wal Fadjri,* February 5–11, 1993). Even former President Léopold Senghor, an ethnic Serer who authored several articles on Wolof linguistics, made occasional slips. A widely recounted anecdote has it that once during a radio speech on agricultural policy when he meant to address the problem of brush fires (*daay*), he unwittingly raised the issue of bowel movements (*day*). These gaffes suggest that, at a minimum, not all bent meanings are the result of deliberate calculation.

Be that as it may, the shifts in meaning from *démocratie* to *demokaraasi* should not be seen solely as consequences of specific word choices; they emanate from the general nature of translation, a process that inevitably involves some loss, addition, or skewing of meaning (Nida 1959, 13, 19). Diouf, Savané, and Bathily relied on a set of cultural premises grounded in the everyday life of the unschooled populace because the presuppositions that provide meaning to the French term *démocratie* are missing in Wolof. The transfer of meaning from French to Wolof involves a shift of reference points and corresponding metaphors. The absence of equivalent cultural frames in Wolof has, in short, required the various factions of the Senegalese political elite to generate new frames of interpretation that fit the cultural frameworks of non-French-speaking Wolofones (Nida and Reyburn 1981, 14, 17, 25).

The evidence presented in this chapter thus suggests that the Wolof concept *demokaraasi* as used by the political elite is something other than the French term *démocratie* pronounced in accordance with the phonetic rules of Wolof. The transfer of meaning from French to Wolof entails a shift of cultural reference points, a shift that bends the original meaning of the concept. The question remains, though, how non-Francophones assimilate and transform these meanings, and whether *they* have any coherent understanding of the concept.

# 3

## *Demokaraasi*: The Mother of Twins

It was on a hot, dusty September afternoon that I interviewed Modou Ndiaye under the welcome shade of an acacia tree planted near the edge of Thiourour, a village located about two hundred kilometers northeast of Dakar, in the northern end of the wide zone known as the peanut basin. It is in this basin, about the size of West Virginia, that most Senegalese rural people live, cultivating peanuts for sale in the world market and growing millet and beans for their own consumption.

This northern portion of the peanut basin lies within the Sahel, a transitional band of savanna and sparse woodlands that bridges the Sahara Desert to the north and the more verdant tropical regions to the south. Rainfall in this zone varies greatly from year to year, and Modou remembers vividly the devastating drought that lasted from 1968 to 1974.

Thiourour is a slightly larger-than-average Wolof village of about 380 inhabitants. Like most villages of its size, it has no electricity or running water. It consists of thirty-five compounds built around a central square. Each compound typically contains both cement-brick houses and grass huts and is separated from other compounds by millet-stalk fencing.

Modou, the eldest son of his now deceased father, is the head of his compound. At fifty-two years of age, he has already surpassed the average life expectancy for Senegalese men by about six years. He has two wives and ten children. In his compound also live an unmarried younger brother and the wife and children of another brother, Souleymane, who has gone to Dakar to work as a journeyman mason. The family's cash income derives mainly from Souleymane's irregular earnings of about 75,000 CFA francs per year ($289) and from the 85,000 CFA francs or so ($328) that the family has received each year for its peanut crop.[1]

Modou has no formal schooling and speaks only Wolof.[2] Like almost all the inhabitants of Thiourour, he is a member of the Mouride brotherhood, one of Senegal's three major Sufi sects.[3] Modou does not belong to any political party. Nonetheless, like most other adults of Thiourour, he voted for the incumbent President Abdou Diouf in the elections of 1988, and he attended a few meetings of the president's party, the PS, in the regional capital of Louga.

I was introduced to Modou by a common acquaintance in the weekly market of a nearby village. I explained to Modou that I was researching politics in Senegal and asked if he would mind meeting with me for a few hours the following day. When I arrived, he was lying on a straw mat in the courtyard of his compound, reciting verses of the Koran he had learned as a child.

We talked about his family history and his village, and Modou shared his views of Abdou Diouf and other political leaders. At one point I asked him if he thought there was *demokaraasi* in Senegal. "Yes," he responded. "You cast your ballot for the party you choose. Abdou Diouf said, 'Here's the mosque, whoever wants can call people to prayer.' That is our *demokaraasi*. That is what brought seventeen parties to Senegal." He then went on to give an example:

> Here, if there are a hundred people, ninety of them will share the same opinions. Before long, those who disagree end up joining the majority too. A while ago there were two politicians who were candidates for office. When they came to this village, we got together and asked one another, "Which candidate do you prefer?" Some chose the first candidate, others the second. When we saw the first candidate had more support, those who had initially chosen the second candidate immediately joined the majority to make things run better. That is our *demokaraasi* here in this village. *Demokaraasi* is important because "what one person can do, two can do better." Twenty people can do more than five. That's how it is here in Thiourour. We have several associations. In each one the money is managed by all the members together. We deliberate and make common decisions. *Demokaraasi* means that the group is united in wanting good and refusing bad.

What is puzzling about these statements is how Modou's village example seems to contradict his initial assertion. How could *demokaraasi* mean voting for whoever one wishes and yet require people to change their votes in the interest of group solidarity? Modou presents two ideals that Americans normally

---

[1] These exchange rates reflect the value of the CFA franc toward the end of 1991, when the interview was conducted.

[2] Here, and in what follows, I use the terms "schooling" and "educated" (or "unschooled" and "uneducated") to refer to training received (or not) in the French-language education system. An unschooled farmer may well have received religious training in Koranic school, as did Modou.

[3] The other main Islamic brotherhoods are the Tidianes and the Qadiriyas.

see as contrasting—individual electoral choice and group conformity—as if one flowed naturally from the other.

Of course Modou may simply be giving voice to tensions already present in the Wolof discourse of the political elite. As we saw in Chapter 2, the mosque metaphor contains explicit ideas of individual choice layered over implicit notions of communality. But the communality embedded in the mosque metaphor is couched in images of religion and common worship. It is a spiritual communality based on the adoration of a single God. What Modou has to say, in contrast, seems flatly secular and utilitarian. Group conformity is important because it "makes things run better." This functionality does not seem to be a mere playing out of religious themes. Nor does the association of *demokaraasi* with communal agreement appear to stem completely from connotations borne by *fal* and *folli*, concepts that denote the choosing or rejection of leaders. In Modou's statement, *demokaraasi* gets expanded to encompass a form of consensus building that extends beyond the selection of leaders to include consensual decision making on financial issues in various village economic associations.

Indeed, it appears that part of the contradiction stems from the way Modou draws on ideas that do not emanate directly from the Wolof-language discourse of the political elite at all. Modou's experience of village social interaction leads him to recast ideas from the elite's discourse. Talk of Abdou Diouf and national political parties gives way to discussions of community associations and local electoral politics. If French-language discourse on *démocratie* is anchored in the political struggles of vying factions of the political elite, what Modou has to say seems rooted in the soil of village social life.

Yet the way Modou describes *demokaraasi* in his village is strikingly different from the way social scientists usually characterize local-level electoral politics in Senegal. Whereas Modou stresses community-wide solidarity and reconciliation, outside observers highlight the bitterness of struggles waged between competing political factions.

These factions, known locally as *clans* or *tendances*,[4] are diffuse groups of people aligned behind a leading notable or family that offers cash or favors in exchange for electoral support (Cottingham 1970; Barker 1973; Cruise O'Brien 1976; Foltz 1977). Most *tendances* exist within the ruling party, since opposition par-

---

[4] The vocabulary of factional competition has been undergoing a slow evolution in Senegal. Through the 1960s factions were, in French, called *clans*. In the 1970s PS leaders began making modest efforts (which continue to this day) to depersonalize factional competition within the party. This strategy entailed the introduction of new terminology and new distinctions. In PS documents, *clan* has come to refer to a faction organized around personal allegiances while *tendance* describes the ideal intraparty organization, one that coheres around shared ideas and ideology. This distinction has, however, become blurred in everyday talk. It is today common for Francophones (and some non–French speakers) to refer to personalized factions interchangeably as *clans* or *tendances*. For an example of this PS literature see Diom 1986 and Ka 1986.

ties are generally too weak and resource poor to develop extensive patron-client networks. (The only exception is the PDS, which appears to be developing factional rivalries, especially in Dakar and a few other urban centers where its support is strong.)

In Thiourour, partisans of the opposition are few, and villagers are aligned with one of two different *tendances* that operate within the ruling PS. The larger of the two supports the chief of the largest village in the local-level administrative zone (called rural community) in which Thiourour is located. The other is organized around the chief of another village in the same zone.

People adhere to *tendances* less as a result of ideology or policy commitment than out of a desire to share in the spoils of patronage. Loyal clients receive from political patrons extra income, government employment, privileged treatment by the civil services, and protection against legal sanctions (Schumacher 1975, 28). Rivalry between patrons sparks bitter intraparty clan conflict. The political survival of national leaders depends upon their ability to create a personal power base among competing clan leaders.

The fiercest factional competition in Thiourour is for control of the rural community council, whose membership is elected by the voting-age population of fifty-two villages that make up this administrative zone. Because opposition candidates rarely run for these positions, the real competition takes place before election day during the intraparty process of selecting PS candidates. At times this selection process and the bitter factional competition to which it gives rise can turn violent. In 1992 factional conflict within the PS left four dead in the city of Vélingara and several wounded in Mbour and Fatick.

None of these elements of factionalism, though, enter prominently into Modou's description of *demokaraasi*. He speaks mostly about villagewide unity and solidarity. Perhaps Modou is wishfully describing an ideal world of *demokaraasi* where divisiveness or competition is minimal. Or perhaps clan rivalry and factiousness do not figure into *demokaraasi,* or stand outside its conceptual boundaries.


## Consensus

There is some evidence to support this latter interpretation, for in the minds of many Wolofones with little or no education, the term *demokaraasi* has come to mean, at times, simply the achievement of agreement. Consider these statements:

> There is *demokaraasi* in our village because each time we disagree, we straighten things out [*juboo*], we mend things.
> —Mouride blacksmith in the town of Coki, male, 38 years old

*Demokaraasi* means ironing out disagreements [*juboo*] between you and those in your community.
                    — Tidiane street vendor in Dakar, female, 43 years old

*Demokaraasi* is to agree [*déggoo*], to form "one." Even if you are many, to be able to form a bloc and work together. To form one is to support one another, to discuss among yourselves. Even if agreement is difficult, you need to do all you can to reach a consensus.
                    —Catholic unemployed teenager from Dakar, male

*Demokaraasi* means coming to agreement [*déggoo*].
                    —Unemployed Mouride in the city of Touba, male, 23 years old

*Demokaraasi* is nothing other than mutual understanding. I argue with him, before leaving this place a third person will reconcile us [*jubale*]. And when we leave, the dispute is finished [*ñuy ànd*].
                    —Mouride farmer from the city of Mbacké, male, 43 years old

There is *demokaraasi* in Senegal because everybody agrees [*ànd*], people are content, everybody is talking about unity [*ànd*].
                    —Peanut farmer in the town of Coki, male, 65 years old

If everyone comes to agreement [*déggoo ci kaddu*] there is *demokaraasi*.
                    — Tidiane carpenter in Dakar, male, 65 years old

These statements, from a diverse group of informants, share the sense that *demokaraasi* involves agreement. Yet in these statements, and in the Wolof language more generally, speakers distinguish different types of consensus.

## Déggoo

Formed from the root *dégg* (to understand) plus the suffix *-oo*, which denotes reciprocity and simultaneity, *déggoo* means "to agree, to reach an understanding." It connotes mutual understanding and absence of antagonism, a natural agreement flowing from intimate understanding of one another.

## Juboo

Composed of the root *jub* (to be straight) and the suffix *-oo*, *juboo* means "to reconcile, to agree, to reach an agreement." Unlike the agreement achieved in *déggoo*, the understanding reached in *juboo* presupposes prior disagreement. What is important is the "straightening out" of differences.

## Maslaa

From the Arabic term *maṣlaḥa* (that which is beneficial), *maslaa* marks the establishment or maintenance of an outward appearance of consensus and civility despite the persistence of real disagreement below (Mouradian 1963, 86).

## Ànd

*Ànd* means literally "to be or go together," and by extension it also means "to agree." The agreement connoted by *ànd* is reached in the spirit of solidarity; it entails going along with the majority for the sake of conforming. This type of agreement undergirds the following two Wolof proverbs cited by a peanut farmer to illustrate his understanding of *demokaraasi*. The first: "Hyena says: 'What everyone says—that is the truth'" (Bukki ne na lu ñëpp wax mooy dëgg); and the second: "He who is in conflict with everyone else is the one who is wrong" (Ku dëngo ak ñëpp ya dënga).

The kind of agreement associated with *demokaraasi*, then, can take several forms. It may reflect deep mutual understanding; it may be the product of compromise ironed out between hostile camps; it may be a surface veneer that masks hidden discord; or it may arise from a desire to conform to social norms. The quality of the agreement matters less than the fact itself of having achieved some kind of consensus.

These connotations pull the concept *demokaraasi* from its moorings in Western political tradition. It is not that democracy cannot involve deliberation or have a consensual quality. Several prominent political scientists (Dahl 1956; Key 1961, 27–53; Rustow 1970, 337–63) have, in fact, pointed precisely to an underlying societal consensus that makes democracy possible.[5] Critics of contemporary American democracy (Pateman 1970; Mansbridge 1980; Pitkin and Shumer, 1982) are also attracted to ideas of consultation, deliberation, and consensus building, and often incorporate them into models of "unitary," "participatory," or "deliberative" democracy. But while consensus can be a precondition for, or part of, the democratic process, few Americans would argue that democracy is, *tout court*, the achievement of agreement, which is what the Wolof concept *demokaraasi* has come to mean to the people who made the above statements. Shorn from *demokaraasi*, in other words, are the ideas of governance and collective decision making that provide the context for deliberation

---

[5] For instance, Dahl (1956, 132) writes that "prior to politics, beneath it, enveloping it, restricting it, conditioning it, is the underlying consensus on policy that usually exists in the society among a predominant portion of the politically active members. Without such a consensus, no democratic system would long survive the endless irritations and frustrations of elections and party competition."

and consensus building in American scholarly theories of democracy. Two friends who fight and then reconcile have achieved *demokaraasi* but not democracy, even in any of its usual metaphorical senses.[6]

Viewed in this light, electoral competition appears to afford an opportunity for village solidarity to be reaffirmed. Indeed, from Modou's perspective, *demokaraasi* was achieved in Thiourour the moment everyone ended up agreeing on a candidate. The act of choosing—the key element of democracy in his statement—seems less important. The essence of *demokaraasi* appears to lie in the final consensus achieved and the social peace it ensures. Through the act of voting, villagers reinforced their ties of solidarity.

## Solidarity

This community solidarity seems to lie at the heart of many uneducated Wolofones' understanding of *demokaraasi*. Consider the statement made by an elderly farmer in Ngabu, a village about one hundred kilometers south of Thiourour: "When there is work to do, we come together to do it. When someone falls ill, we come together to cultivate his field. If something happens to one of us, everybody helps him out financially. When someone is sick, the women go to the well to fetch him water. That is our *demokaraasi* here in Ngabu." A comment made by a Tidiane farmer in Kaolack (the southernmost region of Senegal inhabited by native Wolof speakers, some four hundred kilometers southeast of Thiourour) was strikingly similar: "Our *demokaraasi* is everyone being unified. We do our work together. When it rains, we do the same work. If someone is sick and can't cultivate his fields, we all meet to help him. To pay our taxes, we all get together to give our money."

Another farmer in Ngabu explained what he thought the term *demokaraasi* meant: "You are weaving a thatched roof for your hut. Here you can do it out in the field. You place the frame on the ground, you put it together, you plait the straw. You do everything. But you can't lift it yourself. It is too heavy to pick up. You have to call someone to help you. You call one person, you call another. Together you all lift it up. That is our *demokaraasi*."

---

[6] When one understands that *demokaraasi* may mean agreement, whatever its form, otherwise puzzling statements become clear. A Dakar carpenter, for example, explained that "there used to be *demokaraasi* here in the days of colonial rule. The Korité prayer, for example, only took place once. When someone announced the time of prayer, everyone agreed. If everyone looks for the moon and sees it at the same time, that is *demokaraasi*." Korité is the Muslim holy day that marks the end of the fasting period of Ramadan. Ramadan lasts about one month, covering an entire lunar cycle. Korité begins at the first sight of the new moon. Several times, most notably in 1983 and 1991, leaders of the Mouride and Tidiane brotherhoods have disagreed as to whether the moon had indeed been spotted at the end of Ramadan, and on those occasions Korité was celebrated on two successive days. For this Dakar carpenter, then, agreement among religious leaders typifies *demokaraasi*.

City dwellers, even some who received primary school education, express comparable views. A Catholic woman with seven years of schooling explained why she thought *demokaraasi* no longer existed in her Dakar neighborhood: "In the past everyone was united. It is not like that anymore. In the past, the city was not large; everyone knew each other. After Mass we visited each other, spoke with each other. People used to help each other."

For these people, the ideal of *demokaraasi* seems to involve the recognition of mutual dependence and the consequent importance of sharing responsibility for one another's well-being. These people, like Modou, have moved outside the realm of electoral politics. All identify *demokaraasi* with a comprehensive form of community solidarity.

Often this solidarity is expressed in the idiom of the family. Many Wolofones say that *demokaraasi* means that everyone "shares the same mother and father" (*bokk ndey bokk baay*). The solidarity reflected by this phrase is grounded in the metaphor of the nation as family. This familial solidarity is meant to include all the people of Senegal, who are commonly called *doomi réew mi*, literally "the children of the country," a phrase that can also mean roughly "patriots" or "citizens." When political speechmakers address a crowd, they often begin by calling the assembled *mbokk yi*, literally "relatives."[7]

This cultural tendency of infusing political authority with familial images is echoed in the Wolof vocabulary of governance. One word for governing is *boot*, the primary meaning of which is "to carry a child on a mother's back." The term may also mean "to cuddle or comfort" and carries strong connotations of nurturance. Extended to fathers, the term means "to support a family." In the political realm, *boot* means loosely "to govern" but carries the same connotation of parental or familial responsibility. The political leader assumes responsibility for the well-being of the *doomi réew mi* in the same way a mother does her child or a father his family.[8]

*Bokk ndey bokk baay*, we might say, is roughly equivalent to the American idea of fraternity. Both encompass a range of connotations: tolerance, sharing of values and goals, bonds of affection, and mutual obligation are among the most significant. What emerges from both metaphors is a picture of the nation as a community of siblings held together by ties of affection, responsibility, and commonly held ideals and purposes. Yet neither expression should be confused with any simple notion of equality, since both refer to feelings that arise out of a common *subordination* to parents. The interjection of the kinship metaphor also introduces ideas of hierarchy and authority.[9]

---

[7] For a more general discussion of familial metaphors in African political discourse see Schatzberg 1986.

[8] Similarly, the terms *yor* (to carry) and *uuf* (to hold in one's lap) may also mean roughly "to govern" and carry comparable connotations.

[9] On American notions of fraternity see McWilliams 1973.

Beneath these similarities shared by fraternity and *bokk ndey bokk baay,* however, lie important differences. In Senegal, three of every ten married men have more than one wife (République du Sénégal, Présidence de la République 1989, 9). Among the Wolof, almost half of all married men are polygamous (Diop 1985, 185). Many siblings thus have the same father but not the same mother. *Bokk ndey bokk baay* refers to the especially strong ties felt by the children who have the same father and mother. On this topic it is worth recalling that the meaning of most Wolof terms related to siblings can be stretched wide. *Mag,* for instance, may refer not only to an older sibling but also to an older cousin, or any elder whom one wants to address with respect. The same is true of the indigenized French spoken in Senegal and the rest of francophone Africa. In these countries *frère* is often a vague term that may, depending on the context, mean either (1) a male sibling who has the same mother and father as oneself, (2) a male sibling who shares either the same mother or the same father, (3) any male member of the extended family, (4) any male member of the extended family in the same age group, or (5) any male with whom one feels ties of loyalty (Equipe IFA 1983, 156–57). Within the universe of sibling terminology, *bokk ndey bokk baay* is unusually precise and emotionally potent. The American concept of fraternity, in contrast, invokes a diffuse kind of affection more akin to the Franco-African concept *frère*. Like *frère,* "brother" can be used to address not only male siblings but friends, fellow union and church members, and sometimes strangers as well, as in the Depression era song "Brother, Can You Spare a Dime?"

It is also important to note that the Wolof phrase is gender neutral; it does not harbor the masculine or uniquely brotherly overtones of "fraternity." Indeed, the Wolof language contains no words to translate exactly the concept of fraternity. Nor is there a term that refers to brothers in general. Siblings are classified first by age. One may have an older sibling (*mag*) or younger sibling (*rakk*). The older sibling may be male (*mag bu goor*) or female (*mag bu jigeen*), as can the younger sibling (*rakk bu goor/rakk bu jigeen*). One word that is sometimes translated to mean "brother" is *càmmiñ,* but only women may use this term, in reference to their male siblings.[10]

One consequence of this difference is that *bokk ndey bokk baay* is more inclusive than "fraternity" in that it includes siblings of both genders. The Wolof expression, however, reinforces images of inequality in a way that "fraternity" does not. In Wolof all siblings are classified immediately and automatically as older or younger. Not only is there subordination to parents, but a rank order-

---

[10] The absence of a general term for brotherliness, incidentally, posed problems for nineteenth-century Catholic missionaries who tried to generate a suitable Wolof vocabulary for Bible translation. At least one of them (Guy-Grand 1923, 267) resorted to coinages that lost something in translation: *cofeel ga doomi ndey soppante* (love that a mother's children feel for each other), *cofeel gu takku* (loyal love), *déggoo bu mat* (complete understanding).

ing of siblings reigns as well. The solidarity of *demokaraasi,* in short, is one graded by hierarchy.

## Evenhandedness

The relation of *demokaraasi* to hierarchy is complicated further by the fact that many Wolofones identify *demokaraasi* as containing something roughly equivalent to the American concept of equality. These Senegalese people often allude to the type of equality associated with *demokaraasi* by invoking the Wolof term *yemale.* This word implies an equality grounded in action, an equality that rests specifically on treating others as equals, the key word being "treating."[11]

*Yemale* does not mandate that all enjoy equal status. The equality of *yemale* — and thus of *demokaraasi* — preserves hierarchies in age, gender, caste, and religious authority (just as democracy preserves certain inequalities, such as those that differentiate Donald Trump and a secretary — more on this later). *Yemale* and *demokaraasi* require only that a man treat his wives equally, that an Islamic marabout treat his disciples equally, or that a mother treat her children equally. Consider this statement made by the son of a marabout: "*Demokaraasi* means *yemale.* If you have two bowls for two people, if you intend to put food in one, you need to divide it up equally. One should not get more than the other. That shows that *demokaraasi* prevails, because you treated the two people the same. As we say in Wolof, the mother of twins lies on her back.[12] To permit each infant to suckle a breast as it likes, when it likes — that is *demokaraasi.*"

A farmer in the village of Keur Moussa expressed a strikingly similar idea: "*Demokaraasi* means that when you have two wives, you have to do everything possible to avoid arguments in the household. If you have something, you need to distribute it equally." Or take this assertion made by a religious teacher in Coki: "There is *demokaraasi* in the household because the father of the family treats everyone equally to maintain peace. If you are polygamous, you have to treat your wives equally in terms of food and clothes. That is what God ordered." A farmer in the village of Darou Lo explained *demokaraasi* in similar terms:

The marabouts here in Senegal make us live according to Islam, and Islam is *demokaraasi.* That is to say, our marabout Cheikh Lo gave birth to *demokaraasi* here in Darou Lo. Any villager is as much a child of Cheikh Lo as the marabout's own natural child. Today we sit on the same bed. We eat the same food. The marabout

[11] We can contrast *yemale* with two other words — *nawle* and *moroom* — that also denote equality but that are not consistently used in talk about *demokaraasi. Nawle* applies to people who share the same caste and are thus equal in caste status; *moroom* applies to someone who is an equal in physical attributes or character.

[12] In Wolof: "Ndey ju seex, jaaxaanaay lay tëddee."

Cheikh Lo teaches us the same things. We have the same desires. The same things are prohibited to us both. Here, whatever we do, we do it together. Whatever is forbidden, we all forgo it together.

Clearly neither *yemale* nor *demokaraasi* requires that an abstract, equal status reign universally. The religious teacher quoted above explained it this way: "Your rights must be pegged to your capacities. Neither *demokaraasi* nor *yemale* means that everyone is equal in all respects." What these concepts do require is that a caretaker or guardian treat the people under his or her care or authority evenhandedly, without partiality or favoritism—despite any hierarchies of age that may exist among wives, siblings, and villagers.[13]

How did *yemale* come to be associated with *demokaraasi*? In one respect it brings to mind images of *demokaraasi* that we saw in Landing Savané's Wolof speech in Chapter 2. His repetition of *nguur*—a word meaning government, power, or reign that bears connotations of fulfillment and indulgence—seemed unwittingly to transform *demokaraasi* from a redistribution of power to a redistribution of pleasure and benefit. That is, *demokaraasi* shifted from meaning that everyone should rule to meaning that everyone should experience gratification. We might think of *demokaraasi* in the sense of *yemale* as this (evenhanded) redistribution of benefits.

Yet absent from *demokaraasi* are the connotations of kingly pleasure or exploitation so pronounced in *nguur*. Only partially, therefore, do popular notions of *demokaraasi* echo messages disseminated by the francophone political elite, as less educated or unschooled Wolof speakers reground *demokaraasi* in the immediacy of family, neighborhood, and village relationships—between husband and wives, marabout and follower, mother and child.

## Some Statistics

Interview data show considerable uniformity in the way Senegalese who speak little or no French understand *demokaraasi*. Of the seventy-eight people who had fewer than nine years of education, or no formal schooling at all, fifty-

---

[13] It is worthwhile to note that *yemale* also means to stop at a certain point, as in "We'll stop the discussion at this point" ("Fii lënuy yemale sunu waxtaan"). The term used in this way applies to setting not only temporal but spatial and moral limits. *Yemale,* in all its uses, carries the connotation of placing constraints that should not be lifted or defining boundaries that should not be trespassed. These boundaries or constraints are at times self-imposed. *Yemale* can refer to regulating what one says or acting with tact and discretion; thus a Wolofone might say that a respectable man should *yemale* (measure) his words ("Muskàllaf dafa war yemale i waxam"). At the same time, some constraints are clearly imposed by a higher moral authority, be it husband, father, or marabout—in short, by a *kilifa*.

nine understood the concept to involve, beyond references to voting and elections, one or more of the three ideals discussed above: consensus, solidarity, or evenhandedness. Of the remaining nineteen respondents, five did not know what the term meant, eight provided answers that did not clearly reflect their understanding of the term, and six used *demokaraasi* in ways that echoed PS notions of *démocratie* as freedom of expression. These last six respondents had nothing obvious in common beyond their understanding of *demokaraasi*. They proclaimed different political loyalties, lived in different parts of the country, and had different types of occupations (two were market vendors; one was a farmer, one a tailor, one a retired factory worker; and one was unemployed). That they all understood *demokaraasi* in ways advantageous to the PS suggests that the ruling party's efforts to shape Wolofones' understanding of the term have not been totally in vain.

Only four of twenty-two people who had more than nine years of education, in contrast, understood *demokaraasi* (or *démocratie*) to mean either consensus, solidarity, or evenhandedness. The first was a Mouride marabout and businessman, the second a retired rural development worker, the third a hawker, and the last an employee of a state enterprise. None of these four respondents had any postsecondary education, so that all were less well educated than most other schooled respondents. Three lived in rural areas or small towns in the interior of the country; only one, the hawker, lived in Dakar. One voted for PDS candidates in the 1988 elections, another was a local-level PS cadre, and two did not vote in 1988 or profess any political leanings. These facts do not reveal any striking similarities among the four informants. Perhaps none of them understood French particularly well, or perhaps they moved primarily in Wolof-speaking circles; in either case, they would have been insulated from the messages disseminated by the francophone elite. Or it may be that meanings common to the unschooled population are beginning to enter the vocabulary of more educated Wolofones.

There is some evidence to support the latter hypothesis, for *demokaraasi/démocratie* as used by Francophones has taken on a meaning of distributive equality in some contexts. One such context is tea drinking. The Senegalese often get together to drink tea; it is a very social occasion. One person is in charge of brewing and distributing the tea, which is served in three rounds. If the brewer neglects to serve one of his or her guests, it is possible for the forgotten person to ask, if speaking Wolof: "Xanaa fii amatul demokaraasi?" (Is there no longer *demokaraasi* here?). It is a playful way of asking, "Where is *my* glass of tea?" A meaning of distributive equality is also revealed in particular choices of image or metaphor made by Francophones. A cartoon that appeared in the satirical weekly *Le Cafard Libéré* on August 3, 1990 depicts *démocratie* as a bowl that contains enough food to provide a hearty meal for leaders of both the ruling party and the opposition. This image appears to draw on food metaphors that pervade talk about *demokaraasi*, and it brings to mind the statement made about apportioning food to nursing twins. In this cartoon, *démocratie*, like *demokaraasi*, is a full bowl that provides sustenance for all.[14]

## Alternative Hypotheses

The three meanings of *demokaraasi*—consensus, solidarity, and evenhanded-ness—appear interrelated, for they all seem to involve a sense of community-wide interdependence. Jointly they constitute what we might describe as an idea of mutuality. This cluster of meanings, it bears repeating, does not emanate wholly from messages disseminated by the political elite. While ideas of voting, solidarity, and distribution are contained in images of *demokaraasi* projected by French-speaking politicians since the mid-1970s, many Wolof speakers with lim-ited educational backgrounds, in addition to a small number of better-educated people bilingual in French and Wolof, appear to root their understandings of *demokaraasi* in the moral ground of local community life. The result is what we might call a folk concept of *demokaraasi* that differs in important ways not only from views of *démocratie* or *demokaraasi* generated by the French-speaking elite but also from the American concept of democracy.

If the cluster of meanings here labeled "mutuality" cannot be traced wholly back to the francophone elite's Wolof discourse of the past two decades, from what does it derive? I have stressed the role of Wolof speakers themselves in generating meanings pertinent to their own life conditions. Before we investi-gate this idea further, a few alternative hypotheses are worth exploring.

One obvious possibility is that notions of mutuality—especially its senses of solidarity and evenhandedness—originate in a long-standing French political tradition rooted in Rousseau's vision of communitarian *démocratie* and the egal-itarianism of the French Revolution.[15] To evaluate this hypothesis it is essential to investigate the historical diffusion of the concept from France to Senegal. I therefore examined available Senegalese newspapers, party organs, and political tracts dating from the mid–nineteenth century to the present. Because a signifi-cant amount of print material has been lost, especially from the earlier periods, this survey was necessarily incomplete. My examination turned up little evi-dence that egalitarian notions of *démocratie* were ever widespread, with two no-table exceptions.

The first exception dates to the 1940s, when talk of *démocratie* was subsumed within debates about expanding France's policy of assimilation. Assimilation, as

---

[14] Similarly, a cartoon picturing *démocratie* as a fruit-bearing tree can be found in *Le Cafard Libéré*, April 25, 1990.

[15] For a conceptual history of *démocratie* in France see Rosanvallon 1995.

nineteenth-century French theorists conceived it; entailed the notion that France's colonial possessions should become integrated into the *métropole*, the mother country. "Its ideal," one proponent wrote, "is an increasingly intimate union between the colonial territory and the metropolitan territory" (Girault 1895, 54). Assimilation, as such, was a vague concept that allowed for a variety of interpretations. It often included some notion of administrative assimilation, whereby colonial possessions would become overseas departments; political assimilation, whereby colonial subjects would become French citizens; or legal assimilation, whereby the laws of France would be applied to overseas territories. More broadly, the term also meant assimilation to "French civilization" generally, and entailed the adoption of the French language, Catholicism, and "civilized" customs (Lewis 1962, 131–32).

France never unambiguously pursued assimilation, even in the Four Communes where the policy was perhaps most vigorously applied, since the influence of assimilationist thought was closely tied to the unsteady fortunes of republican government (Girault 1895, 55). Furthermore, even during times of assimilationist zeal, the French people evidenced considerable anxiety over the prospect of being outnumbered in their own polity by Africans, Arabs, Southeast Asians, and others.

Debates about assimilation and the resultant wavering of colonial policy formed the backdrop for the assertion of political muscle by the black citizens of the four Senegalese communes. In 1914 they rallied to elect Blaise Diagne the first African deputy to the National Assembly. Among his keenest supporters were members of a political movement called the Young Senegalese, a group of teachers, clerks, and low-level bureaucrats who advocated full application of assimilationist ideas (July 1968, 399). Diagne's major accomplishment in his twenty years as deputy was the Law of September 29, 1916 (the Loi Diagne), which preserved voting and citizenship rights for Africans in the Four Communes at a time when some people in France sought to weaken them (Markovitz 1969b, 26; Johnson 1971, 168). Diagne thus established a role that his successor Senegalese deputy, Galandou Diouf (who served from 1934 to 1941), and his onetime protégé and later opponent, Lamine Guèye, would follow. As a distinguished historian of this period remarked:

> In Senegal the citizens had to fight to retain their privileges against an administration that came increasingly to regret the privileges it had granted the Senegalese in the first fine flush of colonial expansion in Black Africa. Thus until the outbreak of the Second World War one had the paradoxical situation of the French regretting their assimilationist policy and the Senegalese citizens asking that it be applied more liberally. This is one of the main reasons why the activities of French Africans, particularly in Senegal, were channelled not towards the attainment of independence but the assertion of their fundamental equality with the French. (Crowder 1962, 15)

After the Second World War, Lamine Guèye would himself become deputy to the National Assembly in Paris; and he too would attach his name to laws extending the assimilationist ideal. The first Loi Lamine Guèye, passed in 1946, granted citizenship rights to all inhabitants of the French overseas community. The second Loi Lamine Guèye of 1950 stipulated that African and French civil servants were entitled to the same rights (Markovitz 1969b, 33–34; Bernard-Duquenet 1977, 164).

It is interesting that when Guèye speaks in his memoirs about *démocratie* during the colonial era, he refers to the second rather than the first Loi Lamine Guèye: "What we were asking—with all the democrats of France and Africa—was simply to make everyone admit that an African and a European who completed the same studies, obtained the same diplomas and professional qualifications to become doctors, professors, magistrates etc., have the same rights to the same salary and benefits for people of the same rank and seniority within the same civil service branch" (Guèye 1966, 101). Guèye links here the ideal of *démocratie* to the fight for equal treatment.

This statement is typical of the way Senegalese leaders framed the issue of *démocratie* during the 1940s and early 1950s. At that time, discussion of *démocratie* was subsumed within the larger issue of political and administrative assimilation and sometimes meant quite narrowly the equal treatment of African and French civil servants by the colonial administration.[16]

It was perhaps during this period that the word *demokaraasi* was introduced into Wolof as Senegalese leaders explained the issues of the day to their unschooled constituents. This understanding of *démocratie* as equality of treatment by a higher authority may partially explain why so many Wolofones today link *demokaraasi* with *yemale*. Just as *démocratie* once required that the colonial administration treat African and French civil servants as equals, so *demokaraasi* today means that the mother of twins should lie on her back to allow both infants equal access to her breasts.

Such conclusions, however provocative, are nonetheless problematic. One theme that emerged in Chapter 2 is that the transfer of meaning from the francophone elite to the non-French-speaking populace is hardly free of distortion. Channels of communication are narrow, and meanings are prone to mutation. That such a meaning should remain virtually intact and unchanged for so long would be somewhat surprising. Moreover, there is no record of *demokaraasi* in any written sources dating from this period. Nor, as we shall soon see, did the term occur in the spoken language of uneducated Wolofones recorded over the course of the 1960s. We can only conclude, then, that it is unlikely that the meaning of

---

[16] See, for instance, the speeches made by Léopold Sédar Senghor to the French National Assembly on September 18, 1946, and June 30, 1950 (reproduced in Senghor 1971, 19–28, 74–80); Gaye Jacques Ibrahima, "Démocratie et colonisation," *L'AOF,* May 30, 1947; and Massata N'diaye, "Pour une démocratie plus vraie," *L'AOF,* March 30, 1948.

*demokaraasi* can be traced to eighteenth-century French ideas or colonial-era debates.

The second exception dates to the early years of independence in the 1960s. It was at this time that Léopold Sédar Senghor, president of the new republic, popularized the notion of a uniquely African *démocratie* based on discussion and unanimity. As Senghor told the parliament of Ghana in 1961:

> African democracy [*démocratie*] is essentially founded on the *palabre*. The *palabre* is a dialogue, or better yet, a colloquium, where each has the right to speak, where everyone takes the floor to express his opinion. Formerly, even the dead were consulted. But once every opinion was expressed, the minority followed the majority to manifest their unanimity. This unanimous opinion was then vigorously applied without deviation. (Quoted in Markovitz 1969a, 195)

Perhaps the meaning of consensus borne by *demokaraasi* originated in Senghor's notion of African *démocratie*; indeed, Senghor here sounds much like Modou.

The problem with this explanation is that the word *demokaraasi* itself had not become integrated into the linguistic repertoires of uneducated Wolof speakers until sometime after the 1960s. Linguists recorded a corpus of 500,000 words from the speech of adult Wolofones all over the country between 1963 and 1968 (Diop et al. 1968–72). In the 365,000 words of the corpus that are available for analysis,[17] *demokaraasi* occurs only twice, in the speech of two informants. The linguists provided no educational or linguistic information about these particular informants, but judging from the other loan words the two used, both appear to be schooled Wolof-French bilinguals.

There were in the corpus, then, no unambiguous uses of *demokaraasi* by non-Francophones. Furthermore, the word appeared infrequently in comparison with other political loan words, such as *dippite* (from *député*), *meer* (from *maire*), *góornëmaa* (from *gouvernement*), and *politig* (from *politique*). *Politig,* for instance, occurs twenty-eight times in the analyzed part of the corpus, in the discourse of thirteen speakers.[18] The recurrent use of *politig* and its phonetic assimilation into Wolof led one linguist to conclude that this French loan word was by that time fully assimilated into Wolof. He reached no such conclusions about *demokaraasi* (Dumont 1973, 101–76). There is evidence, in other words, that a fair number of French political loan words were in common use in the 1960s but no evidence that *demokaraasi* was used widely.

That *demokaraasi* had not been introduced into Wolof discourse in the 1960s may be a consequence of Senghor's choice of audience. He formulated his ideas primarily to legitimate a strong presidency and single-party rule to potential

[17] I could not locate a copy of vol. 2.

[18] The educational backgrounds of only four of these informants were recorded. None of them had any formal education.

donors and allies abroad, as well as to intellectuals and other members of the francophone political elite at home. As Senghor himself put it, "a democratic policy pays dividends. . . . This is excellent propaganda" (1964b, 52). Senghor thus raised the topic of *démocratie* while speaking in other countries, in French-language party organs and reports, and at press conferences.[19]

It was not possible to determine whether Senghor or anyone else spoke of *demokaraasi* in speeches or radio broadcasts aimed at the domestic non-French-speaking population, since I could find few Wolof-language sources from the 1960s. But tellingly, the earliest written occurrence of the term appeared in a 1972 issue of *Kaddu,* a Wolof-language journal published by the filmmaker Ousmane Sembène and the linguist Pathé Diagne—both vocal critics of Senghor.

To conclude, French egalitarian political traditions, colonial debates about assimilation, and Senghor's notion of unanimous *démocratie* are all plausible but unlikely explanations of the way *demokaraasi* came to mean mutuality. A more likely explanation dates to recent times: first to the use of this term in speeches made by politicians in the post-1974 era of multiparty politics and to the deformation of meaning that resulted when the French concept was translated into Wolof; and second to Wolof speakers who themselves assimilated the concept and transformed its meaning.

## Mutuality and Economic Uncertainty

Norms of mutuality are not unique to Senegal. Students of precolonial and preindustrial societies have noted the importance of "mutuality" to seventeenth-century Japanese farmers (Smith 1959, 149, 53–64), of "mutual support" to nineteenth-century Hausa villagers (Watts 1984, 127), of "mutuality" and "moral solidarity" to early-twentieth-century Vietnamese and Burmese peasants (Scott 1976, 43), of "mutual assistance" to mid-twentieth-century Nuer communities (Evans-Pritchard 1940, 85), and of "reciprocity" to present-day Basarwa households in Botswana (Cashdan 1985).

Such norms appear to be common among groups of people who experience what James Scott has called an "existential dilemma" of economic uncertainty (1976, 25). When barriers to collective action are not too high, material precariousness leads vulnerable populations to adopt some form of community-wide insurance (Posner 1980; Fafchamps 1992). Peasants reduce the risk of food shortage by participating in a range of customary social arrangements—ritual

---

[19] See, e.g., Senghor 1964a; Senghor, "La démocratie négro-africaine," *L'Unité Africaine,* November 26, 1964; and Senghor's reports to the 1961, 1963, and 1967 UPS Congresses, reproduced in Senghor 1983.

gift exchanges, patron-client relations, communal land tenure systems that guarantee access to land and diversify plot locations (for an overview of the literature on these topics see Platteau 1991). An ethic of mutuality provides the "emotional cement" required to maintain these protective arrangements (Wynne 1980, 44).[20]

Researchers have observed that industrialization and colonialism tend to erode such insurance schemes, along with the emotional cement that holds them together. Taxation, cash cropping, and monetization draw self-sufficient communities into the market economy, thereby encouraging the growth of individualistic economic strategies (Watts 1984, 133–37; Platteau 1991, 158–59). Still, there is evidence that an ethic of mutuality and various collective social security arrangements have survived in the market economies of Japan (Smith 1959, 148–52, 208–12), India (Das Gupta 1987), Colombia (Ortiz 1967), and Mexico (Halperin 1977).

In Senegal too there is considerable market activity. Participation in the monetary economy provides essential resources to buy rice, tea, sugar, clothing, and household utensils, to pay taxes and school fees, and, for urban dwellers, to meet the costs of food and rent (Ames 1962, 29–60; Waterbury 1987, 47–73). Full participation in this economy entails heavy risk, however. For farmers the risk involves fluctuating prices, high input costs, uncertain returns, and predatory state interventions (Bates 1981; Lofchie 1985).[21] For urbanites the major risks are unemployment and falling wages.

Of course, neither urban nor rural populations are economically homogeneous, and exposure to risk is thus unevenly distributed. A survey of 435 rural households in the Kaolack region was conducted from 1982 to 1987. It found that while 44 percent of those interviewed received a maximum of 60,000 CFA francs ($225 in 1987) for their peanut crops, one of every ten received five times that amount (Diop 1992, 39–42). Rural elites, most notably the leaders of the religious brotherhoods, are substantially better off than even the richest peanut farmers included in the survey, and are sometimes impressively wealthy in comparison to other inhabitants of Senegal. In 1966, the year for which the best data are available, forty-nine Mouride marabouts received from the sale of peanuts somewhere between $2,200 and $8,400; twelve between $8,400 and

---

[20] The existence of collective insurance arrangements in some communities does not mean that such arrangements exist in all preindustrial and precolonial communities, that all participants in these arrangements are equal, that free-rider problems have been fully resolved, that these arrangements continue to function well during times of prolonged crisis, or that community members refrain from seeking individual or household subsistence guarantees. On these points see the (sometimes overdrawn) analyses in Popkin 1979 and Haggis et al. 1986.

[21] It should be noted that where profit incentives are strong, risks few, and government actions negligible or benign, urban and rural capitalism has expanded in Africa. As René Lemarchand (1989, 58–60) rightly argues, the growth of cocoa farming in Ghana and southern Nigeria in the nineteenth century are cases in point.

$36,300, and two important leaders over $83,700 each (Cruise O'Brien 1971, 216).[22] Marabouts also receive income from business ventures and cash offerings from their followers. In urban areas as well the spread between rich and poor is large. The average annual salary of a civil servant in 1989 was more than eleven times higher than that of a well-paid domestic worker (Berg 1990, 4; Graham 1994, 126). Looking at the country as a whole, we find that the poorest fifth of the population earned 4 percent of the national income while the richest fifth earned 59 percent (World Bank 1995b, 301).

By one definition of poverty (an inability to maintain a daily intake of 2,400 calories per adult per day) about 33 percent of the population were poor during the 1992 harvest season. Estimates are that during other seasons and during years of bad harvest the poverty rate climbs to 60 percent (World Bank 1995a, 1–2). While by this definition a majority of poor people live in rural areas, many urban dwellers are also vulnerable. Structural adjustment programs, put in place in the early 1980s, have hit urban areas hard. Privatization and the lowering of protectionist barriers led unemployment rates in Dakar to jump from 16.6 percent in 1976 to 24.4 percent in 1991 (ibid., 18). They also led the real income of wage earners to decline. Between 1981 and 1988 civil servants saw their earnings fall by an average of about 40 percent (Berg 1990, 192–95). It is common for such wage earners, despite their dwindling resources, to support between ten and fifteen family members each (Somerville 1991, 165).

Those urban and rural dwellers who are poor or vulnerable (and those who perceive themselves as such) seek ways to maintain some level of security. Farm households diversify their income by sending one or more members (such as Souleymane, Modou's younger brother) to work as wage laborers in the city (Frankenberger and Lynham 1993, 83). Farmers and traders evade burdensome government controls by participating in informal markets beyond the state's reach. Indeed, in 1985 only about one quarter of the national peanut harvest was sold through officially condoned channels (Gersovitz and Waterbury 1987, 2).

In addition to these market strategies, farmers balance their production for the market with subsistence agriculture. When the market for their produce is particularly depressed, farmers may reduce commercial production sharply. One student of Senegalese agriculture describes how rural cultivators reacted to a difficult period of drought made more onerous by increased state demands for rural revenues: "The peasants responded . . . by withdrawing from rural development services, intensifying noncompliance with administrative regulations and laws, and shifting from peanut cultivation to subsistence farming. Be-

[22] In addition to the more than $83,700 the leader of the Mouride brotherhood received from peanut fields worked by his followers, he also received an estimated $39,000 from pilgrims to an annual religious ceremony (called *màggal* in Wolof) in the holy city of Touba. Other sources of income are government grants and cash gifts from rural followers and urban associations. None of these dollar amounts are adjusted for inflation (Cruise O'Brien 1971, 124, 139).

ginning with the severe drought of 1968, governmental officials reported sharp increases in the production of millet for local consumption in acreage previously devoted to peanuts" (Schumacher 1975, 184). In 1986, the Senegalese government estimated that about 60 percent of all agricultural land was used for the cultivation of food (as opposed to cash) crops (Goetz 1992, 729).

Poor and vulnerable populations also employ a variety of social strategies to ensure a measure of economic security. In Wolof and Serer farm communities customary land tenure arrangements require the head of each compound to allocate land to compound members for their own use. The peanuts that are usually grown on these fields provide many female, elderly, and poor family members their own cash income. Additionally, informal lending and borrowing of land between compounds enable farmers to maximize the number of plots on which peanut and millet crops can be rotated, a practice that helps maintain soil productivity and crop yields (Golan 1994).

Some strategies are common to both rural and urban dwellers, such as trying to find patrons in the system of clientelism that permeates the country's political, economic, and religious institutions. Another shared strategy is to turn to networks of kin, friends, and neighbors. Farmers may engage in various forms of collective agricultural work, such as *santaane* (obligatory cooperative work organized by an individual), *dimbali* (voluntary cooperative work), and *nadante* (reciprocated work) (Copans et al. 1972, 227; Venema 1978, 147–56). They may also participate in cooperative groups (*xamba* or *kompin*) that work the fields of local notables in exchange for money or goods, resources used to ease the burden of costly ceremonies such as weddings and baptisms. These cooperative groups will also work the field of a member who falls ill, or help in arduous tasks such as house building. As one anthropologist noted, the function of these groups is to "provide mutual aid in labor and economic 'insurance' for their members" (Ames 1959, 224).

Urbanites have their own cooperative groups. Muslims belong to urban religious associations known as *dahira*, which, beyond their specifically religious aims, collect fees from members that are put aside to be used for mutual assistance (Diop 1982; Cruise O'Brien 1988, 139; Samb 1989; Villalón 1995, 150–62). Women often belong to neighborhood mutual-aid groups called *mbootaay*, which collect contributions from their members to be used in times of emergency or to organize familial ceremonies (Ndione 1992, 22, 30). Another type of association, known as *mbaxal*, collects money from members to finance regular get-togethers (Mottin-Sylla 1987, 8). City dwellers also take part in the rotating credit associations known as tontines, which provide each member in turn with a sum of money that would ordinarily lie beyond his or her possibilities (1–7). Other, similar associations exist as well (for an overview of the various types see Odeyé-Finzi 1985; Fall 1994; Antoine et al. 1995, 173–96).

Tontines, *mbootaay, mbaxal, dahira,* and the like do not merely satisfy short-term financial needs. They also serve to solidify a wide web of social bonds that may be counted upon in times of trouble. It follows, as one researcher with long experience studying women's associations in Dakar observed, that "what counts is the circulation of money through neighborhoods or social networks under various pretexts: familial ceremonies, gifts, loans, economic activity. This fluidity of money permits the formation of alliances, to multiply one's partners and to diversify sources of income" (Ndione 1992, 17). Thus even in urban areas, market activity is not the sole means of survival. Indeed, unique reliance on individual economic activity may threaten one's welfare: "Counting exclusively on individual economic activity leads to a rupture with one's solidarity network, to isolation, to inertia and impasse. In contrast, to multiply one's contacts, by enlarging the social networks in place through continued investment in relationships, constitutes a more sure guarantee of survival in the peri-urban environment" (63). Investing in relationships provides a kind of security and wealth unattainable from individual action. The person who is socially isolated is thus often seen to be more at risk and poorer than the person who has few economic resources but many social ties. As a Wolof proverb puts it: "Poverty is not the lack of clothing; the person who is truly poor is the person who has nobody" (cited in Ndione 1987, 154).[23] Putting all one's resources in market activity is risky, then, not simply because of fluctuating prices and state interference. Many Senegalese must balance any potential gains from the monetary economy against the risk of loosening or severing the social bonds that form their safety net.[24]

It should perhaps be stated explicitly that these webs of reciprocal social relations are incorporated within a broader pattern of moral obligation that stresses the importance of mutual assistance. These bonds are, of course, functional for the individual's self-interest insofar as they are essential strands in the community safety net, but they are also objects of respect and consideration. The upkeep of these bonds is a matter of loyalty (kollëre), honor (ngor), and dignity (fulla) (Ly 1967, 285–326; Sylla 1978, 170–82). These bonds are, in short, embedded in a deeper set of cultural values. This may explain why an ethic of mutuality persists even among a certain number of better-off Senegalese.

However strong these bonds may be, social safety nets sometimes fail. Failures affecting whole communities result from prolonged drought. The failure of individual or family nets most commonly results from a reliance on resource-poor or inadequately diverse solidarity networks. In such cases, those affected cut down on food consumption, forage for food in the wild or in garbage dumps, or turn to crime and prostitution (World Bank 1995a, 11–13).

Because welfare and notions of mutuality associated with the concept of demokaraasi are so closely linked, it may not be coincidental that this Wolof term calls up images of sharing or apportioning food—be it the mother of

---

[23] In Wolof: "Rafle, du ñakk yëre, waaye ki rafle mooy ki amul nit."
[24] In surveying a wider literature on Africa, Lemarchand (1989, 58) makes a similar point.

twins who lies on her back, or the host who divides food equally between two bowls. Sharing food, after all, is a concrete way to establish trust and bonds of solidarity.[25] One Bayfall disciple[26] seemed to have these connections in mind when he explained that "eating together . . . , sharing is typically Senegalese. If you arrive somewhere you say 'peace unto you,' the host replies 'come eat.' This has always existed here. And it is this that has created *demokaraasi*. Yes, take the beggar—he goes around with his bowl asking for food. Every house he goes to gives him rice. That is pure *demokaraasi*." Pure *demokaraasi* means giving on demand to someone needy who has nothing to offer. It is a willingness to share, even if one gets nothing in return. It is not by chance that the Bayfall disciple used the idiom of food to convey this idea: sharing food is an important metaphor for *demokaraasi* because an important purpose of *demokaraasi* is to ensure material security through mutual community assistance.

The notions of *demokaraasi* held by many non-French-speaking Wolofones appear, then, to be conditioned by the repertoire of normative and institutional strategies used by this largely poor and vulnerable population to respond to their precarious life conditions.[27] This conclusion, of course, begs the question why the concept *demokaraasi* in particular has become associated with norms of mutuality. This is the question to which we now turn.


## Mutuality, Economic Security, and Elections

Why do so many Wolofones with little or no schooling make a connection between mutuality and economic security, on the one hand, and the concept of *demokaraasi,* on the other? The most plausible explanation seems related to the fact that Wolofones who lack the language skills to grasp elite-generated meanings of *démocratie* have learned from Wolof-language broadcasts that *demokaraasi* has something to do with elections, as well as with religious communality and distributive generosity. These meanings dovetail with the lived experience of many Senegalese insofar as elections—the institutional referent of *demokaraasi*—provide an important occasion to attain solidarity and material goods. But uneducated Wolofones also sever from this concept the religious and royal connotations attached to it (for the most part unintentionally) by the Francophone elite, while preserving meanings that are consistent with their

[25] Several case studies show the same to be true elsewhere in Africa. See, in particular, Price 1975, 116–20; Goody 1982, 88–93. A more theoretical discussion can be found in Sahlins 1972, 215–19.

[26] The Bayfalls are a sect of the Mouride brotherhood which believes that work in the service of a marabout may substitute for prayer. In this case, the Bayfall disciple lives with and works the fields of his marabout.

[27] Poverty is strongly correlated with a lack of formal education and thus also with French-language skills (World Bank 1995a, 8).

economic predicament and the electoral strategies they use to ensure collective security.

In an electoral system shot through with clientelism, many Senegalese citizens regard participation in the electoral process as a form of economic exchange in which political patrons offer money or food in return for votes. This was the view of the elderly woman in Dakar whose statement we examined in Chapter 2. For her, *demokaraasi* meant the exchange of political support for rice, sugar, or money. Another woman, a gas station attendant in the same poor Dakar neighborhood, explained why these exchanges are so important: "If you don't belong to the party [the PS] you are nothing. You can't resolve any of your problems. Life is expensive and there is no money."

Procuring benefits may sometimes require the efforts of an entire urban neighborhood or rural village. In the city of Pikine, residents organize themselves into *tendances* in search of PS patrons who can provide them with communal fountains, an essential public good in an area where virtually all dwellings are without running water. The political patron can expect, in return, votes on election day and demonstrations of popular support at local rallies and meetings (Salem 1992).

If the benefits derived from participation in the electoral system are sometimes immediate and tangible, at other times they are more diffuse, serving instead to cement community bonds necessary for collective long-term security. Recall how the essence of *demokaraasi* for Modou appeared to lie in the unanimity achieved in his village and in the social harmony it ensured. Through the act of voting, the villagers reinforced their ties of solidarity and strengthened their safety net.

To sum up, the elite's Wolof-language messages are only partially responsible for the way uneducated Wolofones today understand *demokaraasi*. Also important is the way vulnerable populations respond to their life conditions. Economic uncertainty, the ethic of mutuality to which it gives rise, and the use of elections to promote collective security are all important elements for explaining how and why *demokaraasi* has come to mean mutuality.


## *Demokaraasi*'s Opposite: *Politig*

A discussion of one final dimension of *demokaraasi* is warranted. Mutual trust betrayed, reciprocal obligations snubbed, social bonds abused, and *demokaraasi* thwarted are, in Wolof, called *politig*, a term that derives from the French noun *politique*, which American English speakers usually translate as "politics." How this situation came about requires a brief explanation.

Like the French *politique*, the Wolof term can mean many things depending on the context. Several of its meanings resemble closely those of its French progenitor.[28] *Politig,* like *politique,* is often used to refer in a general way to the activities of governments, political parties, and leaders. Both can also mean "policy." We can, for example, translate both *la politique agricole* and *politigu mbey* as "agricultural policy."

Yet Wolof speakers, even those who speak no French, draw a sharp distinction between "French" and "Wolof" meanings of *politig,* a difference that is most clearly seen when *politig* is used as a transitive verb or adjective. A farmer living in a village without a single French-speaking resident explained that "in French, *politig* means that those in power do all that they can to create good, to bring together intelligent people to lead the country. But in Wolof, *politig* is a foul word. We think immediately of deception. If you say something that seems false, we say that you are trying to *politig* us. *Politig* is to lie, to trick." A non-francophone farmer in a different village expressed similar ideas: "*Politig,* in French, means to build the country. *Politig* in Wolof is different. I go to a tailor. Instead of sewing my shirt with tight, solid stitches, he does shoddy, careless, *politig* work; work that should have been done well, but is done poorly, intentionally so." For Wolofones, then, the "French" meaning of *politig* carries a range of positive connotations; the "Wolof" meaning, in contrast, is strongly pejorative and indicates a variety of dishonest or deceitful behaviors.[29]

Many Senegalese associate this Wolof meaning of *politig* with the self-serving lies politicians tend to tell in search of votes and support. A tailor offered the following allegory about politicians: "I will explain to you what *politig* is: when their car breaks down they call you, ask you to push it, and promise you a ride in return. When it starts, they wave goodbye and drive away. You are left standing in the road." The reference is to how politicians make false pledges when they ask for votes, with no intention of giving their electors anything in return. They manipulate voters' expectations of reciprocity and solidarity for their own advantage. Central to the meaning of *politig* is this underhanded exploitation.

Members of the Senegalese political elite are well aware of these pejorative meanings of *politig.* Several intellectuals and politicians I interviewed thought its origins dated to the late 1940s or the early 1950s, when the French colonial

[28] The French term *politique* can be used in a variety of contexts. As a noun it can be feminine (*la politique*) as well as masculine (*le politique*). In its feminine form, we can distinguish at least two different usages. It can mean "line of conduct" or "policy," as in *la politique coloniale* (colonial policy) and *la politique de gauche* (left-wing policies). In other contexts it denotes involvement in public life as a career or activist. Thus we might translate *faire de la politique* as "to be a political activist" or "to be in politics (as a career)." We can also identify two usages of the masculine form of the term. It can refer to a person involved in *la politique* as a career (a politician) and it can also mean "politics, the political side of things."

[29] The French language does, in fact, have a verb (*politiquer*) and adjective (*politique*) that derive from the noun *politique.* The verb is always intransitive, fairly neutral, and often used informally to mean, variously, to be interested in, to talk about, or to engage in politics. The adjective has a range of meanings that, depending on the context, correspond roughly to the English "political" or "diplomatic."

administration extended suffrage to all adult Senegalese. For the first time politicians campaigned in rural areas and made wild promises to peasants unlearned in the workings of the new electoral system.

Evidence shows that *politig* was indeed used in its pejorative sense at that time. In a 1950 party organ one political commentator, writing in French, discussed the unique meaning of *politig*, or, as he spelled it, *poleutique*:

> In Wolof, the word *politique* does not have an equivalent. The corresponding word is *poleutique*, a term that does not find its origins in any African dialect, and is in fact derived from the French word. This word *poleutique* has, and can only have, a pejorative meaning. It signifies wiliness and insincerity; a game dominated by guile, a game in which the most cunning dupes the most foolish; a game one needs to know how to escape. The Wolof has a good laugh when one tries to make him understand that *politique* is a social service destined to guarantee the primacy of the general interest, to improve the material conditions of the masses, to transform the face of the country. He has only seen men who today find black what yesterday they presented as white; men who, if the occasion arose, would tell you without batting an eye that nobody is infallible, and nevertheless continue to fatten themselves on the stupidity of their neighbors. All this, in time, has conferred great credibility on the bamboozlers and professional hoodwinkers who know how to bellow in front of crowds and shed tears out of pure *poleutique*. (*Condition Humaine*, March 28, 1950)

Yet references to a particularly Wolof understanding of *politig* date back much further. In 1914 a mulatto merchant named Louis Pellegrin, a candidate for the legislature that year, wrote: "In 1896 I returned to the colony I had left when I was four years old. . . . I noticed at once that our old colony was still in its childhood and that the politique that was applied to it seemed to be purely administrative. To give you an idea of the impression held by the native-born of the old *politique*, consult with me the Wolof language. The word *politique*, taken from French, means in Wolof: circumlocution, lies, falsehoods" (Pellegrin 1914).

At that time electoral competition was restricted to Europeans, mulattoes, and a limited number of Africans living in the Four Communes. In 1914 a total of 4,863 people voted, and only a fraction of them were Africans. The vast majority of urban and rural Senegalese—that is to say, the mass of Wolof speakers—were formally excluded. Nevertheless, some of these excluded Senegalese were becoming more politically engaged (Johnson 1971, 218). Thus it is difficult to determine whether the *politig* known to most Wolof speakers at that time was closer to "policy" or "electoral politics"—whether it was the policies of colonial administrators or the practices of indigenous political candidates and elected officials that were riddled with lies, deceit, and circumlocution.[30]

---

[30] Pellegrin himself emphasizes the preponderance of policy in the turn-of-the-century colony when he writes that the *politique* that had been applied was "purely administrative." Certainly there was plenty of deception in Senegalese electoral competition at the time. The 1908 legislative elec-

Wherever its origins lie, this Wolof concept of *politig* has been extended to a wide range of contexts. Indeed, Wolofones use *politig* pejoratively in situations that American English speakers would not consider to be political at all. As we saw earlier, a tailor can do "*politig* work." Or consider an artisan who tries to pass off as gold a ring made of brass. In Wolof the ring would be called a "*politig* ring." In this context *politig* means fake or phony. A Dakar jeweler explained: "The way I see it, *politig* means hidden lies. If I take a ring, and I want to use it to *politig* you, I will tell you that the ring is gold when it is really brass. That ring, you can sell it for five thousand CFA, even though it sells for only ten CFA in the market. In our eyes that is *politig*." The use of *politig* here places the emphasis on the injurious intentions of the seller who has broken the bonds of trust with his client. "To *politig*" is to abuse the confidence someone has placed in you. It refers to an act committed for the purposes of duplicity and betrayal.[31]

Thus the way Wolofones distinguish what "is *politig*" from what is "not *politig*" looks very different from the way American English speakers distinguish what counts as politics from what does not. What is salient to Wolof speakers is a distinction between actions that undermine mutuality (and by extension collective security) and those that promote it. *Politig* belongs to the former category and *demokaraasi* to the latter. A farmer summed up the situation well. "For us Wolof," he explained, "*politig* is a vile word because it means to fool, to exploit, to betray. But *demokaraasi* is a good thing. It strengthens the country. It is something that can lift a person up, support him."[32]

---

tions were annulled, for example, partly because one of the French candidates made the fraudulent promise to his African electorate that he would rescind all house taxes if he were elected mayor, something only the governor had the authority to do (Johnson 1971, 117, 121).

[31] Contrary to popular opinion in Senegal, the Wolof term *politig* is not unique in meaning any kind of exploitive lie or trick. In the Africanized French of Congo and Cameroon, *la politique* can also refer broadly to various forms of deception. In Rwanda, *les politiques* has come to mean gossip or false rumors (Equipe IFA 1983, 299). Some bilingual Mende in Sierra Leone translate the English word "politics" with the Mende *kabânde* — a term that, in the words of one student of Mende culture, "refers to rhetorical tricks of deception and evasion" (Murphy 1990, 34). The Bambara term *politigi* also carries negative connotations and, like the Wolof *politig*, can be used as a verb to mean "to trick" or "to fool" (John Hutchison, personal communication, December 1991). This may explain why linguists in Mali were moved to coin a Bambara neologism, *nyetaasira*, to translate *la politique*. *Nyetaasira* translates roughly as "the path of progress" (Calvet 1987, 236–38).

[32] In one respect, the Wolof and American concepts *are* similar: the opposition between *demokaraasi* and *politig* is parallel to the opposition, in some contexts, between "democracy" and "politics." This parallel results from the fact that democracy and *demokaraasi* are both freighted with positive connotations, as politics and *politig* are with pejorative ones. Thus an American populist may laud "real" democracy while attacking politics and politicians, just as this farmer praises *demokaraasi* while assailing *politig*. Still, the content of this opposition in the English language is somewhat different from that in Wolof. For the American populist, the opposition seems to have something to do with citizen autonomy vs. outside control — usually by politicians in Washington (see, for instance, Garry Wills, "The New Revolutionaries," *New York Review of Books*, August 10, 1995). For the Wolof farmer, the opposition has something to do with actions that promote mutuality vs. those that undermine it.

## The Meaning of *Demokaraasi* Revisited

It may be helpful at this point to sum up what we have learned about *demokaraasi*. The term derives from the French concept *démocratie* and probably entered the lexical stock of most Wolof speakers sometime after the reintroduction of multiparty politics in 1974. At that time, intense rivalries developed between the ruling party and the opposition, prompting each to define this French concept in ways beneficial to its interests. While the ruling party has argued that true *démocratie* is simply the right of political parties to organize freely and proclaim their agendas openly, the opposition has insisted that the concept also entails fair rules of electoral competition and party turnover.

In their rivalry to lend exclusive legitimacy to their understandings of *démocratie,* both ruling and opposition parties have tried to disseminate their opposing views to the broader, mostly non-French-speaking population. To reach these non-Francophones, political leaders have chosen, by and large, to speak Wolof, for Wolof is the most widely spoken language in the country. *Démocratie,* however, has no direct equivalents in Wolof. Members of the political elite have thus tried to communicate their views by extending established Wolof words to novel political contexts or by using metaphors to render this foreign concept intelligible to Wolof speakers. These projections and metaphors have carried with them meanings embedded in popular culture that added connotations of religious harmony and kingly generosity, connotations that contributed unintentionally to the creation of *demokaraasi* as a distinct Wolof concept.

Non-francophone Wolof speakers, in turn, have adapted this word to their own culture and conditions. For them, *demokaraasi* has continued to be associated with elections, voting, and multipartyism, associations that correspond most closely to those of its French progenitor. The word has, however, taken on added meanings of consensus, solidarity, and evenhandedness, meanings derived in part from the Wolof discourse of the political elite and in part from an ethic of mutuality rooted in a pervasive condition of economic precariousness.

It appears that notions of voting and elections have become linked to ideas of mutuality because for many voters, participation in the electoral process has ensured collective economic security. Most important, elections are occasions to build relationships with electoral patrons and to obtain material rewards from them, as well as occasions to reinforce ties of solidarity that may be called upon in times of crisis. It follows that the opposites of *demokaraasi* are disruption, discord, exploitation, egoism, and greed—in short, *politig.*

## *Demokaraasi* and Democracy Compared

We are now in a position to compare systematically the meanings of *demokaraasi* and "democracy" and to determine the degree to which the ideal aspects of the two concepts overlap.

At the broadest level of comparison, both *demokaraasi* and democracy are concepts that belong to the realm of human interaction, concepts that involve people's conduct with and among other people. To borrow a phrase from Hannah Arendt (1958, 7), both relate to the "human condition of plurality."

Both concepts, furthermore, refer to patterns of interaction that are generally deemed good or desirable in their respective societies. That is, both concepts carry strong positive connotations. *Demokaraasi* represents an ideal associated with collective economic security, an ideal that I have labeled "mutuality." Wolof speakers contrast this ideal with the egotism and greed associated with *politig*. Similarly, democracy entails an ideal of widespread participation in governance, which encompasses ideals of equality, meaningful participation, and the availability of choice.

For both Wolof and American English-language concepts, furthermore, these ideals apply both to electoral politics and to a wider range of situations. The meaning of democracy thus ranges from universal suffrage to inclusive participation in such activities as basketball and dancing; from the elimination of social or economic inequalities that infringe on electoral participation to the leveling effect of activities such as riding the subway and eating ice cream; from the availability of meaningful electoral options to the availability of choices to consumers, be it among electronic mail systems or diner menu selections.

Similarly, the meaning of *demokaraasi* ranges from agreement among villagers to vote for a particular candidate to the agreement of religious leaders on what day to begin a lunar-based holiday, from the reciprocity of voter and elected patron to the solidarity of villagers who come to the aid of an ill neighbor, from the fair distribution of electoral spoils to the evenhandedness of a nursing mother of twins.

As we have seen, many nonpolitical uses of "democracy" in American English are metaphorical extensions of literal political ones, though it is not always easy to distinguish between the two. The same may be true of *demokaraasi*, although such a distinction is even more difficult to recognize, for mutuality is so diffuse a notion that many kinds of agreement, solidarity, and evenhandedness may, in fact, be relevant to building a social network that can be called upon in times of crisis. As a result, it is all the more difficult to determine where literal usage ends and metaphorical extension begins.

Still, taken in their more restrictive electoral contexts, democracy and *demokaraasi* are similar insofar as both contain ideals that are collective goods. In other words, both widespread participation in governance (in the case of democracy) and material security (in the case of *demokaraasi*) are goods that are social, goods that can be realized only in a collectivity. The two are different insofar as one is related most directly to a concern for autonomy, the other to a concern for welfare. This difference is, however, easily blurred in practice. For those who participate in democracy, concern about material well-being provides an important motive for taking part in collective decision making; and for those who participate in *demokaraasi,* an important way to guarantee collective welfare is through electoral participation.

Be that as it may, central to both concepts are elements of choice and decision making, for the achievement of each collective good is a social undertaking, one that requires many people to act together, to make decisions, to choose among options. But whereas democracy (when used literally) requires the opportunity to choose among meaningful options in the service of governance, *demokaraasi* requires only agreement on a particular option chosen in the service of social harmony. Whereas democracy requires that decision making on matters that affect the community be made inclusively, *demokaraasi* requires that such decisions be made with an eye to reinforcing bonds of solidarity.

In addition, basic to both concepts (in electoral and nonelectoral contexts alike) is some notion of equality, whether it takes the form of social equality (the equality of maid and stockbroker riding the same subway train), distributive equality (the equality experienced by the secretary who can eat the same ice cream as Donald Trump), or fairness (the equality of a mother nursing her twins without partiality). The leveling or homogenizing democracy of the subway or gourmet ice cream converges with *demokaraasi* used in the sense of fair treatment.

The equalities of democracy and *demokaraasi* are the same insofar as both are only partial. In *demokaraasi,* there is no leveling of status between a mother and her nursing infants, between a religious leader and his disciples, between a polygamous husband and his wives, or between a homeowner and beggars. What is important is that guardians and benefactors treat the people under their care or patronage evenhandedly. In democracy, hierarchy exists as a kind of background condition. It makes sense to speak of the democratizing effect of the subway only if the stockbroker and the maid were in some meaningful sense unequal before they began the ride. And of course, this inequality still exists while they ride, or while the secretary eats the same ice cream as Donald Trump. The stockbroker and the maid share only subway inconveniences; Mr. Trump and the secretary share only ice cream. It is, in effect, the leveling of particular inequalities that counts as democracy.

Differences between the equality entailed by the Wolof and American English concepts do appear, however, when we examine how their respective ideals apply to the context of electoral politics. The equality of democracy requires that social or economic inequalities be prevented from undermining equal participation in the selection of leaders or policies (thus the importance of the slogan "one man, one vote"). In other words, both the stockbroker and the maid must each have, among other things, the right to one (and only one) vote and the right to run for office, whatever other inequalities may exist between them. The evenhandedness of *demokaraasi,* in contrast, requires that benefits acquired by elected officials be distributed fairly among the voters who elected them, just as the mother must nurse her twins fairly. The equality of democracy is an equal right to participate in decision making; the evenhandedness of *demokaraasi* is a fair distribution of material benefits.

Finally, the American English and Wolof concepts are similar insofar as both evidence a duality of form and function. That is, both concepts are used to refer not only to ideals but also to institutions, most notably electoral institutions, that can or do realize these ideals.

It should be stressed, however, that this overlapping of institutions is only partial. *Demokaraasi* may be used to refer to many institutions that American English speakers would not usually consider democratic. One such institution is the Mouride brotherhood. Its hierarchical internal structure, the spiritual and temporal guidance provided by religious leaders to their followers, and the integral place of religious commands (*ndigal*) and acts of submission (*jébbalu*) make it arguably an undemocratic institution. Yet many uneducated Wolof speakers see the brotherhood as an institution infused with *demokaraasi* because it offers economic security, whether from participation in its offshoot associations (*dahira*) or from reciprocal exchanges with religious clerics.

Other institutions that have the potential to realize *demokaraasi* include various urban and rural mutual aid groups, revolving credit and cooperative work associations, and the state agencies that distribute seed and credit. Insofar as a given institution functions to preserve or enhance collective economic security (or at least fosters consensus, solidarity, and evenhandedness), it may be associated with *demokaraasi*. Of course, American English speakers may consider some of these same institutions to be democratic, but only to the degree that they allow meaningful, widespread participation in governance, or at least involve some kind of inclusive participation or social equality, or make available some kind of meaningful choices.

Thus many kinds of institutions may or may not be democratic, may or may not embody *demokaraasi*. Actors and outside observers are, in fact, able to judge whether particular institutions or situations are instances of democracy or *demokaraasi* only because they have standards for doing so.

We are now in a position to compare these standards. When deeming something to be an instance of democracy, American English speakers ordinarily consider the thing in question to actualize at least one of the ideals on the left side of Table 1. When deeming something to be an instance of *demokaraasi*, Wolof speakers with little or no education ordinarily consider the thing in question to actualize at least one of the ideals on the right side of Table 1. Despite these apparent differences, there are various points of commonality, most notably the presence of collective goods, the centrality of partial equality, and the importance of choice and decision making.

We can also identify, more specifically, standards used by American English and Wolof speakers to judge the presence or absence of democracy and *demokaraasi* in electoral institutions. A summary of these differences can be

*Table 1.* Some standards for judging the presence of democracy and *demokaraasi*

| Democracy | Demokaraasi |
|---|---|
| Widespread participation, which requires one or more of the following: | Mutuality, which requires one or more of the following: |
| Availability of meaningful choices and freedom to decide among these choices | Consensus (the achievement of various types of agreement) |
| Inclusive participation | Solidarity (reciprocity between people who have a sense of shared responsibility for one another) |
| Economic and social inequalities diminished or irrelevant for inclusive participation | Evenhandedness (guardians or caretakers treat those under their care or authority fairly) |

found in Table 2. Of course, these are only conceptual standards. In reality, other consequences may ensue. In Senegal, electoral institutions are the loci of clan rivalries and the occasional violence that results, while in the United States, money politics often makes economic inequalities count heavily in electoral outcomes. Thus electoral institutions in the United States may or may not be democratic, just as electoral institutions in Senegal may or may not realize *demokaraasi.* Conversely, electoral institutions in the United States may act as conduits for the exchange of votes and material goods and thus, perhaps, be a good example of *demokaraasi,* just as the presence of meaningful political options in Senegalese electoral politics may, perhaps, be a good example of democracy. Table 2, to repeat, shows only *standards* for judging whether particular electoral institutions count as instances of democracy or *demokaraasi.*

*Table 2.* Some standards for judging the presence of democracy and *demokaraasi* in electoral institutions

| Democracy | Demokaraasi |
|---|---|
| Widespread participation in governance, which requires one or more of the following: | Mutuality, which requires one or more of the following: |
| Availability of meaningful political choices (between candidates, policies, etc.) and freedom to decide among those choices | Agreement on choices (candidates, policies) among voters in same social network (family, village, neighborhood, religious community, etc.) |
| Inclusive participation in decision making; many people vote and rotate the holding of offices | Reciprocal solidarity between voters and elected officials (exchange of votes for material goods) and among voters (facilitated by consensus) |
| Economic and social inequalities diminished or irrelevant for inclusive participation in decision-making process (e.g., voting, running for office) | Evenhanded distribution of benefits by elected officials (whether or not public channels are used) |

To sum up, then, "democracy" and *demokaraasi* are related in meaning, which is not surprising since they are linked historically by way of *démocratie*. In their institutional aspects, they are related insofar as both refer centrally to electoral institutions but may also refer to a wider range of institutions and situations. In their ideal aspects, they are related insofar as both project a socially valued state that can be achieved only through collective action, the making of choices and decisions, and some notion of partial equality.

The concepts do, however, differ in one critical way. The ideal of democracy, used literally, requires collective participation in decision making; used metaphorically, it requires inclusive participation, availability of choice, or diminished inequality. The ideal of *demokaraasi* is best realized through the attainment of collective economic security via mutuality, or at a minimum through the achievement of consensus, solidarity, or evenhandedness. As a result of these differing standards, the two concepts point toward institutions and practices that are only partially overlapping. Let us explore some consequences of this partialness.

# 4

## *Demokaraasi* and Voting Behavior

Having compared *demokaraasi* to democracy, we are now better prepared to investigate aspects of electoral participation in Senegal that might be deemed too hazy for study if one relied exclusively on a Schumpeterian strategy of inquiry, or might go unnoticed if one were restricted to a Dahlian concern about democratic competence. My goal here is to identify those contexts in which we can learn something important about the electoral participation of Wolofones by taking into account their own conceptual schemes.

### A Thought Experiment

To help identify such contexts, we will engage in a thought experiment whose lessons will become clearer as it proceeds. Imagine now a social scientist who discovers a functioning democracy among the Senegalese even though the Wolof language has no term that translates "democracy" exactly. To contemplate what such a discovery would entail, it may be useful to distinguish between:

1. The American English word "democracy" and the standards or ideals it encompasses.
2. The Wolof word *demokaraasi* and the standards or ideals it encompasses.
3. The institutions that English-speaking Americans associate with the word "democracy."

4. The institutions that Wolof-speaking Senegalese associate with the word *demokaraasi*.
5. The actual political institutions of Americans.
6. The actual political institutions of the Senegalese.

Using these distinctions, let us recast the issue as follows: What would it mean for our social scientist to find significant overlap between the institutions that Americans associate with the word "democracy" (level 3) and the actual political institutions of the Senegalese (level 6), even though important differences exist between the English word "democracy" (level 1) and the Wolof word *demokaraasi* (level 2)?

Looking for a correspondence between the institutions of some alien country (level 6) and the institutions Americans normally consider democratic (level 3) is, of course, a strategy common among social scientists today, especially among those who stand under the long shadow of Schumpeter. Such a strategy entails accepting various electoral institutions as democratic and allowing that these institutions sometimes operate imperfectly (thus the gap between what Americans normally consider democratic [level 3] and how their actual institutions function [level 5]).

Using this strategy, our imaginary social scientist might conclude that Senegal is a democracy if she found most or all these institutions in that country. If she found, instead, that Senegal has some but not all, she might conclude that the country is only partially democratic. And if she found that Senegal lacks them entirely, she might conclude that real democracy does not exist there at all.

Whatever conclusions she reaches, there is an advantage to posing the question in this way: focusing on institutions facilitates large-scale comparative analysis. This advantage, however, is counterbalanced by problems. Most important, designating particular institutions as central components of democracy presupposes standards by which to judge whether such institutions are in fact democratic. That is, our social scientist can identify the institutional features of democracy (in Senegal, the United States, or elsewhere) only if she first recognizes a certain set of institutions as somehow integral to the project of democracy.

This realization might lead her to consider, additionally, the meaning of democracy and the standards it encompasses (level 1). From this perspective, she might ask whether the actual functioning of Senegalese institutions (level 6) meets American standards of democracy (level 1). This is the question a scholar such as Dahl is likely to ask.

To address this question our imaginary social scientist might look at the observable context and consequences of the participants' actions. She would want to know whether involvement in these institutions brought about meaningful, inclusive participation in governance in some observable way; that is, in the case of electoral institutions, whether people actually voted, and whether their voting was really consequential in the process of collective decision making. Thus if Senegalese voters were obviously coerced in making their electoral choices, or if those choices clearly had no impact on policy or selection of leaders, she would surely be suspicious of claims that electoral institutions in Senegal were substantively democratic.

Reliance on such observations, however, entails an important assumption: our imaginary social scientist must accept that voting is an act of registering preference, regardless of what the person actually understands or intends by placing the ballot in the box. Yet there are surely times when she would want to know whether the person placing a piece of paper in a box is actually registering a preference, especially when she wants to inquire about the meaning of the vote. From this perspective, intentions matter.

Our social scientist can, of course, sometimes glean intentions by simply observing contexts and behaviors. Imagine that a person, broom in hand, walks into a polling station late at night on election day, after the poll workers have left and the results have been announced, and sweeps up from the floor dozens of crumpled ballots and shovels them into an empty ballot box, along with some rotten fruit and other debris. It seems reasonable to assume that by so doing this person did not mean to vote or register a preference. The context suggests, rather, that this person was simply cleaning up.

Drawing conclusions about intentions from observable behavior and context, however, is not always so easy. Marking an $X$ on a ballot and dropping it in a ballot box may count as voting in the right context, but what does it reveal about the person's actual intentions? At this point our social scientist would like to ask the ballot caster, "Why did you mark the ballot in that way and put it in the box?" The person might respond, "Because I am voting."[1] Probed further, the person might add, "Because I liked candidate $J$," and give a variety of reasons for registering a preference for candidate $J$ over candidate $K$. On the basis of such answers our social scientist might infer that this person understands what it means to vote and participate in a democracy. But what would she make of a person who cast a ballot without possessing basic knowledge about the connection between casting ballots and choosing candidates; of a person who dropped a green slip of paper as opposed to a blue slip of paper into the ballot box only because an uncle or religious leader instructed him to do so? Our social scientist might determine that this person is, to return to Dahl's formulation, an incompetent voter in the service of democracy. Of course, she will not know unless she questions the ballot caster, until she asks how he understands the purposes of voting and participation in elections.

---

[1] Of course, this question has many possible answers, depending on what the respondent assumes the asker does not know, or needs to know. Other answers might be "Because I'm late," "Because I made a mistake," "Because I only had a pencil," "Because I'm left-handed." To ascertain how the person comprehends the purpose of voting, then, one may well have to ask further questions.

To figure out whether Senegal is a democracy, then, our social scientist may well need to examine voter intentions, for through such an inquiry she might determine (in ways that observation of nonverbal conduct cannot) the degree to which voters see themselves as involved in democratic governance.

There are problems, however, with gleaning intentions from questions such as "Why did you vote?" and "Why did you vote for candidate *J*?" Such questions assume that voters can articulate their intentions, an assumption that may be false to the extent that people do not themselves know their true motives. Still, our social scientist is more likely to learn something about these motives by asking such questions than by relying on observation of nonverbal conduct alone.

Additional problems arise when such questions are posed in foreign languages. Our social scientist cannot assume, for instance, that language *Z* has a word that corresponds exactly to, say, "vote." She thus wants to be sure that the ballot casters do not misunderstand her questions and that she does not misinterpret their answers, that she does not conflate her understanding with what makes sense to them.

It is at this juncture that an alternative circle-closing strategy becomes important. Returning to the case of Senegal, we must consider *demokaraasi* (level 2) and the institutions that Wolof speakers associate with the word (level 4). Analysis of *demokaraasi* and related institutions, after all, provides insight into the shared cultural frames that Wolof speakers use to understand electoral institutions, insight that (1) might not be obtained by observation of nonverbal conduct alone and (2) is essential for making sense of ballot casters' responses to such questions as "Why did you vote?"

What counts as evidence for democracy in Senegal, then, depends on the assumptions that our social scientist is willing to make: Is she willing to accept as democratic the simple presence of fair and free elections, as a Schumpeterian might? Is she willing to see voting as an act of registering preference, no matter what the person actually understands or intends by placing the ballot in the box? The less she is willing to assume, the more important it becomes to study intentions and conceptual schemes.

This imaginary exercise has implications that extend beyond the borders of Senegal. It suggests that different assumptions are appropriate to different research agendas. In the comparative study of democracy, the exercise suggests that it is most important to be wary of explanations that rest on unexamined assumptions about the aims of voters when such assumptions (1) are pivotal to what is being explained and (2) pertain to individuals from substantially different cultures.

This point can perhaps be made more forcefully if we consider an example drawn from the work of real social scientists. Take the writings of scholars who see a positive causal link between mass political participation and accountability, a link, not incidentally, that today provides one of the theoretical underpinnings for many American and World Bank governance and democracy-building programs in Asia, Africa, Eastern Europe, and Latin America.[2] In these works, it is a common assumption that the institutionalization of competitive elections makes government operations more transparent. Elections elicit active popular participation, the argument goes, and this participation makes leaders more accountable insofar as public officials are obliged to be responsive to the wishes of the electorate if they hope to remain in power.

This responsiveness, in turn, is said to create norms of accountability that (1) prevent elected officials from appropriating state resources for private use (Nyong'o, 1988, 71–72; Kpundeh 1992, 36); (2) make public agencies less corrupt (King 1981, 500; Goodell and Powelson 1982, 174; Sklar 1987, 713; Landell-Mills and Serageldin 1992, 311); (3) make elected officials more willing to change inappropriate policies and consider a broader range of policy options (Healey and Robinson 1992, 152);[3] and (4) extend trust and predictability beyond interactions based on personalism (Goodell and Powelson 1982, 171).

Of course, these arguments are tenable only if voters do indeed expect elected officials to act in the public interest and in accordance with the rule of law. For this reason, it is important to verify that voters do in fact hold such expectations. The problem, at least with regard to Africa, is that researchers know little about voter intentions, a point emphasized by Tom Young, who, after surveying the literature on African elections, concludes that "our grasp of how electoral processes are perceived and understood in non-Western cultural settings . . . remains relatively slight" (1993, 307).

In the literature on African voting behavior that does exist, it is generally recognized that the factors influencing voting behavior are complex and depend on—among other things—whether elections involve single intraparty or multiparty competition, levels of ethnic polarization, and the breadth of clientelist networks. Still, for those who see voting as being in some sense rational, three general categories of motivation stand out. People vote to:

1.  Influence public policy and the allocation of resources.

Voters may see elections as an opportunity to voice their opinion of particular leaders or parties and the policies they pursue. Voting for this reason is a means

---

[2] Thus the U.S. Agency for International Development (USAID), in justifying the integration of democracy-building projects into its program, explained a few years ago that "fostering democracy is a long-established goal of the United States. Experience has shown that our relations with democratic countries tend to be more constructive and to enjoy more consistent domestic support than our relations with authoritarian regimes. Finally, and perhaps most importantly, there is growing evidence that open societies that value individual rights, respect the rule of law and have open and accountable governments provide better opportunities for sustained economic development than do closed systems which stifle individual initiative. Democracy, therefore, is an economic development issue, as well as a political one" (USAID 1990, 2; see also USAID Africa Bureau 1991, 1–2; World Bank 1989). For an analysis of how the World Bank's interpretation of "governance" implies electoral participation see Lancaster 1993, 10.

[3] Note that Healey and Robinson are not wholly convinced that elections will in fact lead to accountability or, consequently, to a change in policy; cf. Healey, Ketley, and Robinson 1993, 33–37.

to influence public debate over the formation of policies and the allocation of resources (see, e.g., Prewitt and Hyden 1967, 274–77; Moyo 1992, 100–115; Charlton 1993, 336).

2. Advance group interests.

Voters may see elections as competitions between rival kin, ethnic, or religion-based communities for scarce resources or positions of power. Such voters cast ballots out of group solidarity, as a means to further group interests (see, e.g., Lemarchand 1964, 192–97; Dunn 1975, 208; Holm 1987, 139).

3. Obtain material rewards.

Individuals may cast ballots to avail themselves of the resources distributed by political parties and leaders. Votes, in other words, get exchanged for material rewards, often through the conduits of clientelist networks (see, e.g., Bienen 1971, 195–213; Barkan 1979, 265–88; Widner 1994, 127–47).

These motivations are, of course, not mutually exclusive. There may, for instance, be considerable overlap between voting to advance group interests and voting to obtain material rewards. As Denis Cohen remarked, "It can be argued that the tendency for African voting behaviour to be dominated heretofore by ethnic factors results from the fact that ethnic community has continued to be the most stable source of material benefit and security for most voters. Consequently they decide, as individuals, to support a common choice as the best means of protecting and advancing their individual material interests" (1983, 82). While each of these three characterizations is in some sense accurate, then, common sense tells us that reality is often a good deal more complicated.

Unfortunately, most students of African voting behavior have not availed themselves of the conceptual and methodological tools necessary to address the full complexity of this reality. Rarely have scholars conducted voter opinion surveys, and the few surveys that have been used exhibit serious difficulties. Kenneth Prewitt and Goran Hyden (1967), for instance, conducted a large opinion survey in Tanzania in the mid-1960s. One part of the survey asked respondents to select the two factors that most influenced their votes from the following list: the candidate's age, tribe, religion, traditional status, party record, campaign performance, position on issues of government, record and experience in government, and ability to acquire things for his constituency (283). One obvious problem is that multiple-choice questions preselect a particular set of factors while leaving in obscurity a range of other possible influences. Another set of problems was identified by the authors themselves: "We make no secret of the difficulties encountered. Sampling bias, translation problems, inexperienced interviewers, reluctant and bewildered interviewees, vocabulary difficulties, ambiguous coding choices, and related factors can all introduce error into the data" (273).

A certain number of these problems, to be sure, fell outside the control of the interviewers. More troubling are the vocabulary and translation problems referred to by the authors, difficulties that stemmed from translating questionnaires designed in English into Swahili and Luhaya.[4] Take the above survey question. How did the interviewers translate "record," "issue," and "government"? Mapping such words from English onto languages used by populations with divergent cultural traditions would seem difficult and subject to distortion. What value, then, can researchers attach to answers given to that survey question?

Social scientists have traditionally regarded such translation issues as a predicament. Here, however, translation and meaning are the focus of our study. Consequently, we will use our understanding of Wolof concepts to learn something about how Senegalese voters, especially those with little or no education, understand the purposes of their own electoral participation. This strategy will help us think more clearly about the extent to which Senegalese voters seek, through their ballot casting, to hold elected officials accountable.

## Uneducated Wolofones on Voting

How do Wolofones with little or no education perceive elections? It is clear that many voters do hold clearly defined, well-articulated opinions about important political leaders, and vote according to these convictions.[5] One farmer explained why he voted for Abdoulaye Wade, leader of the PDS, in the 1993 presidential elections: "I voted for Abdoulaye because if he came to power he would develop the country. He would help the farmers, the herders, and those who fish. Why do I believe him? [Former President] Senghor provided credit to build grain silos and Abdoulaye said he'll give us a silo. Senghor gave us credit to buy seed and cattle. Abdoulaye said if he comes to power, he'll provide those things too. Senghor was able to do it—that's why I believe Abdoulaye can too." Yet we should not misinterpret this as a statement about Wade's (or Senghor's) policy positions, for it is unclear whether policy is in fact at issue. This farmer could simply be referring to the distribution of patronage benefits. This ambiguity takes on added significance when we recall that many Senegalese cit-

---

[4] To be fair, Hyden showed himself to be quite sensitive to the problems of translation in later works, particularly in his discussions of administrative terminology in Kenya (Hyden 1970, 120–21).

[5] Students of mass political behavior in Ghana, Kenya, Tanzania, and Botswana have similarly found both urban and rural people to be well informed about the identity of government leaders, parliamentary representatives, and important political parties. Indeed, levels of political knowledge on these subjects were comparable to, and in some cases higher than, levels found in the United States. See Prewitt and Hyden 1967, 277–78; Barkan 1976, 452–55; Hayward 1976, 433–51; and Somolekae 1989, 75–88.

izens do regard voting as a service provided in return for economic payoffs, a transaction they see as legitimate and moral.

Of course, not all uneducated voters share this positive appraisal of vote buying. An unschooled resident of the small, poor village of Nguène Cissé described with bitter eloquence the depravity that he saw flowing from government corruption and patronage:

> The government [*góornëmaa*] in place now is like a prostitute. Anyone who pays can have sex with her. The government corrupts people. It is even corrupting our moral leaders [*kilifa*]. If government leaders give you a million francs, you're obligated to look after their interests only. You can no longer even think about other people. You don't even think about where they got the money from—whether they took it from their supporters or stole it from a bank account belonging to Senegal. This is money that the people of Senegal earned through hard work.
>
> The government is like a newborn baby who found huge amounts of money already put aside for it. This baby doesn't worry about wasting it. It squanders it as it likes. This money should serve more important purposes. For many years now we've been poor, we've had drought, yet the government ignores us completely. We no longer have grain silos, provisions, or even wells. We have nothing. Even God is mad at us and no longer gives us rain because of all the lies and wickedness. All we have left is misery.
>
> But look around, every government deputy has money to buy a huge field and transform it into a green garden. He hires people to work for him. He even installs a chicken coop. Then he takes the money he earns and puts it in a foreign bank. He's done nothing to develop the country or help the poor. He has nine, we have one. He should give us two or three to help us. Instead he does all he can to take our one away and add it to his nine.
>
> This government has seen that there are spiritual leaders [*kilifa diine*] who can sway people's opinions. It gives these leaders money to get them to influence how their followers vote. This government does not think about the interests of the country or its farmers. If we had an irrigation system, we could grow vegetables during the dry season. If we had running water, we could serve you lettuce, potatoes, and macaroni for dinner. But today we can't even offer you a single bean or a grain of couscous. . . . Today I can't offer you anything because I have nothing.

A few themes and images stand out in this powerful statement. The government in place is an irresponsible child that misuses state funds. It is also a corrupting prostitute, perverting all who exchange money (votes) for her sexual attention (material benefits).

Why is this exchange so corrupting? The problem seems to stem in part from the illicit origins of the money and from the way it makes the recipients beholden to the givers. From this perspective, all patronage, no matter who receives it, is unethical and injurious. But part of the corruption also derives from the diversion of scarce money from poor farmers to rich spiritual leaders and deputies. From this perspective, patronage might not be so bad if it were routed to farmers instead, if government leaders only gave villages like Nguène Cissé two or three of their nine. Whether leaders use public channels or private patronage networks to effect this redistribution seems to be inconsequential.

There is a tension, then, in this statement. The farmer is angry that public norms were violated, and he is resentful over a lack of distributive fairness. It is unclear to what extent he is critical of patronage in general, and to what extent merely bitter because few benefits have been channeled his way. To put it another way, this farmer appears to be mixing two moral codes. On the one hand, he seems to be calling for a more open political process in which leaders can be held accountable. On the other hand, he appears to be calling on those who *nguuru* (rule) to provide the resources for all to *nguuru* (be comfortable). In this sense he seems to be expressing a desire for the betrayal of *politig* to be replaced by the solidarity of *demokaraasi*.

Yet calls for public accountability, however mixed and combined with other moral precepts, were not common among interviewees (this is one reason why the remarks of this farmer are so memorable). Many informants just did not distinguish between public and private channels of distribution. Typical was the statement of another farmer: "Here in Kab Gaye, in my opinion, our *demokaraasi* is in the work the government [*nguur*] has done here. The maternity clinic, the town hall, and the gas-powered well that the foreigners built—all this is a result of Abdou Diouf's efforts." To this farmer, the mechanisms of distribution seem unimportant. Kab Gaye received development assistance because of the president's "efforts." Left unspecified is whether these efforts consist of openly formulated public policies or a private channeling of clientelist rewards. What *is* important, and what counts as *demokaraasi,* is the fruit of those efforts, the tangible benefits of the president's attention.

A similar lack of specificity characterizes the statements of many who are critical of the government: "There is no *demokaraasi* in Senegal because those who lead do so for their own self-interest. Those who do not share in the government are left to fend for themselves any way they can." We are reminded here of Khar Mbaye Madiaga's song about *demokaraasi* in which she praises Abdou Diouf for sharing the "benefits" of his office. Doing right consists of distributing goods and favors widely, no matter what channels are used to do so.

The weak or blurred sense of publicness evidenced in these statements pervades the categories Wolof speakers use when they talk about what Americans call the public domain. Things Americans normally designate as public, Wolof speakers often identify as that which belongs to the *buur. Buur,* it will be recalled, are roughly analogous to what English speakers call kings. What Americans call a public road, a public park, and the state treasury, Wolof speakers identify respectively as the *buur*'s road (*mbeddu buur*), the *buur*'s park (*toolu buur*), and the *buur*'s assets (*alalu buur*). In addition, Wolof speakers sometimes call government agents "*buur*'s messengers" (*ndawu buur*) and civil law "*buur*'s law" (*yoonu buur*), although these usages are less common.

Perhaps such expressions are simply artifacts of a past age, as in the case of "the king's highway." This British expression dates to the early fifteenth century and originally referred to roads under the protection of the king (Kuhn 1968, 523). In current British usage, however, it means little more than "public road-way." Few would argue that the British have a weak sense of national public good simply because this expression is still used today.

But the Senegalese case is different. All but one of the *buur* expressions appear to have been coined *after* the destruction of the traditional Wolof states and their *buur* during the French conquest,[6] so they do not appear to be relics of kingly rule. A more likely explanation is that they are metaphoric extensions. Colonial and postcolonial rulers reminded people of *buur,* and, as we saw in Chapter 2, it has been principally the egoism and indulgence of the *buur* that have been mapped onto those who rule today. Those who are in power (the *nguur*) *nguuru*; they act like *buur.* That is, they use their power for themselves or in their own interest. They not only exercise power but gain materially by doing so. Thus parks, roads, laws, and treasuries maintained by the state exist for the pleasure or interests of the (new) *buur,* not of ordinary Senegalese.

Because government at the national level is linked so closely with the self-interest of the ruling elite, a state of affairs regarded as a natural part of ruling (*nguuru*), many Senegalese seem to hold only a weak notion of a national, public good. This, at least, is the conclusion reached by Benoît Ngom, president of the African Jurists Association. Reflecting on his fellow Senegalese, he found that many "do not yet have any clear notion of the 'republic' or of its president; they are still in the mindset of the *buur* and the *nguur*" (Ngom 1989, 40).

A sense of *local* community good, however, is very strong. Every village and urban neighborhood has a *pénc,* a central square that serves as a meeting place where people confer and make decisions about issues concerning the community. In fact, *pénc* derives from *fénc,* a verb that means roughly "to deliberate."

The *pénc* belongs to the local community. It is not imposed or provided by the *buur.* In this context it should be noted that linguists at the University Cheikh Anta Diop have tried to popularize "Deputies' *Pénc*" (*péncum dipite yi*) as a Wolof translation of "National Assembly" (SODEVA-CETAD 1991, 26). This neologism, however, has not caught on among the wider population, perhaps because people do not generally perceive the national assembly as a deliberative body, or perhaps because they do not perceive national institutions as the proper locus of deliberation.

Voters with little or no education perceive elected officials qua *buur* as unaccountable. From this perspective, involvement in the electoral process is not aimed at making the people in power more accountable. It provides, rather, an

---

[6] *Ndawu buur* is the only term included in any of the available early Wolof-French dictionaries. It appears in RR.PP. Missionaires 1855, 10; and in Kobès 1923, 217.

opportunity to benefit tangibly from the power and wealth of the *buur.* Consequently, no clear distinction is made between the public good and private benefit or between corrupt and legitimate mechanisms of distributing the material wealth of the *buur.* What counts is the circulation of goods and favors.

As we saw in Chapter 3, the benefits that accrue from voting are sometimes more diffuse. For my informant Modou, elections provided an occasion to reinforce bonds of community solidarity. A similar outlook can be seen in the reasons an elderly farmer in the village of Kab Gaye offered for voting for Abdou Diouf in 1993, even though he personally strongly supported Diouf's main opponent, Abdoulaye Wade of the PDS: "I voted for Diouf because of my relatives and the people with whom I live in this village. Before the elections, everyone got together and decided to vote for Diouf. I voted for him out of respect for that decision." Motivated by deference to his family and neighbors, he implicitly acknowledges the powerful moral obligations imposed on him by the network of reciprocal social relations to which he belongs.

Understanding this set of concerns provides a useful corrective to earlier perspectives on African voting behavior. One of the most perspicacious studies, one that scholars have seen to have relevance beyond the borders of the country in which it was conducted, is that of Ken Post on the Nigerian federal elections of 1959. Post points to the electoral importance of local group solidarity: "For most electors the choice between candidates was not one to be made individually, but as a member of the community. Sometimes indeed . . . it was regarded as something to be made by the community as a whole" (1963, 377). Thus the act of voting "was not in itself a very sophisticated way of participating in the political system. It involved two quite simple things—an appreciation by the individual of where his interests lay, *and the understanding that he was called upon to choose someone to represent these interests*" (390; emphasis added). Electors, then, identified their individual interests with that of the local community, and understood that by voting they were being called upon to choose someone to act as their collective "spokesman," to borrow Post's term, with regard to the government. Electoral solidarity, in short, was primarily a means to ensure effective representation of group interests or to procure government-bestowed benefits.

Post's observations of Nigerian voting behavior do not fit the Senegalese case in one important respect. The statement of the Kab Gaye farmer suggests that for some Senegalese voters, the choice of a candidate was determined not by the likelihood that one candidate would serve the interests of the local community better than another but by the imperative to safeguard the *internal* solidarity of the village or some other social network. This is why for Modou, the actual choice of a candidate seemed ancillary. What was essential was village cohesion.

From this perspective we see that elections can endanger *demokaraasi* and the social survival strategies of which it is a part, by threatening to splinter community solidarity through factious clan rivalries. For this reason, some Senegalese prefer not to participate in elections at all. As one farmer explained:

> I didn't vote for anyone in these past elections because I am a leader in this village. I only watch and observe because I don't want to alienate anyone. Elections cause relations between people to deteriorate. I remain neutral. Everyone likes me and everyone respects me. When I tell people to do something, they do it. So I don't side with any political party. I don't want to be in conflict with anyone, neither the elders nor the young people. Everyone trusts me. The women's association always asks my advice. The youth association, too. Whenever they have to send a representative somewhere, they delegate that responsibility to me. In our village you can't separate voting from other aspects of life. When there is a baptism, you see everyone. If there is any kind of village event, everyone participates.[7]

No community is exempt from discord, jealousy, and distrust. Conflicts can be intense, even deadly. Elections, viewed from this perspective, provide the occasion for *demokaraasi* to be either strengthened or subverted, bringing both an opportunity to reaffirm solidarity and a risk that it will be shattered.

While local communities are often coterminous with villages and neighborhoods, this is not always the case. Some communities are religious, made up of devotees beholden to particular religious patrons. Others are based on family, kinship, or ethnic ties. Still others, such as business and farming cooperatives, are organized around particular activities. There are also urban and rural youth groups and women's associations. Any of these associations may act as support networks; they are solidarity communities that pool their resources and sometimes seek the patronage of party bosses, marabouts, bureaucrats, or wealthy entrepreneurs. It follows that individuals may belong to more than one support network. Indeed, vulnerable populations seek to maximize the number of groups to which they belong as a way to diversify and multiply their sources of security (Ndione 1987, 150–63).

The more important a given solidarity group is to an individual's well-being, the more likely it is that the individual will harmonize his or her (electoral) behavior with group expectations. If the memberships of two or more groups overlap and the groups support the same candidate, the pressure to conform rises. Such seems to have been the case for the farmer from Kab Gaye, who voted for the candidate supported by both his family and his neighbors rather than the candidate he preferred. If an individual belongs to two or more groups

---

[7] A marabout in the city of Fatick offered similar reasons for not voting. As Villalón (1995, 136) tells it, the marabout "states that he should neither belong to a party nor vote, those not being appropriate activities for a religious leader ('Does the pope vote? Or belong to a political party?' he asks rhetorically). He sees his role instead as that of an intermediary with local officials for his disciples, should any of them be in trouble. And since he has *taalibes* [disciples] from all political parties, it would be impolitic of him to affiliate with any. This position, therefore, arises out of a concern to maintain his ties to his *taalibes*."

that are equally important, and each group supports a different candidate, then it is quite possible that the individual will abstain from voting altogether, to avoid alienating anyone. This may have been the situation of the village leader who did not want to alienate anyone in his village, "neither the elders nor the young people," and so simply did not vote. Individuals who belong to several nonoverlapping groups, none of which is essential to their welfare, are likely to feel less pressure to conform their (electoral) behavior to the expectations of any one group. Since opportunities to participate in such networks are generally more numerous for urbanites than for villagers, city people might be expected to show more independence in their electoral choices than farmers. And in fact it is in the largest urban areas that support for opposition candidates has been the strongest.

The electoral motives of uneducated Wolofones, then, are complex. Voting is an opportunity to express satisfaction or displeasure with leaders, to influence national policies, to benefit from the wealth of government leaders, and to reinforce bonds of solidarity in a variety of communities. Voting mixes moral codes of public accountability, private exchange, and social cohesion.

We can also draw more specific conclusions. First, it appears that while some voters recognize a national public interest, such concerns often get swamped by the immediate survival needs of the local community. The need to secure benefits for family, association, or village and the pressure to reinforce bonds of mutuality overwhelm commitment to the national public good, especially in areas where solidarity groups are few and their memberships overlapping.

Second, many voters perceive the exchange of votes for material benefits as a *moral transaction*. While such voters often value the exchange of material benefits and votes for the immediate relief it brings, they also tend to see such transactions as proper, ethical, and praiseworthy. Patron-client arrangements involve reciprocal obligations and benefits, and this reciprocity cements bonds of mutuality. This is not to say that such exchanges, or clientelism in general, cannot also have a coercive character. Indeed, we shall see precisely this aspect shortly.[8]

Finally, it seems that voters do indeed cast ballots out of group solidarity as a means to further group interests or to obtain government benefits, as Post observed in Nigeria. Yet voters also cast ballots to protect and preserve the *internal solidarity* of neighborhood, village, kinship, or religious groups. Vulnerable populations that rely heavily on group cohesion for their survival may well perceive the risks of social discord occasioned by elections to be so great that the question of whether one candidate or another would best serve the interests of

---

[8] Anthony Hall (1977, 511–12) distinguishes between "patrimonial" and "repressive" forms of clientelism. The former is "based on overt acceptance of traditional values by the subordinate"; the latter relies on "cruder forms of social control." But these forms are not exclusive; they can and do coexist.

the community is inconsequential by comparison. As a result, they vote along with the majority, or abstain from voting altogether, to keep their social safety net intact. Thus, to return to Dahl's concerns about democratic competence, what may look like ineptitude (for example, not knowing the names of candidates, not being familiar with issues, voting the way others vote) may in fact be a skillful strategy for ensuring basic material needs, given the larger environmental, economic, and political forces at work. In other words, what Dahl sees as incompetence in the service of democracy may be perfectly competent in the service of *demokaraasi*.

## Public Voting and Community Cohesion

Concerns about community economic security shape the way many Senegalese understand voting. This realization helps explain why many voters with little or no education shunned the institution of public voting introduced by the ruling party in the 1970s, even though this practice appeared to be a natural extension of traditional Senegalese culture.

In 1977 the electoral code was modified to eliminate the mandatory use of voting booths. The ruling party justified voting in public on the grounds that this practice was an integral part of Senegal's cultural heritage. While this assertion has a basis in historical reality, the urban and rural uneducated Senegalese I interviewed by and large rejected the legitimacy of this practice. Their rejection makes full sense only in the light of the social survival strategies of the large underclass to which these interviewees belong.

Until 1977, the use of private voting booths (the "secret ballot") was mandatory in Senegal. This legal provision was first introduced in 1914 by the colonial administration. At that time the franchise in Senegal was restricted to Europeans, mulattoes, and a limited number of Africans in the Four Communes. It had been common for European and mulatto patrons to use public voting to exert pressure on their African clients (Zuccarelli 1987, 107). The aim of the new law was to make the vote both free and secret.

When, in 1914, the African Blaise Diagne opposed the mulatto incumbent François Carpot for election as Senegal's deputy to the National Assembly in Paris, the secret vote proved essential in capturing the African vote, the key to Diagne's victory.[9] African voters openly displayed the ballots of their patrons as they entered the voting booths, but once hidden from view, many substituted

---

[9] Diagne was quite aware of the benefit that mandatory use of voting booths would bring. One of his backers, Jean D'Oxoby, used his newspaper in 1913 and early 1914 to advocate the application of appropriate legislation to Senegal (*La Démocratie du Sénégal*, November 13, 1913; January 1, 1914). Once the decree was promulgated in Senegal, Diagne's election committee made it a priority to teach Africans how to use the new voting booths (*L'AOF*, April 24, 1914).

the ballot for Diagne. The governor general of French West Africa was duly impressed. Reporting on the elections to the minister of colonies in France, he wrote:

> The indigenous voters, even though 90 percent of them were illiterate, understood to a remarkable degree the advantages and utility of the voting booths, which allowed them to take advantage of the ill-advised generosities of each candidate without making known to which side their real sympathies went—that is to say, their ballots.
>
> In almost every voting booth we found after the elections numerous ballots carried with ostentation into the voting hall by the black voters; at the last moment and behind the curtain, these voters slipped into the envelope a different ballot, hidden most often in their babouches. From this point of view, it would not be an exaggeration to say that the Senegalese, from the very start, revealed themselves to be prudent electors, conscious of the small advantages that voting booths offer. (Le Gouverneur Général de l'A.O.F. à Monsieur le Ministre des Colonies, Cabinet et Service de l'A.O.F. et de l'A.E.F., Paris, June 24, 1914, folder 20-G-21, Archives du Sénégal)

The voting booth, in short, made a propitious start in Senegal.

Laws stipulating the mandatory use of voting booths remained in effect throughout the colonial and early independence periods. In practice, however, electors often failed to use them, especially in rural areas, where the franchise was extended piecemeal from 1945 to 1956.[10] This situation did not change until 1974, when President Senghor liberalized the political system by allowing the legalization of three political parties and the reintroduction of multiparty contestation of elections. Not long after that, Senghor's UPS (relabeled the PS in 1976) moved to reverse Senegal's sixty-year legal precedent of secret voting. No doubt nervous UPS/PS leaders wished to preserve their advantage over their new competitors by legalizing the already prevalent practice of public voting. Under the watchful eye of local party patrons, few rural voters would dare vote against the ruling party. A change in the law would provide a juridic defense of the practice. The National Assembly finally passed a law in 1977 that modified the electoral code, stipulating that voters could choose to use or not to use voting booths, as they wished.

The reaction of the opposition (for the most part not yet legally recognized) was bitter. Many agreed with the judgment of the journalist who wrote that

> the secret vote has been removed from the electoral code to create uncomfortable situations conducive to electoral fraud. . . . If you enter a voting booth, it is because you want to shield yourself from the view of others. If you want that, it is be-

---

[10] See, e.g., the report on the elections of March 30, 1952, in *Afrique Nouvelle,* April 5, 1952, and the accusations concerning the elections of November 18, 1956, in *L'AOF,* December 15, 1956.

cause you have something to hide. . . . Since you are hiding something, you are thus suspected of sympathizing with the opposition—that declared "enemy" of the Parti Socialiste. From that moment on, you are put on a blacklist of "enemies" and treated as such. (*Andë Sopi,* January 1978)

In 1978 Abdoulaye Wade, the head of the only legal opposition party at that time, challenged this new provision in court, but with little success.

Senghor resigned in 1981, turning over the presidency to his groomed successor, Abdou Diouf, who immediately opened up the political system by legalizing political parties of any ideological bent. The new political openness required revisions to the electoral code, and the secret vote again became a divisive issue between the PS and the opposition.

In February 1982 eight opposition parties formed a joint commission to study the electoral code. One area of fundamental agreement was the need to restore the mandatory secret ballot (*Le Soleil,* February 12, 1982). The PS remained adamant in its refusal. The political situation, however, had evolved significantly since 1977, when Senghor pushed the original provision for the secret vote effortlessly through the exclusively PS National Assembly. In the legislative elections of 1978, the PDS won 18 of the 100 seats in the National Assembly. When the new electoral code came up for parliamentary debate in 1982, the PS needed a more sophisticated justification for the optional use of voting booths. This task fell to the minister of the interior, Médoune Fall, who presented the administration's proposed legislation to the National Assembly:

As you know, in our country we take pride in political and religious engagement, often manifested by the wearing of various articles of clothing or insignia. This public display is a way for people to prove their attachment to a religious brotherhood or political party. This is part of our ancestral heritage and we did not want to act precipitously against it by indiscriminately copying whatever might be done elsewhere in the world. This is one reason why we have decided, at present, to keep the use of voting booths optional. It is . . . Europe that introduced to Africa the principle of the secret ballot, a principle that does not conform at all to the traditional qualities of courage and pride of our African people. (*Journal des Débats Parlementaires,* 1st sess., April 30, 1982, 143–45)

The minister of the interior thus sought to link the traditionally open, public quality of African moral commitment to the practice of public voting. Casting a ballot, he argued, should be considered an act of public display, grounded in Senegalese values of "courage" and "pride."

To justify public voting, the minister of the interior, like other leaders of the PS, maintained that since traditional political practices involved public exhibition, expressing one's political opinion in full view of others had long been an integral part of Senegalese culture and should be legally sanctioned.

This argument is not without justification. It is noteworthy that "to vote" may be translated into Wolof as *sanni baat* (to cast one's voice), an expression that suggests the oral, and thus public, nature of voting.[11] Moreover, there is also some continuity between public voting and the traditional methods of choosing (*fal*) and deposing (*folli*) leaders discussed in Chapter 2, methods that required the airing of opinions among leaders of noble lineages, not the counting of votes.

By grounding a justification of public voting in the past practices of Wolof nobles, leaders of the ruling party hoped to transpose traditional notions of public display and political commitment onto modern electoral institutions. At least, this seems to have been the strategy of the minister of the interior.

It is interesting to contrast this justification with arguments for retaining the public vote in mid-nineteenth-century Britain. The private vote in British parliamentary and local elections, it should be recalled, was not instituted until 1872. John Stuart Mill, among those opposed to the secret ballot, wrote in 1861: "In any political election . . . the voter is under an absolute moral obligation to consider the interest of the public, not his private advantage. . . . This being admitted, it is at least a prima facie consequence, that the duty of voting, like any other public duty, should be performed under the eye and criticism of the public" (1975, 304). It is doubtful that such an argument would resonate among today's uneducated Senegalese voters, who, as we have seen, generally have a diluted sense of national public interest. It is perhaps for this reason that the ruling elite drew on indigenous notions of commitment and display rather than arguments about public-spiritedness to justify the public vote.

Be that as it may, it is mildly ironic that Médoune Fall emphasized the European impulse behind the introduction of private voting in 1914. While it was indeed the colonial administration that imposed the use of voting booths on the colony, it was the African Blaise Diagne who campaigned most assiduously for the secret vote, and who gained the most from its implementation. African voters also proved highly adept at using the private voting booths to their advantage in this important election, and they apparently had little trouble checking their exhibitive impulses, suggesting that some values in the cultural repertoire of the Senegalese might not be so inimical to secret voting after all.

The proposed legislation providing for the optional use of voting booths became law in June 1982. It is telling that public voting since that time has found its strongest support among PS cadres and stalwart PS partisans, the people

[11] There are other terms for voting. One can also "cast a ballot" (*sanni kart*). In addition, the Wolof *wote,* derived from the French *voter,* is also roughly equivalent to the English "vote." Like "vote," *wote* can be both verb and noun. Unlike "vote," to "*wote* with" (*wote ag*) is to run against someone in an electoral campaign, as in "Abdou Diouf wote na ag Abdoulaye Wade" (Abdou Diouf ran against Abdoulaye Wade). It appears that *wote* had already entered the Wolof language by the late nineteenth century; at least it was given as a Wolof translation of the French *voter* in an 1890 French-Wolof dictionary (Guy-Grand 1890, 781).

who have the most to gain from it. A local political organizer for the PS in the Médina neighborhood of Dakar, for instance, explained her preference for the public vote as follows: "People tell you that they'll vote for you, but on the day of the elections they betray you by voting for someone else. To vote in hiding is no good; it is betrayal. I prefer transparency; that way everyone can see and know." The coercive character of the public vote was lost neither on this organizer nor on ordinary voters, regardless of party affiliation. Many voters, however, resented this form of intimidation. They maintained that voting should be an act of *sutura,* a Wolofized Arabic word important in Senegalese Islam that means, roughly, "discretion" or "privacy." One farmer, a member of the PS, explained that "we need voting booths to ensure discretion. To vote in front of everyone and to be afraid of what you're doing is not normal. If I know that voting for Abdoulaye Wade will create problems for me with Abdou Diouf's supporters, I wouldn't dare vote for Wade for fear of being assaulted."

The debate on public voting thus juxtaposed a moral code based on the values of public display embodied by the noble castes to an ethic of personal discretion prescribed by the tenets of Sufi Islam. The debate over private versus public voting, then, not only opposed European to traditional African practices but also pitted competing indigenous moral codes against each other.

In this competition between moral codes, Islamic discretion appears to offer a more compelling ethical standard for many voters, at least among those I interviewed. These voters value discretion because, as the PS farmer's statement suggests, it secures some level of protection against intimidation by supporters of the ruling party. For this reason, opposition leaders had good reason to believe that public voting caused them to lose elections. Voters, especially in rural areas, did indeed appear reluctant to cast ballots against the ruling party under the watchful eye of influential local party patrons who control the flow of local resources and have the power to intimidate wayward voters.

Yet voters have still other reasons for preferring the discretion afforded by private voting. Most notably, it helps insulate voters from feelings of obligation to family and friends. As a jeweler in Dakar explained, "Imagine that you're my close friend and an active member of the PS. Now imagine that I want to vote for a candidate who doesn't belong to that party. If I see you sitting there, I'll vote for your candidate." A factory worker in Pikine voiced similar thoughts: "Voting should be done behind a screen. When I vote I don't want my brothers or close friends to know who I'm voting for. If I voted out in the open, I could see a close friend that I like very much in the process of voting for someone. That would influence me to vote for that same person, even though it's not the person I prefer." The same idea runs through the statement of a farmer: "Suppose I support Abdoulaye Wade and go to vote for him. There, seated in the polling station, is a friend representing Abdou Diouf. Now this friend has helped me out when things were going badly. Morally, if I see this friend I'll feel a debt toward him and I'll vote for his candidate at the expense of mine."

It appears that these voters prefer the voting booth because it allows them to vote their convictions, regardless of moral obligations to friends and family. Yet also implicit in these statements is the idea that the discretion offered by secret voting minimizes potential conflict and maintains bonds of kinship and friendship.

The importance of community solidarity was expressed more explicitly by a farmer in a village where political loyalties were divided between the PS and the PDS:

> Voting in front of people is not good for everyone. When I go to the polling station, both my child and my nephew are there. One is a member of the PS and the other of the PDS. I greet each one, and they each pay their respects to me. I can't then jump up, take my ballot, and support my nephew only to abandon my child. Nor can I get up and support my child only to abandon my nephew. So I go behind the curtain, take my ballot, put it in an envelope, place the envelope in the ballot box, and go on my way. Nobody knows who I voted for. The fact is, family ties are so important to us that we wouldn't dare offend any of our kin.

Public voting, in the eyes of this farmer, threatens familial solidarity. The significance of this fact should not be underestimated. For vulnerable populations, bonds to kin and neighbors form an essential safety net in times of need.

Considerations of collective security also underlie the conviction of some people that public voting is good and right, an idea hinted at by a young mother in Dakar: "Voting in front of everyone is the right thing to do because that way you can avoid making mistakes. If you vote where nobody can see you, you risk making a mistake. You risk choosing the wrong candidate." The statement implies that the right candidate is identified as such by everyone; that is, by the community. Perhaps this candidate is the right one because of the greater material benefits he or she offers, or perhaps for some other reason. But even apart from such reasons, agreeing unanimously on a single candidate reduces divisiveness and factiousness. From the perspective of community solidarity, then, public voting may well serve a valuable function.

In sum, whether the uneducated voters I interviewed supported or rejected public voting had more to do with considerations of social ties and calculations of economic security than with the traditional ideals of public display extolled by the ruling party.

Legislation providing for the optional use of voting booths remained in effect through the 1980s, and the debate between the PS and the opposition continued to rage. The PS not only aggressively defended the optional use of voting booths but exhorted PS supporters to vote publicly (*Le Soleil*, November 11, 1982; *Takusaan*, February 22, 1983). During the 1988 elections PS leaders heatedly argued that voting in private was sneaky and cowardly. In the words of Thierno Diop, president of the PS parliamentary group in the National Assembly at the time, "For the great majority of Senegalese, to cast a ballot in a voting booth is to vote on the sly. It is a questionable vote because the Senegalese are not accustomed to being discrete in their political choices" (Diop 1988, 31; quoted in Diop and Diouf 1990, 312). At PS rallies, party supporters held high banners proclaiming "No voting booths for the members of the PS" (*Le Soleil: Urnes 88,* February 11, 1988). As for the opposition, the PDS was most vocal in maintaining that the optional-use provision in the electoral code was unconstitutional. The party vowed "to oppose physically" acts of electoral fraud, including the failure to use voting booths (*Le Démocrate,* November 1987; Parti Démocratique Sénégalais 1988). Fragmentary evidence suggests that the use of voting booths was sporadic. It appears that a scattering of men, mostly urban partisans of the opposition, passed behind the curtain. Women and rural voters generally voted in full view.[12]

When the post-1988 crisis subsided and the national consensus pushed by Abdou Diouf emerged in 1991, the PS and the opposition met to reform the electoral code in anticipation of the February 1993 presidential elections. Yielding to the long-standing demands of the opposition—and heeding the recommendations of a delegation sent by the National Democratic Institute for International Affairs (NDI), an American organization called upon by Diouf to furnish a nonpartisan evaluation of Senegal's electoral code (National Democratic Institute 1990, 23–24)—the PS agreed to reinstate the mandatory use of voting booths. The new provision became law in September 1991. The PS lost no time in justifying the reintroduction of voting booths by having Iba Der Thiam, one of Senegal's most respected historians and a former minister of education, remind everyone that voting booths were an old tradition in Senegal, dating back to 1914 (*Le Soleil,* September 28–29, 1991).[13] Colonial traditions thus abruptly supplanted precolonial ones as the reference point for electoral practices, a turnabout that underscores the political opportunism of the ruling party's position on public voting.

The 1993 presidential and legislative elections marked the reintroduction of the mandatory secret vote. This time public voting appears to have been a rare occurrence,[14] even though certain PS deputies (such as Adja Aram Diene of the poor Médina neighborhood of Dakar) exhorted supporters to carry their unused ballots out of the polling station to prove they had voted for the PS presidential candidate. I found no reports, however, that these exhortations were heeded.

---

[12] This conclusion is based on interviews I conducted and on *Wal Fadjri,* March 5, 1988.

[13] Less than a year later Thiam went on to found his own political party—the Convention des Démocrates et Patriotes (CDP). He lost much stature after making outrageous campaign promises during his bid for the presidency in 1993.

[14] This conclusion is based on my experience as an election monitor with the NDI mission, reports filed by forty other NDI observers, and newspaper accounts.

It may well be that with the reintroduction of secret voting, both juridically and, more important, in practice, voters' concerns about the effects of their ballots on community cohesion will lessen in the future. Many voters, after all, may no longer feel pressured to vote in ways pleasing to their solidarity groups if their ballots remain secret. We will consider this possibility in Chapter 5.

For now, let us simply recap what we have learned thus far. Senegal's ruling party, drawing on a moral code of public display upheld by the noble castes, characterized voting as an act of political commitment and exhibition. Yet most uneducated voters that I interviewed appeared to be motivated less by a desire to display their commitment than by considerations of social and economic security. These people saw public voting as a practice that is coercive, punitive, and likely to strain the social bonds necessary for collective long-term security. It is perhaps for this reason that after the PS vacated public voting provisions in 1992, I could find few people who exhibited any nostalgia for this practice.

Recognizing the meaning of *demokaraasi,* then, and seeing how values embodied in this concept get realized through the electoral process deepen our insight into Senegalese voting behavior. It would be difficult to understand why uneducated voters reacted so negatively to the institutionalization of public voting, given its roots in traditional moral codes, without a grasp of the values of social solidarity reflected in *demokaraasi.*

## Islam and the *Ndigal* of the Mourides

Religion adds another layer of complexity to the voting behavior of the Senegalese, particularly those who are Mouride. Islam has become intimately intertwined with Senegalese politics. Such mixing of religion and politics is, of course, not unique to Senegal. Religion has influenced the development of democracy in Europe and the United States in a variety of ways. Early and medieval Christian ideas of redemptive community reemerged in Lutheranism, Calvinist Geneva, Cromwell's Commonwealth, Rousseau's general will, and later theories of participatory democracy. The modern concept of parliamentary representation has roots in the Latin term *repræsentare,* which in the thirteenth century referred to the representation or embodiment of Christ by the pope or his cardinals. The theological egalitarianism formulated in Reformation Protestantism found a more temporal expression in demands for democratic suffrage at Putney in 1647, demands that were sometimes expressed explicitly in the religious idiom and that profoundly affected American colonial thought.

In Senegal, Sufi Islam, a court religion since the thirteenth century, spread rapidly to Wolof of all levels of society in the mid–nineteenth century, as advancing French armies dismantled the traditional states of Waalo, Kajoor, Bawol, and Jolof. Since independence, Islamic clerics have been central actors in Senegalese politics. The maraboutic leaders of the three main Islamic brotherhoods of Senegal are among the most influential political figures in the country; and the language of Islam pervades public discourse as political leaders invoke widely popular religious ideas to legitimize their rule.

Since colonial times, the power of these Islamic leaders derived from the hierarchical internal structure of their brotherhoods, which ensured their spiritual and temporal control over their followers. The weak hold of the colonial administration over the rural population increased the political influence of these saints. Thus early in the twentieth century the founders of the brotherhoods began to play the role of intermediaries between the administrative authorities and their own religious followers—a role their heirs have continued to play in the postcolonial period (Coulon 1981).

Muslim political influence is today multifaceted. At times marabouts intervene in the political process to protect or augment their own fortunes. In return for their political support, powerful marabouts receive direct economic assistance, promises to build mosques, and loans from politicians seeking their favor. To safeguard their holdings, marabouts also exert pressure in the selection of candidates and appointments at all levels of government and resist reforms detrimental to their economic interests (Behrman 1970, 111–28; Foltz 1977, 246; Coulon 1981, 237–50).

Farmers, it is important to note, have benefited from the political patronage procured by their marabouts. Indeed, once or twice the brotherhoods have, in the words of Donal Cruise O'Brien (1979, 223), exercised "a bizarre and theatrical form of trade unionism" in defense of farmers' economic interests. In 1973, for example, the Mouride leadership organized a rural protest against the state's agricultural policies. The government responded by doubling the producer price of peanuts, Senegal's main export crop and backbone of the rural economy (Cruise O'Brien 1979, 223; 1975, 176–77).

Muslim leaders also act as mediators and arbiters of factional disputes within the ruling political party. Most dramatically, the holy men helped determine the outcome of the power struggle between President Senghor and Prime Minister Mamadou Dia in 1962. The marabouts also perform essential roles of linkage and mobilization, providing administrators with a wide audience that would otherwise be unavailable to them (Markovitz 1970, 90–93; Cottingham 1973, 678).

When Diouf became president in 1981, perhaps most crucial to his political survival was his ability to retain the backing of the important saints. The marabouts' support of Diouf was reaffirmed in 1983, when religious chiefs from all the brotherhoods openly and vigorously supported his reelection (see *West Africa*, March 14, 1983), and again in 1988, when the leader of the Mouride brotherhood issued an order (*ndigal* in Wolof) to vote for Diouf. The nature of this intervention sheds light on how notions of Islamic devotion interact with other moral codes in shaping the way Senegalese voters understand the electoral system.

*Ndigal* is unique to the Mourides. It does not exist in either the Tidiane or Qadiriya brotherhoods.[15] The Mouride faithful achieve salvation by submitting themselves to the spiritual guidance of a marabout, who is a bearer of divine grace and wisdom. This act of submission (*jébbalu*) requires the follower to obey the commands of his marabout and other leaders at the top of the brotherhood hierarchy (Cruise O'Brien 1971, 85–100; Coulon 1981, 104–11). In day-to-day life, Mouride marabouts give *ndigal* concerning a range of matters, including religious observances, personal conduct, and familial obligations. By obeying the marabout's *ndigal,* the follower is assured a moral life and ascension to paradise.

Originally, however, *ndigal* was not a religious concept, and it did not always signify an order. It derives from the verb *dig* (to promise).[16] In the nineteenth and early twentieth centuries, *ndigal* meant roughly "advice" or "promise."[17] Available evidence suggests that it was not until sometime between the mid-1920s and the early 1970s that the term took on a primary meaning of "order" or "command."[18] This semantic shift thus corresponds roughly to the period of rapid expansion of the Mouride brotherhood, and the two developments are probably related. Counsel given by Mouride saints could hardly be considered simple advice, given the moral authority and divine grace of the person who issued it. A *ndigal* from a marabout thus carried the force of an order.

While *ndigal* today retains the secular meanings of "advice" and "permission," it has become closely associated with the Mouride sect and the religious commands that distinguish it. The Islamic Movement of Mourides in Europe took *ndigal* as the title of a magazine it publishes.[19] In recent years at least three pop songs titled "Ndigal" have been produced, all of which praised God or the founder of the Mouride brotherhood and his descendants. In one of these songs, Abdou Ndiaye sings to a rap beat:

> *Taalibe,*[20] *ndigal!*
> An obedient child, *ndigal!*

---

[15] In 1988, Mourides accounted for about 30% of the population, Tidianes 47%, Qadiriyas 12%, and Catholics 4% (République du Sénégal, Ministère de l'Economie et des Finances 1990, table 3.08). Despite the larger size of the Tidiane brotherhood, many observers consider the Mourides more influential—in part because of the Mouride leadership's ability to mobilize its community with *ndigal.*

[16] There are several other cognates: *digal* (to proscribe or recommend), *dige* (to promise mutually or agree to something), *ndige mi* (a reciprocal agreement), and *digle* (to give instructions).

[17] Only one (Dard 1826, 117) of the nineteenth- or early-twentieth-century dictionaries, grammars, or phrase books I consulted included "order" as one of the meanings of *ndigal.* Cf. Dard 1825, 33, 132; Roger 1829, 161; Boilat 1858, 373; Descemet 1864, 10; and Kobès 1923, 220).

[18] The earliest written confirmation of this shift in meaning dates to the early 1970s, when Donal Cruise O'Brien (1971, 85) reported that during rites of initiation Mouride marabouts would tell their disciples always to obey the *ndigal* of their marabouts.

[19] The French-language subtitle of the magazine is *L'ordre divin*—the divine order.

[20] *Taalibe,* derived from the Arabic term *ṭālib,* appears to have entered the Wolof language by the eighteenth century and today means disciple of a marabout. On eighteenth- and nineteenth-century references see Mauny 1952, 64.

A good upbringing, *ndigal!*

. . . . . . . . . . .

To obey a *ndigal* is to keep from sinking into vice.

. . . . . . . . . . .

Sëriñ Bamba,[21] giving a *ndigal* was a good thing to do.

. . . . . . . . . . .

I will follow whatever *ndigal* he gives.

. . . . . . . . . . .

To act morally is best, do so in the name of the *ndigal.*

Abdou Ndiaye uses the word *ndigal* in this song to conjure images of the spiritual submission and obedience that lie at the heart of Mouridism. As these lyrics suggest, *ndigal* has become a kind of semantic icon that represents the essence of Mouridism in Senegalese popular culture. Indeed, this icon has become so commonplace that one Mouride entrepreneur even named her roadside grill the Ndigal Restaurant.

It was not until the elections of 1983 and 1988 that the term became linked directly to politics. Before both elections the khalifa general of the Mouride brotherhood, Abdoul Ahad Mbacké, issued a *ndigal* to his two million faithful to vote for President Abdou Diouf. "Any other choice," he said, "would betray Sëriñ Touba"—a reference to Amadou Bamba, the deceased founder of the brotherhood and ultimate source of divine grace (*Le Soleil,* October 14, 1987). The message for believers was clear. If they did not want to forfeit their place in paradise, they had to vote for Diouf.

Leaders of other religious groups also made public statements of support for Diouf in 1988, most notably Cheikh Tidiane Sy of the Tidiane brotherhood and Monsignor Jacques Sarr, bishop of Thiès. Senegalese journalists have glibly referred to such electoral suasion as *ndigal,* but the pronouncements of these Catholic and Tidiane leaders did not carry the obligatory force of the Mouride *ndigal* (*Le Cafard Libéré,* September 15, 1987; *Wal Fadjri,* December 30, 1987).

Nevertheless, supporters of Diouf and the ruling party defend the Mouride *ndigal* as simple "advice" given by saints, who have an obligation to counsel their followers on all matters, religious and temporal. Not all educated Senegalese, however, see the Mouride practice of *ndigal* as consistent with *démocratie.* Opposition leaders who were not fortunate enough to win the favor of the most important marabouts argue that the *ndigal* is a perversion of Islam and *démocratie,* and offer various theological, moral, and political arguments to support their view. An article in the PDS party organ, for instance, urges readers to reconsider carefully the ambiguity of the words pronounced by Abdoul Ahad

---

[21] Sëriñ Bamba is Amadou Bamba, the founder of the Mouride brotherhood. *Sëriñ* is a Wolof word that refers broadly to any Muslim cleric or dignitary, and apparently derives from the Pulaar *seernaaɓe,* the plural form of *ceerno,* a Muslim cleric. *Sëriñ* means more or less the same thing as "marabout" (Monteil 1962, 78; Cruise O'Brien 1971, 23, 106).

Mbacké; specifically it reminds readers that Sëriñ Touba (which means literally the marabout of Touba, the holy city of the Mourides) may refer to either Amadou Bamba or the khalifa general of the Mourides; while only *khādim rasūl* (an Arabic expression that means roughly "servant of the prophet") refers in Senegal uniquely to Amadou Bamba. The author of the article points out that "the khalifa general declared that whoever did not submit to his injunction commanding Mourides to vote for Mister Abdou Diouf in the upcoming elections would renounce Sëriñ Touba. He did not say *khādim rasūl* or Bamba. . . . Therefore, since Sëriñ Touba is actually the khalifa general himself, I will not defer to the demand. His *ndigal* does not bind me because it is a hijacking of power" (*Le Démocrate,* November 1987). One member of the LD/MPT put forward a different theological argument: "Paradise is the property neither of the president nor of the marabouts. One simply needs to do good to be repaid by good" (*Le Soleil: Urnes 88,* February 16, 1988). Meanwhile, a leader of the Parti de l'Indépendence et du Travail (PIT) argued that "there is a *ndigal* when the *taalibe* wants to work to go to paradise, but not when an order is given to support someone who sacrifices his people" (*Le Soleil: Urnes 88,* February 15, 1988). Others were not so subtle in their attack on the *ndigal.* Another leader of the LD/MPT stated bluntly that "to fight against the regime is to fight *for* Islam" (*Le Soleil: Urnes 88,* February 17, 1988).

Yet these debates merely shadow the real-life moral dilemmas faced by many Mouride voters, especially by those who would have preferred to vote for an opposition candidate. A longtime organizer for the PDS and Abdoulaye Wade was visibly pained when he explained with some resignation why he and many of his fellow villagers obeyed the 1988 *ndigal* to vote for Abdou Diouf: "We Mourides, we have only the *ndigal.* During the electoral campaign, Ablaye[22] Wade came to this village and even sat with me here in my hut. Later, we heard our *sërin* say on the radio, 'Whoever believes in Sëriñ Touba will vote for Abdou Diouf.' There are many supporters for Ablaye Wade here and we all obeyed the *ndigal.* Whether that pleased us or not, we all obeyed the *ndigal.*" Another Wade supporter, an unemployed resident of Touba, was more articulate in explaining the feelings he experienced: "It was difficult for me to obey the *ndigal* because through *my* actions Diouf was returned to power. I felt as if I had a contradiction within me, as if I didn't believe in what I was doing." For those who supported the opposition, it appears, yielding to the 1988 *ndigal* caused serious distress.

Voters sympathetic to the opposition dealt with this cognitive dissonance in several ways. Some decided to disregard the *ndigal* and adduced a variety of reasons for doing so. Another Mouride in Touba, in an argument reminiscent of those advanced by the opposition, explained that "I didn't obey the *ndigal* be-

[22] Ablaye is a familiar form of Abdoulaye.

cause it wasn't my immediate *sëriñ* who gave it. It was a *ndigal* from my *sëriñ*'s *sëriñ*. If it had come from my *sëriñ*, I would have obeyed it." A farmer in Thiourour was more prosaic in his reasoning: "I listen to the *ndigal* and follow them if I can. If I can't, I don't obey—but not openly."

As the last statement suggests, those who did not comply with the *ndigal* often did so discretely, a task made difficult by the widespread practice of public voting in 1988. For some people discretion meant simply abstaining from voting. For others, it meant obeying the *ndigal* only partially, as in the case of an elderly farmer who observed the *ndigal* by casting his ballot for Diouf but resisted it by not allowing his wife or adult children to vote.

Nonetheless, many Mouride voters did heed the *ndigal*. Indeed, support for Diouf was strong among those Mourides who actually voted—if official voting returns can be believed.[23] For some disciples, complying with the *ndigal* was simply a matter of good religious practice, of submitting themselves to the moral guidance of saintly marabouts. Voting for these faithful was a religious act, one that brought them closer to paradise. This belief may explain the words of a farmer in Ngabu who otherwise would have voted for Wade: "If Sëriñ Touba orders us to do something, we do it. Even if it pains us, we have to do it because we don't know all the reasons why he asked us to do it. We do it only to obey the *sëriñ*, not for Abdou Diouf." For this farmer, obeying the *ndigal* appeared to fulfill a religious obligation whose purposes he could not know. Yet it is not clear that only theology is at issue here, since the marabout's reasons for endorsing Diouf might have been spiritual, temporal, or both.

Indeed, there is some evidence that *ndigal* may be given a temporal interpretation. Many voters offered reasons for obeying the *ndigal* that had to do less with spiritual obligation than with earthly pragmatism. As a farmer in the small village of Samba Sadio explained:

*Ndigal* is a good thing because *taalibe* don't have the vision or wisdom of the *sëriñ*. It is the *sëriñ* who knows what is right. If you listen to the *sëriñ*, misfortune will not befall you. But if you fail to follow his *ndigal,* you will see suffering. If we voted for the candidate we preferred, we would choose things that were not right. We don't know enough and risk choosing the wrong way. The *sëriñ* knows everything and sees further than us. He knows what is right and follows that path. The *taalibe* should listen to him because therein lies his peace and happiness.

These thoughts were echoed by a farmer in Thiourour who had voted for Diouf:

---

[23] In the six Mouride-majority departments (Mbacké, Diourbel, Bambey, Kébémer, Gossas, and Tivaoane), 50% of registered electors voted for Diouf, as compared to 41% in the other twenty-four departments of the country.

*Ndigal* is important because only those who have eyes can tell you "do this." It's like one person who has wisdom and another who doesn't, like one person who has legs and another who doesn't. The *ndigal* about voting was good because we don't know anything. We are poor farmers. People who have gone to school in Dakar can make choices on the basis of their knowledge. But we need someone to guide us.

Still another Mouride disciple:

If the marabout does not give a *ndigal,* each one of us would vote for the candidate of his choice, and that is not to our advantage. The marabout is the one who sees where our interest lies, and he said, "Vote for Abdou Diouf." If he had let us do what we wanted, that would have been to our detriment. That is why we follow his *ndigal.*

Each of these farmers expresses a lack of trust in his own political judgment. In their eyes, the marabout appears more knowledgeable, more capable of discerning their interests, and thus better able to secure their peace and happiness. This reasoning seems less metaphysical than utilitarian.

Yet one should not take these statements of self-distrust at face value. Disciples, after all, have the power to withdraw their submission from one marabout and give it to another, even if this power is asserted rather infrequently (Diop 1987, 145). Research suggests that such choices, when exercised, are sometimes based on considerations of political affinity. *Taalibe* who support the opposition may choose marabouts sympathetic to their political leanings. Indeed, some marabouts appear to have built their following through just such a process.[24] The exercise of political judgment by some disciples, then, may well be embedded in choices that are outwardly religious.

Still other factors also led Mouride voters to obey the *ndigal.* Some saw it as part of a moral and material exchange between the president and the Mouride community. In the months before the election, President Diouf had provided significant material benefits to the Mouride community by building up the infrastructure of the Mouride holy city of Touba. Many voters appeared to have complied with the *ndigal* because they saw it as a legitimate way for the leader of the Mourides to repay the president. One Mouride voter in the city of Mbacké explained it this way: "The 1988 *ndigal* was Abdoul Ahad repaying Abdou Diouf. What Abdoul Ahad did was right. Water, electricity, paved roads—he got everything he wanted. The *ndigal* was compensation." A farmer stated in similar terms that "the *ndigal* is a payment by Sëriñ Touba to Abdou Diouf for the water, electricity, and roads he brought here. If you give me

[24] This pattern is not unique to the Mourides. For an excellent case study of how a Tidiane marabout in Fatick built his following see Villalón 1993, 80–101.

something I want, I should give you something in return." These opinions were echoed by still another voter in the village of Kanene Khar: "The khalifa general of the Mourides asked for work to be done in Touba. Abdou Diouf came and did it. Since he fulfilled his obligations, we should repay him. It was Abdou Diouf who helped us. So if he has need of us, we should help him too." For these voters, the *ndigal* was justified as an act of remuneration.

It is interesting to note that the legitimacy of the *ndigal* seems to derive, in part, from this ability of the Mouride leadership to secure material benefits for the Mouride community. As Abdou Ndiaye sings:

> Why obey the *ndigal*?
> Because the thirsty can drink, the dirty can wash.
> Bamba built a mosque.
> He extended the railroad to Touba.
> There are trains and automobiles and boats.
> There are planes in the sky.
> And we eat well and sleep on soft beds.
> It is Bamba who brought all this.
> It is he who made our pockets heavy with money,
> And softened our beds,
> And made our women more beautiful. . . .
> He created maids so that we can relax.

Ndiaye's hyperbole imitates the exaggerated style of a traditional praise song, but these lyrics do highlight the fact that one motive for obeying the *ndigal* is gratitude for tangible rewards.

Some reasons for obeying the *ndigal,* finally, relate to the internal cohesion of a village or urban community. As one town dweller remarked, "It was hard for me to obey the *ndigal,* but I knew it was in our interest if everyone in the neighborhood reached a consensus." This reason appeared to have been especially important in communities where political loyalties were divided, as another farmer in the village of Darou Lo explained: "Voting creates ill will between relatives. Some go this way, others go that way. You want to bring them together and create unity. But that is difficult. Some say, 'Whatever the *sëriñ* says I will do.' Others say, 'When it comes to voting I don't have a *sëriñ*.' Hearing this makes you afraid. That's why I voted for Diouf." Voting, for these Senegalese, has less to do with a preference for a particular candidate or even with fulfilling a religious obligation than with enhancing social harmony.

Given these various connections between *ndigal,* material reward, and community solidarity, it is not surprising that many Mouride voters with little or no education consider the *ndigal* to be a cornerstone of *demokaraasi.* As one Mouride farmer put it, "Our *demokaraasi* is to do what our marabout orders." Of course, not all voters share his opinion. A Mouride woodworker in Touba complained that "true *demokaraasi* does not go along with *ndigal.* Everyone should do what is in their heart. As soon as a *ndigal* is given, we are only following the will of one person." Nevertheless, obeying the *ndigal* was more than enacting the will of the marabout or even ensuring one's place in paradise. To comply with the *ndigal* was also to solidify reciprocal relationships, both among community members and between elected officials, clerics, and followers. For this reason, many less educated Mouride voters accepted orders given by religious leaders as not only moral but also integral to *demokaraasi*.

In sum, deciding whether to comply with the 1988 *ndigal* required Mouride voters (and nonvoters) to weigh considerations of religious obligation, material benefit, political commitment, and community cohesion. Moreover, we find yet again that ideals of political commitment are often overwhelmed, be it by devotional duties, remunerative obligations, or considerations of social solidarity.

I have not asserted that the existence of *demokaraasi,* as a concept, directly caused people to shun public voting; nor have I claimed that *ndigal,* as a concept, prompted Mourides to obey the commands of their religious leaders. These concepts do not cause behavior in any simple sense.[25] What I have tried to show is that concepts such as *demokaraasi* and *ndigal* do provide social scientists, as outside observers, unique insight into the intentions of the people for whom they are meaningful and therefore help to explain their behavior.

What we have seen, then, is that the intentions of Senegalese voters are many-sided. In addition to calculations of public good and private interest, these voters must weigh considerations of religious devotion, community cohesion, and material exchange. To examine adequately how these factors get balanced requires a contextual analysis of voting behavior; hence the discussions of public and *ndigal* voting. Among the main findings was that voters' preferences often get swamped by the immediate needs of the community. It follows that what might appear to some observers as democratic incompetence might better be seen as proficiency in a different effort. In an environment dominated by economic uncertainty, vulnerable electors use their votes to make their environment less precarious, whether by exchanging votes for material rewards or by solidifying bonds with religious leaders and community members.

---

[25] Attempts to demonstrate that speaking a particular language or using particular concepts have effects on nonlinguistic behavior—a project closely associated with Edward Sapir and Benjamin Lee Whorf—have by and large failed, with the exception of narrowly focused experiments that investigate how the color vocabulary of a language affects the way speakers group together objects of various colors (Kay and Kempton 1984). To get a sense of how complicated the issue becomes when the behavior in question is not grouping colored objects but engaging in political action, see the study conducted by David Laitin (1977) and critiques of this effort by William O'Barr (1978) and Joshua Fishman (1979).

## Voting and Accountability

It is often assumed that competitive elections make government officials more accountable to the voting public. In this view, responsibility for good government rests ultimately on the shoulders of voters, who must demand accountability of leaders via the ballot box. Evidence presented here suggests that this account is questionable, at least when it is applied to uneducated wolofone voters. These voters' demands for public accountability are diluted by concerns about religious obligation, social cohesion, and collective security. For these voters, casting a ballot is not only, or always, an opportunity to express satisfaction or displeasure with the policies of leaders and their performance of official duties; it is also an occasion to benefit from the wealth of candidates and their backers, to attain salvation, and to reinforce bonds of community solidarity. We thus cannot assume that elections in Senegal ensure "good" government, for voters' concerns about impartial governance are often overrun by devotional beliefs and more immediate welfare considerations.

If the case of Senegal is at all generalizable, it can be concluded that ballot casting in other African societies may not in fact be a way for voters to hold elected officials accountable. And even when officials are held accountable, it is not at all clear that they are held to standards of *public* morality; they may be expected, as in Senegal, to distribute patronage through private channels. Accountability, in other words, may be limited to claims that are strictly personalistic or communal. This tenuous connection between voting and public accountability may bode ill for the anticipated payoffs of the many democracy-building projects sponsored by the United States and the World Bank.

The connection between elections and good government, then, is contingent—in part at least—on how voters understand the purposes of their own ballot casting. Unfortunately for those who see elections as creators of transparency, there is little reason to believe that a purpose of ballot casting is always, or even usually, a desire to impose public accountability upon leaders.

The broader point is that similar institutional arrangements in different cultural contexts are not necessarily imbued with similar meaning. While Senegal shares with the United States the most significant institutional feature of democracy (regular elections), ideals of *demokaraasi* among Wolof speakers depart in significant ways from American ideals of democracy. To disregard ideals altogether (as a Schumpeterian might) or to ignore this divergence in ideals (as a Dahlian might) is to blind one to the fact that many Senegalese voters are playing a different game with different aims and rules. Where a Schumpeterian is likely to see a set of institutions that operate imperfectly, and where a Dahlian is likely to see incompetent democrats, we discover able players of *demokaraasi*, a discovery that changes our understanding of the nature and purpose of Senegalese electoral institutions.

# 5

# Democracy and *Demokaraasi* in Senegal

    The practices of *demokaraasi* are motivated by a set of concerns shared by many poor and imperiled Senegalese and might thus be seen as a game played by the more impoverished and vulnerable populations of the country. In much of this book my aim has been to discern the rules internal to this game. While this analytic move allowed us to distinguish *demokaraasi* from democracy, and thereby deepen our knowledge of the intentions and actions of both voters and nonvoters, it is also important to acknowledge that the game of *demokaraasi* is played within the confines of a larger political system. How democratic is Senegal's political system? In what ways does *demokaraasi* strengthen or subvert its democratic aspects? Under what conditions might the undemocratic aspects of *demokaraasi* be democratized in the future?

    In posing such questions, especially the last one, I risk appearing to suggest that only democracy has global value and importance. I do not believe this is the case. Indeed, Americans might expand their own parochial understanding of democracy by looking at the Senegalese practice of *demokaraasi*. It is interesting that many of the ordinary, nonpolitical uses of democracy examined in Chapter 1 presuppose that democratic situations in American society are unusual. Rich and poor do not usually sit side by side, eat similar food, or get the same opportunities. Democracy emerges only when these normally unequal parties find themselves subject to the same external force, be it a subway, dance floor, or plague. Senegalese *demokaraasi*, in contrast, is intentionally brought about by the efforts of the parties themselves, whether by voting for a candidate, providing food to the destitute, or tending the field of an ill neighbor. American democracy is often the unintended consequence of some other activity; Senegalese *demokaraasi* appears where it is intended. Surely there is a lesson here for American democrats.[1]

Nevertheless, American scholars, policy makers, and citizens are today more interested in advancing democracy than in promoting *demokaraasi*. For this reason it is important to ask questions about the possible democratization of *demokaraasi,* though from a perspective that is less normative than descriptive.

## Scholars on Democracy in Senegal

The degree to which Senegal has been truly democratized since the reintroduction of multipartyism in the mid-1970s is open to debate, and scholars offer wildly different opinions on the question. One asserts that "Senegal has emerged as a full-fledged democracy" (Sklar 1983, 13). Others argue that Senegal is a "quasi-," "partial," "proto-," or "semi-" democracy (Villalón 1995, 261; Diamond 1987, 107; Sandbrook 1988, 243; and Coulon 1995, 524, respectively). Still others maintain that democracy in Senegal does not exist at all (Schmitter and Karl 1991, 82).

Two main factors account for these differences of opinion. First, some of the most positive appraisals, such as those offered by Richard Sklar (1983) and by Robert Jackson and Carl Rosberg (1985), date to the early and mid-1980s, a time when Senegal led other African countries in institutionalizing multiparty rule. From the vantage point of the late 1980s, in contrast, Senegal was a democracy laggard. The vote rigging, rioting, and imprisonment of opposition leaders that accompanied the 1988 elections took some luster off Senegal's democratic reputation. The country's democracy looked even more tarnished in the early 1990s after electorates in Cape Verde, Zambia, and Benin voted their incumbent presidents out of office.

The second factor is definitional. Scholars who apply narrowly electoral definitions of democracy are, on the whole, more impressed by the democratic quality of Senegalese political life than those who employ definitions that encompass civil and political liberties, alternation of power, or extra-electoral mechanisms that promote the ideal of inclusive governance. Thus Robert Fatton (1987, 1) and Jackson and Rosberg (1985), who understand democracy in the strictly Schumpeterian sense of competitive elections, see Senegal as an authentic democracy. Larry Diamond (1987), Richard Sandbrook (1988), Christian Coulon (1995), Samuel Huntington (1991), and Michael Coppedge and

---

[1] I thank Douglas Lummis for this insight.

Wolfgang Reinicke (1990)—who all argue that electoral competitiveness requires, in addition, a range of political and civil liberties—see Senegal as only partially democratic. Philippe Schmitter and Terry Lynn Karl (1991), who focus on the requirement of party turnover, argue that democracy is completely absent from Senegal. Leonardo Villalón, combining an institutional and ideal understanding of democracy, is similarly concerned by the lack of alternation but thinks it nevertheless relevant to consider the ways in which extra-electoral institutions, mainly the religious brotherhoods, act as a "religiously based 'civil society'" and are thus "an important democratic element in the system" (1995, 12, 265).

As I argued in Chapters 1 and 4, there is no right way to define democracy, and thus it may make sense, depending on the research context, to define democracy in either institutional or ideal ways, and to regard Senegal as fully democratic, partially democratic, or not at all democratic. For our purposes here, it is not necessary to determine whether Senegal does or does not reach a particular democratic threshold, or to limit the analysis to purely institutional or ideal aspects of democracy. More important is identifying the major areas of democratic strength and weakness, broadly defined.

## Areas of Democratic Strength and Weakness

Democracy requires widespread participation in governance. As I observed in Chapter 1, this participation may be channeled through a variety of institutions. In Senegal, autonomous unions, civic associations, farmers' associations and federations, and the Islamic brotherhoods all serve to some degree as mechanisms of democratic participation insofar as they aggregate interests and influence government decision making (Cruise O'Brien 1979, 223–25; Lecomte 1992; Lachenmann 1993; Bergen 1994, 665–741; Villalón 1995, 258–65). Yet many of these organizations have less than participatory internal structures, and the influence brought to bear by their rank and file is not always great. A competitive electoral system, though not the only mechanism of democratic governance, is consequently one of the most important and direct ways for the people to make their voices heard.

Most of the legal guarantees necessary for sustaining a competitive electoral system are present in Senegal but are subject to restriction and intermittent violation. The freedoms of speech and the press, for instance, generally allow the plethora of independent newspapers and party organs in existence today to regularly criticize political parties as well as government officials and policies. Still, laws provide the government broad powers to prosecute anyone for spreading "false news" or discrediting the state. These laws, moreover, have been applied several times in recent years. A journalist was imprisoned in 1986 after the publication of an interview in which Abdoulaye Wade accused the president of corruption. The distribution of *Jeune Afrique* was suspended in 1994 after it published an article on the suspicious circumstances surrounding the murder of a magistrate. In 1996, the *Sud Communication* media group was fined about $1 million for defaming the Mimran group in a newspaper article alleging that this sugar-importing company engaged in customs fraud (Article 19 1987; Karatnycky et al. 1995, 500).

Other legal guarantees include the freedoms of assembly and association. These rights empower citizens to create political parties, unions, and other associations, and to hold peaceful meetings. But the law also requires that organizations register with the state and that organizers of public demonstrations secure the permission of government officials, which is sometimes denied. The government banned political rallies in 1994, for example, after violent protests over the devaluation of the CFA franc.

Elections have been held regularly since 1978. But ballot rigging, public voting, and unequal access to the media all reduced the competitiveness of elections held before 1992 (reforms of that year made private voting obligatory, equalized media access, and created mechanisms to reduce the frequency of electoral fraud). Even in the 1993 elections some opportunities for fraud remained, particularly in the issuance of fake voting ordinances, though not enough were distributed to alter the outcome of the contest.

Given the limitations placed on political freedoms and civil liberties along with the shortcomings in electoral administration, the absence of alternation must be considered a democratic weakness. In countries where elections are fair and free, a lack of party turnover is of minor significance. Few would consider Sweden, with its history of reasonably clean elections, to be undemocratic even though the Social Democrats held on to power for forty-four straight years, from 1932 to 1976. But in Senegal, alternation is the acid test of transparency.

While party turnover does not seem imminent, elections in Senegal have nonetheless become more competitive over time, with the 1993 elections reaching a new plateau of openness. Compulsory private voting, the presence of international monitors, laws guaranteeing media fairness, and the participation of opposition parties in the administration of the vote all helped increase the number of votes tallied for opposition candidates.

Higher levels of competitiveness notwithstanding, voter disinterest and alienation are additional areas of democratic weakness, though not as significant as some Senegal specialists, such as Coulon and Villalón, claim. Both scholars are alarmed by the low turnout rate in 1993. In the presidential race, 51 percent of registered voters went to the polls, down from 58 percent in 1988. Coulon interprets this fall as a sign that "the electorate shows less and less interest in the constitutional democratic process" (1995, 510). Villalón similarly attributes it to "voter apathy due to scepticism about the utility of the act" and identifies urban youth in particular as having failed to vote (1994, 185).

Although there is some truth in these assessments, they need qualification. First, while Villalón is correct to emphasize the disaffection of some young urbanites (see Gérard 1993), voting statistics show that abstainers were most concentrated in rural areas and that voter participation actually climbed from 1988 to 1993 in the departments of Dakar, Pikine, and Rufisque, which together constitute the most urbanized area in the country.[2]

Second, the drop in turnout that Coulon and Villalón attribute to growing apathy may reflect, in part, a lower rate of fraud and coercion in 1993 than in elections past. It may be significant that the sharpest decline in voter turnout took place in the heavily Mouride department of Mbacké, where it fell from 67 percent in 1988 to 28 percent in 1993. Though part of this decline is surely attributable to the fact that the khalifa general of the Mourides issued no *ndigal* (order) prior to this election (though "smaller" marabouts did), the reduction of fraudulent and coercive electoral activities may also have been consequential. Mbacké, tellingly, was one of the departments in which opposition leaders most suspected vote rigging in 1988.

Finally, Coulon and Villalón overinterpret abstention as an indication of disinterest or alienation. Many potential voters were no doubt indifferent or cynical, but the same cannot be said of all those who abstained. Many in the Ziguinchor region feared for their physical safety or could not get to polling stations.[3] Other potential voters, even a few who had strong political loyalties, did not cast their ballots for reasons internal to the game of *demokaraasi*. As we saw in Chapter 4, one farmer did not vote because he wanted to keep the emotional cement of his solidarity network in good repair. Others may have abstained in attempts to negotiate conflicts between their own preferences and the directives of their marabout. Still other reasons unrelated to disinterest, physical safety, religious obligation, or solidarity surely exist as well.

---

[2] Voter turnout in 1993 was lowest in the departments of Mbacké (28% of registered voters), Bambey (37%), Linguère (37%), Bignona (33%), and Oussouye (39%). The first two departments are heavily populated by Mouride farmers. Linguère is ethnically and religiously mixed. Bignona and Oussouye were the sites of separatist unrest. Of the five departments, Mbacké is the most urbanized, with 17% of its population living in cities. In contrast, three of the four departments with the highest turnout rates—Dakar (63%), Pikine (57%), and Rufisque (74%)—are the most heavily urban in the country (each is at least 72% urban). The fourth department with relatively high turnout, Mbour (58%), is 34% urban. (Urbanization statistics are from République du Sénégal, Ministère de l'Economie et des Finances 1990, table 3.08.)

[3] This region is located in the southwesternmost area of the country. Its cultural distinctiveness and geographical isolation contributed to the rise of a separatist movement in 1982. The struggle between government and separatists has since resulted in sporadic violence, unlawful detention, and torture (Amnesty International 1991). Violence before and during the 1993 presidential elections forced villagers in affected areas to flee to the regional capital, Ziguinchor, creating confusion about where to vote and whether it was safe to do so. The general effect was to disrupt balloting and to lower voter turnout in that region considerably.

## Governments of National Unity

One development in Senegal's political history is particularly difficult to place on the positive or negative side of the democracy ledger: the formation of successive "governments of national unity" in 1991, 1993, and 1995. Reflection on the origins, justifications, and evaluations of these coalitions will provide the occasion to think more contextually not only about the state of democracy in Senegal but also about the ways in which *demokaraasi* sustains and limits that democracy.

The events that led most directly to the first of these rapprochements between Abdou Diouf and his main political opponents can be traced to the 1988 elections and their immediate aftermath. When Abdou Diouf, the incumbent president and candidate of the PS, was proclaimed the winner with 73 percent of the vote, relations between his party and the opposition took an acrimonious turn. Opposition leaders charged massive fraud and denounced the vote as an "electoral coup d'état." Urban youth took to the streets in mass demonstrations, clashing with police and gendarmes in Dakar and Thiès. The government declared a state of emergency and had Abdoulaye Wade placed under arrest, along with several other opposition figures.

Wade obtained his release from jail after a few months despite his continued contention that he had actually won the election with 56 percent of the vote.[4] By this time Diouf felt considerable pressure to reach some modus vivendi with Wade, the strongest of the opposition leaders, to defuse the explosive situation that threatened to rip the country apart. His very ability to govern the country effectively was in question at a time when structural adjustment was exacerbating the country's deep economic crisis and stirring social discontent.

Both Diouf and Wade felt foreign pressures as well. For the United States and France, Senegal had become an important ally in a region where increasing instability was presenting a mounting danger to Western interests. The Iraqi Baathist regime was establishing closer ties to Mauritania; political instability and social unrest threatened Benin, Togo, and Mali; and civil war engulfed Liberia. With its long airport runways, conservative foreign policy, and willingness to cooperate with French and American military forces, Senegal had become such a strategic partner of France and the United States that its political stability became a foreign policy priority for both countries. Consequently, they pushed hard on Diouf and Wade to reach some kind of accommodation (*Africa Confidential,* April 17, 1992).

On April 8, 1991, Diouf announced that the PDS and the PIT would form a new government of national unity, with ministerial positions going to Wade

---

[4] Wade made this claim in his speech of June 19, 1988, at Thiès.

and other leaders of the two parties. Careful to distinguish this form of coalition from the absorption of opposition parties by a ruling party—a common occurrence over the past thirty years in Africa—Abdou Diouf explained that by the terms of the agreement each party would keep its own identity (*Le Soleil*, September 12, 1991). Still, as members of a coalition, all three parties would be responsible for carrying out policies defined broadly by the president (*Journal de l'Afrique,* April 30–May 6, 1991). The coalition, then, rested on balancing the maintenance of party identities with the implementation of PS policies.

The coalition disbanded in October 1992, as the partners found themselves unable to agree on a platform for the upcoming 1993 presidential and legislative races, only to be reconstituted in modified form a few weeks after the elections. Wade, who won big in the cities, was noticeably left out, perhaps because of his suspected role in the assassination of a senior jurist immediately after the legislative elections. In time, the PS entered negotiations with Wade and other leaders of the PDS, and they reentered the government in March 1995.

## A Consociational Democracy?

The governments of national unity call to mind the theory of "consociational" democracy formulated by Arend Lijphart and others to explain the politics of accommodation and power sharing common to small European democracies such as Austria, Switzerland, Belgium, and the Netherlands. The distinguishing feature of consociational democracy is that, in Lijphart's words, "political leaders of all significant segments of the plural society cooperate in a grand coalition to govern the country" (1977, 25). Consociational democracy is thus characterized by both social cleavages (based on ethnicity, religion, culture, and interests of various sorts) and cooperation in the form of a governmental coalition among the elites of the various segments. One benefit of consociation is to allow decisions to be made consensually on issues of common interest, while more divisive issues are settled autonomously by each segment. Indeed, Lijphart argues that consociation is more democratic than electoral systems based on majority rule, which by definition exclude minorities from power (1985, 6–7). This argument holds particular weight in respect to Senegal, for one cannot assume that power will change hands there soon, and coalitions do provide some measure of power sharing and a more inclusive way to make decisions than might otherwise exist.

However well coalition making among Senegalese elites may appear to fit the consociational model, this West African case deviates in one essential way. Whereas elites in the consociational democracies of Europe represent the interests of segmented groups, elites in Senegal, as currently organized in political parties, do not generally represent any such societal groups. Possible exceptions include Marxist parties such as the PIT, the LD/MPT, and the And-Jëf/Parti

Africain pour la Démocratie et le Socialisme (AJ/PADS), which appeal to union-ized teachers, students, civil servants, parastatal employees, and industrial workers (Bergen 1994, 466–75).[5] But these parties attract few votes. In the 1993 presidential elections, for instance, the LD/MPT and AJ/PADS candidates to-gether received less than 6 percent of the vote. (The PIT did not field a presi-dential candidate, and received only 3 percent of the vote in the 1993 legislative elections.) More than 90 percent of voters cast their ballots for either Abdou Diouf of the PS or Abdoulaye Wade of the PDS. Neither of these two leaders nor their parties enjoy the strong support of sizable class, ethnic, religious, ide-ological, regional, cultural, or linguistic constituencies organized as such.

That the major political parties of Senegal do not represent segmented groups can be explained by the combined effect of three factors. First, the law forbids parties to identify themselves with a race, ethnic group, gender, reli-gion, sect, language, or region (article 2, Law 81–17, May 6, 1981). Second, reli-gious, regional, and ethnic loyalties crosscut one another; these multiple alle-giances make it difficult for national-level political entrepreneurs to manufacture a following along communal lines. Finally, political clientelism causes alle-giances to gel around political leaders who offer material rewards, not class or ethnic ideology.

The making of multiparty coalitions in Senegal is not, then, a mechanism for accommodating the claims of competing societal groups, since elites and their parties do not represent significant societal subcultures. In this respect, Senegal does not meet fully the fundamental criterion of consociationalism. The pur-pose and meaning of coalitions may thus be somewhat different in Senegal than they are in Europe.

## Power Sharing and Hegemony

Power sharing in Senegal, if not a consociational arrangement, may represent the culmination of the ruling party's efforts to retain power by co-opting its most threatening opponents. In an engaging study, Robert Fatton provides a framework for such an argument, even though his book was written in 1987, four years before the formation of the first coalition. He attributes both the reemergence of multipartyism in Senegal in the mid-1970s and the ruling party's impulse toward conciliation and consensus in the 1980s to the "hege-monic project" of the leaders and upper-level cadres of the state and ruling party (1987, 4).[6] Legalizing and broadening the scope of political competition and seeking consensus on divisive political issues such as education policy provided

---

[5] AJ/PADS was formed in April 1991 by the merger of AJ/MRDN with several smaller parties.

[6] Fatton also claims that Islamic marabouts and (to a lesser extent) capitalists were involved in this project, though he adduces no direct evidence.

a way for the ruling class to contain and channel the potentially revolutionary demands of disgruntled peasants, workers, students, and intellectuals, all of whom suffered during the early years of independence from a stagnant economy, and some of whom (students and workers in particular) participated in crippling strikes in May and June 1968 (18, 59–62). The ruling elite hoped that multiparty rule and national unity would "gain the consent of the broad masses" (63). Following Gramsci, Fatton calls this limited democratization from above a "passive revolution."

Fatton argues that the passive revolution succeeded insofar as Presidents Senghor and Diouf were able to secure their political opponents' commitment to the new multiparty system and limit competitiveness by drawing on the support of marabouts and other notables who, through their extensive patron-client relationships, could deliver the rural vote and ensure the continued domination of the ruling party. The distribution of clientelist rewards also served to diffuse mass discontent caused by the protracted economic crisis (76, 91, 94).

But to the extent that patron-client politics dominates political relations, Fatton contends, the hegemonic project has been limited in scope, for clientelism undermines the ideological legitimacy of democratic rule. Patron-client politics "stifles the civic culture, corrupts public life . . . engenders a pervasive political cynicism," and "displaces any notion of the common good" (1987, 96). Consequently hegemony, as Fatton argues elsewhere, "relates principally to the ruling class" and is of only "marginal significance in the process of integrating subordinate classes into the social order" (1992, 30–31). Fatton thus concludes that Senegal's democracy is "crippled" but nonetheless "represents a still fragile foundation on which more profound democratic values and practices may be erected" (1987, 170).[7]

What Fatton gets right—indeed, what is impressively prescient—is his discussion of the intent and success of the ruling party in co-opting the opposition. Abdou Diouf's decision to bring Wade and other opposition leaders into a series of coalition governments in the 1990s may be seen as the culmination of the move toward consensual politics that Fatton discerned in 1987.

Fatton's conclusions regarding the "subordinate classes" are problematic, however. In his account, the ruling party has not succeeded in using limited democratization to win over the broader population. The clientelist nature of electoral politics, he argues, undermines any legitimacy that elections may bestow on the ruling party and generates only cynicism. A major problem with these conclusions is that they do not adequately acknowledge the sometimes successful efforts made by the ruling party to gain the consent of the broader population. One such partially successful effort was the legitimation of the first government of national unity itself. While this event came some years later than

---

[7] Note that Fatton uses "democracy" in two senses. His explicit definition of democracy is electoralist. By more substantive criteria he finds that this democracy is "crippled," as he states above.

Fatton's book, it nevertheless illustrates the importance of thinking about inter-actions between the masses and elites in more nuanced ways than Fatton's framework allows.

Leaders of the PS (and the PDS) went to great lengths to portray the new government of national unity as rooted in Senegal's values and its unique heri-tage of *démocratie*. For instance, Ousmane Tanor Dieng, the president's *directeur de cabinet*, argued:

> We are talking about increasing the efficacy of our democratic model by reconciling its universal characteristics with its national particularities. This is what makes it original. There is agreement that all true national democratic systems have certain features in common, such as the separation of powers, all the political and institu-tional mechanisms that guarantee the exercise of individual and collective liberties, a respect for human rights, and fair and free elections. Our model conserves these basic features while retaining the advantage of being able to draw on a cultural and civilizational reserve in which the practice of consensus and the seeking of peace, dialogue, and unity play an essential role. (*L'Unité pour le Socialisme*, August 1991)

Comparable thoughts were expressed by the PDS in its journal *Sopi*: "It is clear that Africa as a whole will be democratic one day, but each nation will achieve its *démocratie* according to its own history and moral values. Dialogue has always been essential in the resolution of the crises that have confronted Senegal. To ignore that, come what may, would be an act of irresponsibility that the PDS (the hope of all the people) cannot and will not commit" (April 19, 1991). Both the PDS and the PS, then, presented the coalition of their par-ties as the crowning achievement of a particularly Senegalese-style *démocratie*.

Similar arguments were advanced to justify the coalition government to the wider, non-francophone population. In a song that was often played on gov-ernment-owned radio in the summer of 1991, the griot pop artist and strong Diouf supporter Khar Mbaye Madiaga sang in Wolof: "Those who came to join in running the government, they deserve respect because they love their country. Senegal is the place to imitate when it comes to *demokaraasi*. . . . Thank you, Abdoulaye [Wade]. Thank you, Amath [Dansokho, leader of the PIT]. Thanks be to God. Senegal is blessed."

Senegalese *démocratie/demokaraasi* and the multiparty governance it entailed would be the envy of Africa. Whereas the older generation of African leaders (most notably Senghor, Kwame Nkrumah of Ghana, and Julius Nyerere of Tan-zania) drew upon various African traditions of consensual decision making to justify the imposition of single-party rule, the PS and the PDS presented the novel argument that Senegalese traditions could provide the ethical foundation for a uniquely African, consensual *multiparty* political system.

The vast majority of non-Francophones I interviewed accepted the argument that the government coalition was the natural endpoint of *demokaraasi*. *Demokaraasi* to them, after all, means consensus, and what better manifestation of a national agreement than integration of opposition parties into the government? Speaking of the first coalition government, one farmer explained: "What we have seen pleases us because all Muslims have come to agree, and agreement is the only thing that really matters. We now have *demokaraasi* because everyone agrees." A farmer in another village expressed similar thoughts: "Now there is *demokaraasi* in the country because the three parties have come to agree, become united. They share the same ideas and make decisions together. Where one goes, the others follow; nobody is going in the opposite direction."

*Demokaraasi,* in short, was realized in their eyes because the parties came to agree. Whether that agreement represented a wider consensus in society, resulted in the right policies, or provided the people with more say in the way government affairs were managed appeared to these farmers to be inconsequential.

There is also some evidence that more schooled members of the population also thought the coalition a positive development for Senegal's *démocratie.* A large poll conducted among the readers of the magazine *Jeune Afrique* in February 1992, about a year after the formation of the first coalition, found that 60 percent of its respondents believed that Senegal was an established *démocratie.* We must, of course, interpret the results of this poll with caution. The respondents were self-selected, represented only readers of a particular magazine, and left unrepresented people who did not read French and therefore could not read the magazine or participate in its polls—three of every four Senegalese. Still, these results indicate that cynicism was not universal even among the more educated segment of the population.

The most vociferous condemnation of the coalition, interestingly, came from independent-minded intellectuals. They perceived it as a dangerous turn in the development of *démocratie* in Senegal, for it diminished the voice of the electorate and threatened the future possibility of party turnover, principles that Wade himself had long espoused as central to *démocratie.* The distinguished political scientist Babacar Kanté (1994, 103) argued that this form of "elite accommodation" was by its "very nature bound to sully the meaning of elections. Instead of conferring legitimacy on a governing majority, elections serve to gauge the relative support levels of the various candidates or lists of candidates in order to fix their respective places in the composition of the next government." Similarly, a journalist attacked the new arrangement as a "suspicious consensus" that left the vast majority of people without invitations to the "banquet" (*Sud Hebdo,* April 18, 1991). Another commentator warned that "the mechanisms of conciliation compromise the chances for *alternance.* The citizen, the elector, and the free individual arbiter are bridled. . . . Democratic turnover, the voice and the responsibility of the people, remains unexplored" (*Options,* April 1991). An editorialist for the journal *Wal Fadjri* lamented that "we are witnessing the weakening of the political counter-power so indispensable to *démocratie*" (August 28–September 3, 1992).

The coalition government complicates Fatton's picture of relationships between the elite and the masses as mediated primarily by clientelism and characterized by cynicism. In the first place, both ruling and opposition parties have exerted more effort than Fatton acknowledges to disseminate ideas advantageous to their respective interests. Both factions of the political elite seek to set the terms of the debate about *demokaraasi* and thereby shape the broader population's perception of what counts as legitimate leadership. Elites thus do not seek compliance though instrumental or maraboutic means alone.

More important, the cynicism that the formation of the first coalition generated appears to have been most pronounced among the highly educated segments of the population. The people who did not speak French, at least those I interviewed, were enthusiastic. And a majority of *Jeune Afrique* readers still thought Senegal was a real *démocratie*.

The coalition government complicates any simple conceptualization of elite-mass relations in one other respect: it shows that ideas do not always move in a unilinear fashion from the elite to the masses, as Gramsci himself recognized (1985, 363–64). Elites sometimes incorporate elements of mass culture in their attempt to legitimate their rule. A careful tracking of *démocratie* and *demokaraasi* reveals such an incorporation of ideas by leaders of the ruling and main opposition parties in Senegal, who justified the coalition in terms of consensus and other values important to the broader population of the country.

There appears, in fact, to be a circulation of ideas between the francophone elite and the non-French-speaking wolofone masses. *Demokaraasi* entered popular Wolof discourse because of struggles between factions of the francophone elite to define *démocratie* in ways beneficial to their interests. Vulnerable wolofone populations transformed these elite-generated ideas to fit their own life conditions. These Wolof meanings then reentered the discourse of the francophone political elite and today shape the way members of the elite justify their new government coalitions to the broader population. The end result is to make it easier for the elite to sell the coalition to the non-francophone population.

Many Senegalese, consequently, regard the governments of national unity as good and right, or at least they did as of 1993. Whether one considers this a positive or negative development for democracy in Senegal depends on one's evaluation of the governments of national unity, and the evidence here is mixed. On the one hand, the coalition parties do not represent large, identifiable constituencies. The governments of national unity thus do not make political decision making significantly more inclusive. Nor do they appear to be making the political system more competitive insofar as the identification of these coalitions with *demokaraasi* weakens the connections that voters make between elections and party turnover.

On the other hand, the coalitions may be creating more trust between the ruling party and the opposition. By agreeing to participate in coalitions, both the PS and opposition parties have tacitly recognized one another as legitimate participants in the political process, and acknowledged the legitimacy of the multiparty system itself. As a result, the commitment of member parties to play by the rules of the game seems to be increasing. Concrete evidence of this commitment can be found in the new, fairer electoral code negotiated in 1991 (see Linz 1978, 27–38, for a more theoretical discussion of these issues). What is true of the elites is also true of the broader population. To those Senegalese who think the coalitions are examples of *demokaraasi* in action, multipartyism is rendered more legitimate, though not necessarily as an institution of democracy.

## Some Effects of *Demokaraasi* on Democracy

The effects of *demokaraasi* on the democratic aspects of Senegal's political system are not limited to legitimating government by coalition. When we think about these other effects, it is helpful to distinguish between nonelectoral and electoral practices of *demokaraasi*. The former encompasses networks of mutuality formed by players of *demokaraasi*—the tontines, *mbootaay*, *mbaxal*, and *dahira* described in Chapter 3. The latter refers to the casting or withholding of ballots to strengthen solidaristic relationships (what we will call solidaristic voting) or the casting of ballots in return for the aid of political patrons (clientelist voting). Though these two types of voting overlap when affective ties to patrons are strong, such is not always the case.

One important consequence of both solidaristic and clientelist voting is to make electoral participation an activity that is both relational (calculated to reinforce personal attachments and allegiances) and economic (performed in return for or anticipation of aid and assistance). This kind of electoral participation is detrimental to democracy to the extent that it reduces the input of voters in political decision making. Those who might otherwise wish to signify their preferences for candidates and policies are diverted from doing so by the more immediate necessity of harmonizing their votes with those of other community members, of abstaining as a way to remain neutral in a divided community, or of using their votes to secure the assistance of political patrons. These voters, like the Mexican voters studied by Jonathan Fox, "exchange . . . political rights for social benefits" (1994, 153). Mutuality displaces citizenship as voters sacrifice their political rights to sustain and protect their networks of social security.

At the same time, it is important to recognize that not all players of *demokaraasi* experience solidaristic or clientelist voting as involving such a trade-off. That is, they do not conceive of voting as an act of political consequence. These voters are not renouncing their democratic rights, for they do not perceive themselves as having such rights to relinquish. The sacrifice made by these voters exists only in a systemic, functional sense.

In either case, clientelist voting serves as a mechanism for holding elected officials accountable to their ballot-casting clients only in ways that are personalistic or communal, while solidaristic voting does not hold them accountable at all. The effect is to create a political system in which the meaningful participation of large numbers of voters in public governance is minimized, at least through electoral channels. *Demokaraasi,* from this perspective, makes political decision making in Senegal less participatory, less inclusive, less democratic.

Yet not all consequences of *demokaraasi* are deleterious to democracy, even in the realm of elections. People who vote, even for solidaristic or clientelist reasons, remain "engaged" with the state (Bratton 1994). Those who become disaffected, especially in the largest urban areas, are prone to violent confrontation, as the riotous aftermaths of the 1988 elections and the 1994 devaluation indicate all too well. The continued electoral involvement of large segments of the population arguably holds greater potential for future democratic transformation than other alternatives. After all, the electoral machines of many late-nineteenth- and early-twentieth-century American cities eventually broke down and gave way to less clientelistic patterns of voting. England's patronage-driven electoral system underwent a dramatic change in the latter part of the nineteenth century. The continued electoral participation of the Senegalese makes such a transformation possible in their country, too.

The nonelectoral practices of *demokaraasi* also have effects on democracy. Tontines, *mbootaay, mbaxal, dahira,* and other types of solidarity networks often operate outside the electoral arena and outside the immediate control of candidates and state administrators. In fact, for some Senegalese, *demokaraasi* and the solidarity networks to which this concept refers are important precisely because they provide protection against abusive politicians and bureaucrats. Referring obliquely to the power of such officials, the gas station attendant we encountered in Chapter 3 explained that in her opinion, "*demokaraasi* is good, because when you're united, nobody can do anything to you. If you take one twig from a broom, it's easy to snap it in two. But if you take all the twigs together; they're hard to break." A farmer, drawing on a similar metaphor for solidarity, describes the changing relationship between bureaucrats and farmers:

> Long ago we had *demokaraasi* here in Senegal, and it was useful. We were poor; government agents helped us when the rains were bad. When the seeds were distributed, they gave them to us on credit, to be paid back after the harvest. This form of aid was our *demokaraasi*. But that no longer exists now.[8] They use us, then throw us aside in the same way an insect gnaws at a peanut. We farmers, we want

---

[8] Rural credit institutions began to break down in the early 1980s. For details see Casswell 1984; Berg 1990, 65–66.

*demokaraasi* because if we can work together, everyone will be happy. If we pull our desires and thoughts together, God will help us. You need to come together, be like a bundle of sticks tied together; like this nobody can do anything to you.

The bundle of sticks may remind some readers of the fasces used as a symbol of fascism. The fasces was a bundle of rods with a protruding ax blade carried before ancient Roman magistrates as an emblem of state authority. It symbolized social unity (the bundle or rods) subordinate to political authority (the ax). For the peanut farmer the bundle of sticks is also a symbol of social solidarity, but it is a solidarity that poor farmers use to defend themselves against a state that gnaws at them.

Both the farmer and the gas station attendant evidence a cynicism reminiscent of the contemptuous distrust expressed by some informants in earlier chapters. Two who stand out are the farmer who spoke of government as corrupting and whorish and the tailor who described the *politig* of politicians who leave their supporters "standing in the road." This is cynicism born of broken promises, coercion, and exploitation. While neither this farmer nor the gas station attendant specified what they feared, other informants did. One spoke of police officers who demanded bribes and payoffs, another of party officials who failed to provide assistance to their backers, still another of state agents who stole or diverted fertilizer and seed meant for area farmers.

An important function of mutuality networks, it seems, is to shield vulnerable people from harm, including harm caused by state officials and party bosses. It might be argued that these networks constitute a kind of (fragmented) counterweight to the power of officialdom. This is an interpretation favored by Fatton, who argues that generally in Africa "the subordinate classes comprising the unemployed, the poor, and the underpaid people of rural and urban areas are seeking to constitute a popular civil society of basic networks of survival to counter the devastating impact of predatory rule" (1995, 85).

Solidarity networks—to the extent that they successfully constrain the exercise of power by the state and ruling party—may contribute to the pluralization of power and widen the space for unions, civic associations, and the national leaderships of farmers' organizations and the Islamic brotherhoods to act on and with the government. In this way the solidarity networks that make up the nonelectoral side of *demokaraasi* may strengthen the democratic aspects of the country's political system.

It is difficult, however, to assess how effectively these solidarity networks actually limit state power. To be sure, they enable groups of individuals to evade laws and participate in the informal economy; but such networks can also seek benefits from the state, as whole neighborhoods did in Pikine in their quest for a better water supply (Salem 1992). However eagerly the farmer and gas station attendant seek protection against the predations of politicians and bureaucrats, these two informants both acknowledge their desire for party and state assistance. The farmer speaks nostalgically of the government support he and his fellow villagers received in the 1970s. The gas station attendant joined the PS, for, as she explained in Chapter 3, only the PS has the resources to "resolve" her problems. State and party are capable of both the mutuality of *demokaraasi* and the exploitation of *politig,* a fact that creates ambivalence for these two informants about their relationships with state agents and party officials.

*Demokaraasi,* it appears, plays a dual and contradictory role in sustaining current power arrangements. *Demokaraasi* among neighbors, disciples, and kin protects against the *politig* of officials and may thereby be conceived as a form of resistance or a "weapon of the weak," to borrow the felicitous wording of James Scott (1985). At the same time, these networks mobilize to seek out aid and assistance offered by the state and the party. The struggle for survival thus leads people to participate in the electoral practices of *demokaraasi,* usually to the benefit of PS candidates. This kind of participation secures the perpetuation of this party's domination but also holds a potential for future democratic transformation. How likely is it that such a transformation will actually take place?

## Under What Conditions Might *Demokaraasi* Be Democratized?

Prospects for the further democratization of Senegal's political system depend in part on how local populations understand and make use of the electoral system. By making electoral institutions the playing field of *demokaraasi,* voters undermine their own power, mute their voices, and render the system less democratic. This insight makes one wonder whether and how the electoral practices of *demokaraasi* may be democratized in the future. An individual, we might suggest, may be moved to forsake the mutuality and personalism of *demokaraasi* for the rule-governed, self-interested, and civic-minded behavior of democracy by any of five factors: civic education, French-language education, economic security, the secret ballot, and extensive networking.

### Civic Education

Civic education projects targeted at unschooled voters are today in vogue among many democratization experts. In 1991 the United States earmarked part of its foreign aid to Senegal for democracy-building programs. A substantial part of these funds went to producing, in several indigenous languages, educational booklets on Senegal's constitution and electoral laws. The assumption was that uneducated voters would act as competent democrats if they could only be taught the purposes of democracy and the rules of the game.

This assumption is faulty. Learning the rules and purposes of democracy does not alleviate the existential dilemmas and material insecurities faced by most Senegalese, nor does it lessen the need to make use of electoral institutions—in

ways Americans would not consider democratic, to be sure—to guarantee collective well-being. Such voters may be poor democrats, but they are adept players of the game of *demokaraasi,* and civic education alone will do little to per-
suade them to play a different, more risky game. (Nor should we overlook the
fact that relatively few Senegalese are literate in any of the indigenous languages
anyway, so these booklets had very limited circulation.)

### French-Language Education

If civic education in Wolof or other indigenous languages is likely to have little effect on voting behavior, what of French-language instruction in the country's formal educational system? Not only does French-language education
allow access to a wide range of political opinions broadcast and published by
the French-language media, it is also a principal avenue of social mobility. A
World Bank study found that Senegalese who have an upper secondary education have expenditure levels 42 percent higher than those with no education
and 25 percent higher than those with lower secondary education (World Bank
1995a, 8). More democratic behavior may thus follow from both exposure to
new ideas and some degree of material security.

It is important to recall, though, that the number of people thus affected is
limited. Only about one-quarter of the population has completed enough education to be literate in French. There is also reason to believe that some factions
of the francophone elite are at best ambivalent about promoting universal
French-language literacy. Leaders in the ruling party benefit from mass illiteracy
insofar as it excludes most of the population from active participation in politics and reduces potential opposition to government actions. Ruling and opposition party officials profit from mass illiteracy to the extent that it generates demand among non-French speakers for francophone political entrepreneurs who
can operate in the official language of government. Finally, mass illiteracy is advantageous to civil servants and workers in the modern sector of the economy
because it reduces competition for high-paying jobs (Laitin 1992, 94–95).

The elite's use of French for communication thus creates linguistic barriers to
the social mobility of people who speak only indigenous languages. The result
is what Carol Myers Scotton (1990) calls "elite closure," the maintenance of
elite political and economic power through linguistic exclusion. Hard proof
that elites have deliberately pursued a strategy of closure in Senegal is scant,
though there is limited evidence that formal education is not a high government priority, at least in comparison with the educational efforts made by other
countries on the continent. Among forty-nine African countries, Senegal
ranked fourteenth in GNP per capita in 1990 but only thirty-sixth in adult literacy (Griffiths 1994, 222–23). Between 1980 and 1986, almost every other country for which data are available had a higher rate of growth in public expendi-

ture on education than Senegal, which ranked twentieth out of twenty-five countries (UNESCO-UNICEF 1990, annex 5.1).

There is little reason to expect that government officials in Senegal will make education, university education in particular, a higher priority any time soon. Unemployment among university graduates is so high that a word has been coined for out-of-work students—*maîtrisards* (for a more general account see Diop and Diouf 1990, 187–203). To make things worse, the implementation of structural adjustment programs contributed to the loss of an estimated 20,000 jobs—14 percent of salaried positions—between 1981 and 1989 (Diouf 1992, 74). As a result, the government feels pressure to slow the growth of university enrollments. In recent years it has tried to tighten university admissions requirements and has been impeded only by the strong reaction of student and teacher unions. French-language education, it appears, is unlikely to play a leading role in the widespread democratization of *demokaraasi* in the near future.

### Economic Security

The achievement of economic security (by means other than French-language education) might also lead more and more people to stop voting for solidaristic or clientelist reasons. Several students of big-city politics in the United States attribute the decline, or at the least transformation, of political machines in this country to economic growth in the late nineteenth and early twentieth centuries. The increased affluence that resulted reduced the voters' dependence on the petty bribes and favors of ward bosses and created a middle class that became the champions of reform. This dependency was further weakened by federal welfare programs established by the New Deal in the 1930s (Greenstein 1964; Lotchin 1981).

The likelihood that Senegalese clientelism will wither away in a similar fashion is slim. First, the prospects of Senegal's achieving rapid and sustained economic growth in the near future are bleak. From 1968 to 1988, GNP per capita (with prices held constant) declined by over 13 percent (Berg 1990, 3). From 1988 to 1993, real annual GDP growth, at only 1.7 percent, was overcome by an increase in Senegal's population of 3 percent per year (World Bank 1995c, 462). Structural adjustment programs, put in place to improve economic performance, have not strengthened the economy noticeably. A major evaluation commissioned by USAID concluded that "it is hard to see in Senegal's growth data, or in other economic outcome data, evidence that some basic change has occurred that has moved Senegal onto a higher growth path, or made the economy more flexible or productive" (Berg 1990, 210). The 1994 devaluation of the CFA franc had some positive effect on the economy in 1995, but it is too early to gauge its long-term consequences (Creevey, Vengroff, and Gaye 1995, 676).

Second, although many programs created by government agencies and international donors have been designed to improve the living conditions of the poor and, starting in the 1980s, to alleviate hardships caused by structural adjustment, most have not been targeted at the most needy members of society. Carol Graham, who undertook a study of poverty programs in Senegal, explains:

> Senegal's first public housing project, implemented in 1964 . . . was designed for the military and civil service *fonctionnaires*. . . . Credit programs have either targeted the skilled or the educated, as the DIRE [Délégation à la Réinsertion et à l'Emploi] did, or require guarantees that the poor cannot provide. . . . Even most donor-sponsored programs do not target the poorest. U.S. AID's Agence de Crédit pour l'Entreprise Privée (ACEP), for example, has achieved a 98 percent repayment ratio, but only on loans to individuals who can provide guarantees. Clearly, these are not the poor. Agetip [Agence d'Exécution des Travaux d'Intérêt Publique contre le Sous-Emploi] and the Caisse Central, for example, have taken steps to sponsor microenterprises, but, again, these efforts are on a relatively small scale and have had little effect on the poor, who in Senegal are clearly the majority of the population. (Graham 1994, 127–28)

Although Graham is critical of the microenterprise component of Agetip, she is, on the whole, impressed by the effectiveness of this government agency. Its major function is to fund the employment of unskilled youth by private firms in public works projects. But, as she notes, its small scale has limited its impact. In 1990–91 it created only about 11,000 temporary jobs (117, 133, 145).

Third, even if economic conditions do improve or if aid programs are targeted more intensively at the poor, the voting behavior of the formerly vulnerable may change little, for the poor are not alone in seeking clientelist benefits. Well-off farmers, tradespeople, shopkeepers, industrial workers, and civil servants still need various kinds of licenses, permits, residence certificates, land titles, and other official documents (Villalón 1995, 94–96, 103). They desire protection to participate, free from harassment, in the black market. They want jobs for their kin, access to educational opportunities for their children, and more. Patrons may no longer be able to buy votes for a kilo or two of rice, but other kinds of assistance become important to more wealthy clienteles. Of course, the same is true in the United States. For this reason some political scientists do not concur that political machines broke down as a result of affluence or the New Deal (Stave 1970; Boulay and DiGaetano 1985); others point out that political machines endure in places like New Haven and Chicago (Wolfinger 1972, Shefter 1983).

In addition, the ideals that guide vulnerable Senegalese voters' understanding of and participation in electoral institutions have become integrated into a larger moral system. Solidarity, consensus, and evenhandedness are functional not only in a strict economic sense; they are valued as the moral fibers that bind together local communities and social networks. We must allow for the possibility that cultural change will not mechanistically follow economic change (should economic change occur). An ethic of mutuality has survived in Japan, one of the wealthiest nations on earth. Solidary ties and the voting behaviors they engender may similarly outlast their social security functions in Senegal. Mutuality may have originated some time ago as a response by vulnerable populations to material insecurity, but increasing security today does not ordain the demise of this collectivist ethic.

The Secret Ballot

The introduction of the secret ballot in 1914 caused immediate and profound changes in the electoral behavior of indigenous Senegalese voters. Blaise Diagne successfully used the secret ballot to break the ties that bound black Africans to their erstwhile French and mulatto patrons, who would never again play a pivotal role in Senegalese electoral politics.

Is it possible that the return to secret voting in the 1990s will have effects as dramatic as those in 1914? Certainly no such dramatic effects were evident in 1993. Though support for opposition candidates grew, the PS still won the presidency with 58 percent of the vote and 84 of 120 seats in the legislature.

When we attempt to anticipate the consequences of private voting over the longer term, it may be helpful to examine the effects of a switch to the secret ballot elsewhere in the world. Nineteenth-century England provides a useful point of comparison, for electoral politics there, as in Senegal, were highly clientelist before the introduction of the secret ballot in 1872. In 1870 a select committee reported to Parliament that "in many boroughs great corruption prevails at Municipal Elections. In some boroughs it appears that a considerable class of voters will not vote unless they are paid; and the fact that the power at the election is mainly in the hands of such persons, prevents respectable persons from becoming candidates, or taking part in voting" (Hanham 1969, 285). The Ballot Act of 1872 put an end to public voting and apparently to the most flagrant forms of vote buying. More subtle forms of bribery were then invented. Indeed, subsequent elections were corrupt enough to prompt the passing of the Corrupt and Illegal Practices Act in 1883.

Gary Cox, in a penetrating study of electoral behavior of that period, argues that bribery declined as a result not of the secret ballot but of an increase in the size of constituencies. "When Parliament sought to deal with bribery that had become too extensive, their method was often simply to expand the offending borough's boundaries so as to include more electors" (1987, 56). Enlarging the electoral unit just made vote buying too expensive.

Interestingly, Harold Gosnell, in a postscript to his classic 1937 study of Chicago politics, attributed the survival of that city's political machine well into the 1960s in part to the small size of its election precincts (1968, 233). "If election precincts were made larger," he argued, "the total number of election officials would be reduced and it would be harder for political bosses to manipulate each tiny unit of the electorate" (190). Secrecy, we might expect, would be most likely to alter behavior in larger constituencies.

But in Senegal constituencies were effectively made smaller, not larger, for the 1993 elections. The government increased the number of polling stations from 3,537 to 8,220 to make voting less burdensome for people who previously had to travel far. As a result, an average of only about 175 voters actually cast ballots at each polling station in the presidential elections.[9] At the end of the voting day, ballots were counted at each station and the results immediately posted for all to see, as stipulated by law. So while the electoral choice of each individual elector remained secret, the aggregate results for each (larger) village or group of (smaller) villages did not. Consequently, local-level political patrons were still able to gauge the effectiveness of their efforts and the overall compliance of relatively small groups of voters. The secret ballot simply forced patrons to devise new methods of (collective) surveillance, made easier by the decentralization of polling and ballot counting.

Increasing the number of polling stations may also have muted the effect of the secret ballot on solidaristic voting in 1993. Though the secret ballot reduced the community pressure on an individual level, the small number of voters at each polling station maintained it at the collective level. Everyone would know that *somebody* voted for the opposition—but who? Suspicion and divisiveness may have lingered, especially in rural areas where the village constituted the primary solidarity network. It is perhaps for this reason that in 1993 some voters, like the elderly farmer in the village of Kab Gaye whom we met in Chapter 4, continued to weigh considerations of community cohesion more heavily than a preference for this or that candidate.

### Extensive Networking

Far-reaching clientelism in Senegal has caused state resources to be appropriated according to a political as opposed to an administrative or economic logic (on Africa more generally see Sandbrook 1986). As a result, many state offices and agencies have been so impaired that they are unable to carry out basic tasks. State operations have been further disrupted and curtailed by the privatization of various parastatal agencies in the 1980s and 1990s, a reform mandated by Senegal's international donors.

Many services once provided by the state are consequently now performed by autonomous grass-roots associations. For example, the dissolution in 1980

---

[9] The maximum number of registered voters that each polling station (*bureau de vote*) could accommodate was limited to 600, although most polling stations had in fact far fewer registered voters on their rolls. The national average was 303 (République du Sénégal, Ministère de l'Intérieur 1992). The number of actual voters was lower still. A parallel vote count conducted by NDI found that in 241 randomly selected polling stations in five departments the average voter turnout in each polling station was 175.

of the main rural development agency in the peanut basin, the Office Nationale de Coopération et d'Assistance au Développement (ONCAD), has led farmers to make their own collective arrangements for the provision of credit and seed and for marketing their peanut crops. The Fédération des Organisations Non-gouvernementales du Sénégal (FONGS), founded in 1978, is an umbrella organization for twenty-three such farmers' associations. In 1991 it had 100,000 members in more than 850 villages. Beyond taking up the responsibilities of the now defunct ONCAD, these associations have made provisions for their own food supply by establishing granaries and cereal banks (Lachenmann 1993, 81–83). Similar associations have been formed by rice growers (Lecomte 1992).

Associations have arisen in urban areas, too. The decay of neighborhoods in Dakar and in other cities gave birth to the *set setal* movement. This Wolof expression means, literally, "be clean, make clean." It refers to the loose network of neighborhood youth associations spontaneously formed in the summer of 1990. *Set setal* encompasses hundreds of associations, almost all of them directed at improving and beautifying the cityscape. One group of *set setal* associations in Rufisque, for example, took it upon themselves to clean out a blocked, putrid canal that cut through their neighborhoods. They cleared obstructions, dredged sand, and washed it clean (*Le Soleil,* April 26–29, 1990). More typically, *set setal* associations repair potholes in the streets, clean up garbage-strewn parks, and paint murals over soiled walls. Funding for materials initially came from "taxes" levied on passing cars.[10]

The disengagement of the state has led to an increase in the number of associations, like those that make up FONGS and *set setal,* that are geared toward the provision of basic, sometimes essential services. There are at least two potential consequences of this trend. First, if the number of associations continues to grow, and if people come to rely more and more on them, such associations may supplement in a significant way the solidarity networks on which urbanites and villagers already depend. And as we saw in Chapter 4, more extensive networking may lead to more independent voting. Second, participation in associational life may inculcate democratic values and induce more civic modes of behavior. This Toquevillean argument is today championed by Robert Putnam, who maintains that dense networks of "horizontal" (nonhierarchical) associations in northern Italy have created high levels of generalized social trust, deeper civic engagement, and ultimately more efficient government. As he pithily summarizes it, "good government in Italy is a by-product of singing groups and soccer clubs" (1993, 176).

Whether associational life may have similar civic effects in Senegal is open to question. For one thing, age, gender, caste status, wealth, and education often stratify the exercise of associational authority. Many local associations are not

---

[10] More detailed discussions of this movement can be found in Enda 1991 and Niane, Savané, and Diop 1991.

horizontally ordered (Ndione 1987; Patterson 1996). It is also uncertain that the number of associations in Senegal will continue to grow. *Set setal*, for instance, is already in decline, mostly because of local government intervention. Neighborhood associations in Dakar began to receive funding from city hall in mid-1990. By the end of 1991 the total had risen to almost 35 million CFA francs. Many associations have also become tied to the municipality through its Coordination des Associations et Mouvements (de Jeunes) de la Communauté Urbaine de Dakar (CAMCUD). About five or six hundred associations were expected to participate in a cleanup drive initiated by CAMCUD in November 1991 (*Sud Hebdo,* November 7, 1991). It is not surprising that government officials would want to gain control over this (initially) autonomous movement of potentially volatile youth. By most accounts the government appears to be succeeding. For this reason many observers are already proclaiming the demise of *set setal.* Cause of death: "assassination" by politicians (*Le Cafard Libéré,* September 18, 1991; *Le République,* September 2, 1991). It is questionable, then, whether *set setal* and similar associations will survive and, if they do, whether they will assume important civic—or welfare—functions.

We cannot point, then, to anything that foreordains the persistence or the breakdown of the electoral practices of *demokaraasi.* Nevertheless, when I consider that among the people I interviewed, those who appeared to be the least likely to vote for solidaristic or clientelist reasons generally were the most educated and most affluent or had the widest set of solidarity networks, it seems that at least some of those five factors may be relevant to the voting behavior of at least some people. But without more sophisticated polling and statistical analysis, it is impossible to assign relative weights or to rule out any particular factor.

In any event, it does not appear that *demokaraasi* will disappear soon. Moreover, we have seen that its effects on democracy are multiple and countervailing. *Demokaraasi* plays important roles in legitimating governmental coalitions, in making public decision making less participatory, in maintaining people's engagement with the state, in contributing to the pluralization of power, and in perpetuating the privileged position of the ruling party. These complexities make it difficult to speak of *demokaraasi's* overall effect. But the fact that *demokaraasi* has such a range of consequences is itself important. It suggests that to gauge more fully the long-term prospects for democracy in Senegal (and in other places and contexts), we need to examine more carefully how popular ideals and practices such as *demokaraasi* both support and frustrate the consolidation of democracy.

# 6

## How Distinctive Is *Demokaraasi?*

Since students of electoral politics in other countries around the world will surely find similarities in what has been described in this book about Senegal, it might be profitable to reflect on what is and what is not unique about *demokaraasi*. When we take up this question, it is useful to draw a distinction between *demokaraasi* as a concept and *demokaraasi* as a set of practices. As a concept, *demokaraasi* combines references to collectivist ideals of welfare and the formal institution of elections. As a set of practices, *demokaraasi* includes participation in solidarity networks as well as solidaristic and clientelist forms of voting.

Many of the practices of *demokaraasi* are certainly far from unique. Urban and rural populations of many countries form and participate in solidarity networks. Work groups, rotating credit associations, religious societies, kinship alliances, and the like exist throughout Africa and elsewhere. Clientelist voting, especially in its least affect-laden forms, is also common. In the past few years, publicized instances of widespread vote buying have occurred in Japan, Malaysia, Thailand, Taiwan, the Philippines, Zimbabwe, Papua New Guinea, Brazil, Mexico, and Lebanon, among other places. Cases of vote buying have also been documented in the United States. In Clinton County, Kentucky, a candidate for sheriff in the 1993 Republican primary pleaded guilty to charges of purchasing votes for between $25 and $50 apiece (*Louisville Courier-Journal,* August 30, 1994); the mayor of Rockport, Indiana, was sentenced to prison after his conviction for buying votes in 1982, 1984, and 1986 (*Indianapolis Star,* June 30, 1990).

As for solidaristic voting, rational choice theorists have long recognized the importance of "relational benefits" (Uhlaner 1989, 259) or "solidary incentives" (Moe 1980, 615) in the voting decision. Patrick Dunleavy explains that "in all liberal democracies the private costs of supporting a particular party can be significant (especially having to declare to politically aligned friends, workmates or neighbors that you voted another way)" (1992, 88). Empirical confirmation that such private costs are significant, however, is hard to come by. Reviewing research on American voters, Stephen Knack concludes that "there is little or no solid evidence in the turnout literature that interpersonal pressures matter" (1992, 138). And as we saw in Chapter 4, students of electoral politics in Africa have not fully explored the nature and effects of solidarity considerations on voters. How important solidaristic voting actually is in Africa and other parts of the world remains to be determined. Still, we have little reason to suspect that Senegalese voters are in this respect unique.

It is at the conceptual level that questions of uniqueness and similarity become more complicated. Certainly *demokaraasi* and democracy share the institutional referent of elections. Even in respect to ideals, *demokaraasi* overlaps with democracy in its inclusion of some forms of equality. *Demokaraasi* departs from the American English term, however, in coupling participation in electoral institutions with ideals of social welfare and extending participation to a range of institutions that promote collective economic security.

Since many practices associated with *demokaraasi* exist elsewhere in the world, might a rough equivalent of the term in another language bear a similar set of meanings and have a similar set of relations to democracy? Without empirical evidence, it is difficult to say. Even other African societies are too heterogeneous, their languages too different, and their histories too divergent to permit any facile generalizations. The one empirical study conducted elsewhere in Africa—a study of Luganda, the language of the Baganda people of Uganda—shows both similarities and differences between the roughly equivalent Wolof and Luganda concepts.

## *Eddembe Ery'obuntu* in Uganda

Mikael Karlström (1996) finds that rural Bagandans routinely translate the English word "democracy" with the Luganda *eddembe ery'obuntu*. *Eddembe* means, roughly, the freedom to do something without interference, and *obuntu* is taken to mean civility in both governance and individual conduct. Together, the words mean something like "civil liberty," with an emphasis on the civil conduct of both ruler and ruled. The concept is thus used to refer to freedom from political disorder and its destructive consequences; the freedom of subjects to have their complaints and opinions heard by rulers; and evenhanded treatment by power holders. The meanings of this concept appear to have been colored by the Bagandans' nostalgia for the well-ordered monarchy of the preindependence era and by their more recent experience of the despotic, sometimes murderous regimes of Milton Obote and Idi Amin during the first twenty-three years of independence.

While *eddembe ery'obuntu* is similar to *demokaraasi* in its emphasis on hierarchical egalitarianism and acting in ways that are socially responsible, it is also different in fundamental ways. Its focus on freedom from oppressive disorder contrasts with the freedom from exploitation and egotism that marks *demokaraasi*. In addition, *demokaraasi* goes beyond the reciprocal rights and obligations of ruler and ruled embodied by the Luganda concept to encompass a wide range of interactions among kin and community members. The two concepts also differ markedly in that elections "virtually never figured in" Karlström's informants' remarks about *eddembe ery'obuntu* (1996, 493).

These differences are most likely attributable to the divergent historical experiences of Wolof and Luganda speakers. Contrast the long, mostly peaceful experience of multiparty elections in Senegal with the reign of terror in Uganda from 1971 to 1985. Failures of *demokaraasi* in Senegal have led to exploitation and threatened economic welfare; breakdowns of *eddembe ery'obuntu* in Uganda have led to chaos and genocide. Also surely important are the circumstances under which the French and English words were introduced into Wolof and Luganda. The use of *demokaraasi* by politicians to speak of the return to multipartyism and the other words and metaphors they chose shaped non-Francophones' understanding of the concept in significant and sometimes unplanned ways. The conditions under which the English word "democracy" was introduced to Luganda and the way Bagandans connected it with *eddembe ery'obuntu* are also surely important, though Karlström does not explore these topics.

Looking beyond sub-Saharan Africa, scholars have examined the uses of *dimuqrāṭiyya, ra'ā'iyya,* and *ḥurriyya* in nineteenth-century Arabic writings of Egyptian and Lebanese government officials, journalists, and chroniclers (Ayalon 1989), the meanings of *démocratie* in speeches made by Moroccan political leaders during the 1977 electoral campaign (Bel Cadi 1986), and the way Malaysian political leaders rendered "democracy" into Malay after World War II (Omar 1993, 171–90). All these studies, however, focus exclusively on elite discourse; and as we have seen, elite and folk conceptions sometimes differ markedly.

## *Minzhu* in China

The one non-African term whose elite and folk meanings have been investigated, though in sometimes frustrating ways, is *minzhu,* a Chinese word normally rendered by translators and lexicographers as "democracy." *Minzhu* combines the characters *min* and *zhu.* L. Wieger, an expert on Chinese etymology, writes that *min* is used to refer to "the people, the mass, the common multitude." This meaning appears to be a metaphorical extension, for *min* signified at one time "a creeping plant with sprouts, that is proliferous." As for *zhu,* it originally represented "a lamp-stand with the flame rising. By extension, a man who spreads light, a lord, a master." Today its most usual meaning is "master" (1965, 217, 269).

*Minzhu* has been an important concept in Chinese political discourse at least since the nineteenth century, when Liang Qichao, a journalist, activist, and later cabinet minister, wrote a series of essays on important Western political thinkers. The noted sinologist Andrew Nathan (1985) explored the content and legacies of Liang's thought. Unconcerned with the kinds of issues raised here about language and translation, Nathan does not use the term *minzhu* at all, preferring instead "Chinese democracy." Whether "Chinese democracy" is an appropriate translation of *minzhu* is a question to which we will turn shortly. For now, let us refer to Nathan's "Chinese democracy" as *minzhu* to keep from projecting onto this Chinese term connotations borne by the English "democracy."

According to Nathan, Liang thought of *minzhu* primarily as a way for the government to communicate with the people, to educate them (1985, 49). The purpose of this education was to "unleash energies that [would] contribute to the collective welfare; it would not—as a Westerner might see it—enable individuals to pursue personal interests that might be competitive with that welfare" (51). Nathan points out that there is a strong Confucian element in this argument: "This faith in the innate potential harmony of human beings in the social order was a tenet of the Confucianism in which Liang was trained. During centuries when Western philosophers labored over the question of how humanity's selfish nature could be reconciled with life in society, Confucian thinkers instead discussed ways of educating people to follow their instincts for social cooperation" (58). Liang thus saw *minzhu* and political participation as a means to achieve national unity. The main obstacles to its realization were the people's ignorance (thus the need for education) and the bureaucracy (which disrupted the natural harmony of rulers and ruled) (67).

The idea that *minzhu* entailed both elite supervision and misgivings about bureaucracy carried over to the thought of Mao Zedong and other leaders of the Chinese Communist Party (CCP). As Nathan explains, Mao meant by *minzhu* that "the masses [should keep] watch over the bureaucracy under the monocratic guidance of the national leader" (1985, xii). These ideas were taken up later by Deng Xiaoping, who in the 1980s instituted local-level elections and other measures to restore what Nathan calls the "means of popular supervision of the bureaucracy" (80). "The party," Nathan concludes, "was once again the reliable vanguard, and democracy [*minzhu*] meant participation under its dictatorship, to discourage bureaucratism and promote the common social interest" (86).

How does the broader population speak of *minzhu?* The best research on nonofficial conceptions comes from studies of the *minzhu* movements of 1978–79 and 1989. David Goodman, who examined unofficial publications from 1978 and 1979, regularly translates *minzhu* as "democracy." This choice creates some conceptual puzzles in his analysis and leads him to find some "amazing contradictions" in the unofficial writings. In the following passage, uses of "democracy" that seem more accurately rendered as *minzhu* appear in italics.

> *"Democracy"* had different meanings for different people, and in many ways merely replaced "Revolution"—predominant during the decade of the Cultural Revolution from 1966 to 1976—as the shibboleth in the new language of politics. According to one commentator in the unofficial press, it implied the immediate "withering away" of party control in basic-level organizations. Others conceived of it as Liberal Democracy, Capitalism, or Christianity, and even, as in one case, all three together. Both the United States and Yugoslavia were suggested as models of *democracy* for emulation. Wei Jingsheng defined it in terms of maximum individual freedom and non-Marxist socialism. . . . One somewhat surprising (given its association with the "Gang of Four" during the [Cultural Revolution]) definition that was suggested was the Paris Commune. However, for the most part any future *democracy* was conceived of as being under the leadership of the CCP, even though at times this might entail some amazing contradictions. (Goodman 1981, 7–8)

As we have seen, there is little contradiction between *minzhu* as conceived by Liang, Mao, and Deng on the one hand and these ideas of Party leadership on the other. The contradiction, it seems, arises when Goodman tries to accommodate these Chinese ideas to his own notion of democracy. Still, we learn from Goodman that despite a diversity of opinion in the unofficial press, most authors use *minzhu* in ways that echo their leaders.

The student activists who participated in the 1989 Tiananmen Square demonstrations also spoke of *minzhu.* In a study more attentive to language than most, Joseph Esherick and Jeffrey Wasserstrom write:

> The Western press and Chinese dissidents abroad usually characterize the events of China's spring as a "democracy movement." There is no question that *minzhu* was frequently invoked in the protesters' banners and slogans, but it would be hasty to associate *minzhu* (literally, rule of the people) with any conventional Western notion of democracy. Consider, for example, Wuer Kaixi's words in the televised dialogue with Li Peng on May 18. Early in the meeting, Wuer Kaixi explained what it would take to get students to leave Tiananmen Square: "If one fasting classmate refuses to leave the square, the other thousands of fasting students on the square will not leave." He was explicit about the principle behind this decision: "On the square, it is not a matter of the minority obeying the majority, but of 99.9 per cent obeying 0.1 per cent." This may have been good politics—and Wuer Kaixi certainly made powerful theatre—but it was not democracy.

The hunger-striking students in Tiananmen Square had adopted a position designed to preserve their unity and enhance their leverage with the government. But
in elevating the principle of unity above that of majority rule, they were acting
within the tradition of popular rule (*minzhu*) thinking in modern China. (1994, 34)

This usage of *minzhu* also seems to reflect official understandings in its stress on
unity and elitism. Still, it may be more difficult to attribute a meaning to
*minzhu* based on Wuer Kaixi's words than the two authors acknowledge. It is
possible, for instance, that the students may have felt it necessary to use non-
*minzhu* tactics to press their demands for *minzhu* from the government. There
may also have been a gap between the ideals of *minzhu* espoused by the students and their actions.

These nonofficial usages of 1979–80 and 1989 are thus suggestive but open to
interpretation. They also come from the language use of only a narrow slice of
the Chinese population. Any conclusions based on them can only be tentative
and of restricted applicability. It does seem, nevertheless, that some of the
popular uses of *minzhu* share important points of similarity with elite understandings. Furthermore, there are areas of overlap between these elite and
popular uses of *minzhu* on the one hand and "democracy," *demokaraasi*, and *eddembe ery'obuntu* on the other. Like "democracy," *minzhu* seems to involve some
notion of popular political participation. Like *demokaraasi*, the Chinese concept
appears to denote unity and harmony. Like *eddembe ery'obuntu*, *minzhu* seems
to require a rightly ordered, elite-guided polity.

## Family Resemblances

We might think of the network of partially overlapping characteristics shared
by the Chinese, American English, Wolof, and Luganda concepts as a set of
"family resemblances," a metaphor used by Wittgenstein to think about the in-
terrelationships of different meanings of a word. An example provided by
Wittgenstein himself explains best the nature of family resemblances:

Consider . . . the proceedings that we call "games." I mean board-games, card-
games, ball-games, Olympic games, and so on. What is common to them all?—
Don't say: "There *must* be something common, or they would not be called
'games'"—but *look and see* whether there is anything common to all.—For if you
look at them you will not see something in common to *all*, but similarities, relationships, and a whole series of them at that. . . . —Look for example at board-
games, with their multifarious relationships. Now pass to card-games; here you
find many correspondences with the first group, but many common features drop
out, and others appear. When we pass next to ball-games, much that is common is
retained, but much is lost.—Are they all "amusing"? Compare chess with noughts

and crosses. Or is there always winning and losing, or competition between play- ers? Think of patience. In ball games there is winning and losing; but when a child throws his ball at the wall and catches it again, this feature has disappeared. Look at the parts played by skill and luck; and at the difference between skill in chess and skill in tennis. Think now of games like ring-a-ring-a-roses; here is the element of amusement, but how many other characteristic features have disappeared! And we can go through the many, many other groups of games in the same way; can see how similarities crop up and disappear.

And the result of this examination is: we see a complicated network of similari- ties overlapping and criss-crossing: sometimes overall similarities, sometimes simi- larities in detail.

I can think of no better expression to characterize these similarities than "family resemblances"; for the various resemblances between members of a family: build, features, colour of eyes, gait, temperament, etc. etc. overlap and criss-cross in the same way. (1972, par. 66–67)

What I suggest here is that we think of family resemblances as existing not only between uses of the same word but as describing the pattern of overlapping and crisscrossing similarities we have seen between the ways in which roughly equivalent words get used in different languages. "Democracy," by this concep- tion, is unique in the particular combination of its features; but each individual feature may still have analogues in other languages and cultures.

It follows that while there may be a complex pattern of overlapping and criss- crossing similarities shared by "democracy" and its relatives in other languages, there may be no essence common to all members of this family. That is, there may be no universal notion of democracy. Thus to speak of *demokaraasi* as "Wolof democracy," of *eddembe ery'obuntu* as "Ganda democracy," or of *minzhu* as "Chinese democracy" obscures much, for each of these games may be unique in its particular combination of aims (ideals) and rules (institutions)—just as Senegalese belote, that card game I learned before the rally in Thiès, is both similar to and different from other card games.[1]

Differences between the games of democracy, *demokaraasi, eddembe ery'obuntu,* and *minzhu* are important because they provide players with different sets of values and concerns, different sets of criteria for distinguishing what is just from what is unjust, different repertoires of actions, and different ranges of mo- tivation and purpose. When these games involve elections, identifying these differences can help researchers determine what aims voters pursue in voting, whether and how their actions are endowed with virtuosity or ineptitude, and whether and how these actions are principled, unethical, or totally outside the realm of moral judgment.

---

[1] Senegalese belote, as I later learned, is a variant of a game popular in France, which itself re- sembles American pinochle (Parlett 1990, 280–98).

The kind of clientelist transactions that Wolof speakers associate with *demokaraasi* may call up images of the machine politics that dominated the cities of post–Civil War America, or the clientelism that political scientists report pervading the electoral systems of any number of Asian, African, and Latin American countries. To most Americans in the post-Reform era, this constitutes "corruption." But to many Senegalese, vote buying is not corrupt, or an aberration in or perversion of *demokaraasi*. Whether or not similar beliefs are held in other countries, they are not common in the United States today. Politicians in a few U.S. cities may at present control electoral machines, and some political scientists may argue that these machines perform important functions, but few Americans would argue today that they represent democracy at its best. They represent, rather, the baser side of American democracy, a departure from what is right. Candidates who give money and those who receive it keep quiet. It is one of the nation's "dirty little secrets" (Sabato and Simpson 1996). Many Senegalese voters and some politicians, in contrast, openly discuss what they exchange and with whom, for the reciprocation of aid and vote between political client and patron is the ideal, the paradigm of *demokaraasi*; it is principled and just.

If students of democracy aspire to understand the meaning, social context, and democratic implications of the behaviors they observe, they cannot assume that their own ideals of democracy (or *démocratie, demokracie,* etc.) are universal. It is risky to equate democracy with what Chinese speakers call *minzhu*, what Luganda speakers call *eddembe ery'obuntu,* or what Wolof speakers call *demokaraasi,* for the ideals and practices that infuse American institutions are not universal. Even when democratic ideas are diffused throughout the world, local communities assimilate imported ideas selectively and transform them to fit their own life conditions. Social scientists thus need to take culture and cultural differences seriously. That is, they need to make explicit the presuppositions of their own behavior as well as those of the Chinese, Ugandans, and Senegalese—an undertaking to which a close attention to language and translation has much to contribute.

# Bibliography

## Unpublished Speeches

Bathily, Abdoulaye. 1988. Radio and television broadcast, presidential electoral campaign, February 7.

Diagne, Bassirou. 1988. Radio and television broadcast, presidential electoral campaign, February 25.

Diouf, Abdou. 1993. Radio and television broadcast, presidential electoral campaign, February 6.

Ndiaye, Fara. 1983. Radio and television broadcast, electoral campaign, February.

Niane, Abdoulaye. 1988. Radio and television broadcast, legislative electoral campaign, February 25.

Savané, Landing. 1988. Radio and television broadcast, presidential electoral campaign, February 25.

Sow, Daouda. 1988. Radio and television broadcast, legislative electoral campaign, February 9.

Wade, Abdoulaye. 1988. Third Ordinary Congress of the PDS, Dakar, January 2–3.

Wade, Abdoulaye. 1988. Thiès, June 19.

## Books, Articles, and Manuscripts

Agar, Michael H. 1980. *The Professional Stranger: An Informal Introduction to Ethnography.* New York: Academic Press.

Almond, Gabriel A., and Sidney Verba. 1963. *The Civic Culture: Political Attitudes and Democracy in Five Nations.* Princeton: Princeton University Press.

Ames, David W. 1959. "Wolof Co-operative Work Groups." In *Continuity and Change in African Cultures,* ed. William Bascom and Melville J. Herskovitz. Chicago: University of Chicago Press.

——. 1962. "The Rural Wolof in the Gambia." In *Markets in Africa,* ed. Paul Bohannan and George Dalton. Evanston, Ill.: Northwestern University Press.

Amnesty International. 1991. *Senegal: An Escalation in Human Rights Violations in Casamance Region.* New York: Amnesty International.

Antoine, Philippe, et al. 1995. *Les familles dakaroises face à la crise.* Dakar: IFAN, ORSTOM, CEPED.

Arendt, Hannah. 1958. *The Human Condition.* Chicago: University of Chicago Press.

Article 19. 1987. *Freedom of Information and Expression in Senegal.* London: Article 19.

Austin, J. L. 1979. "A Plea for Excuses." In *Philosophical Papers,* 3d ed., ed. J. O. Urmsom and G. J. Warnock. Oxford: Oxford University Press.

Ayalon, Ami. 1989. *"Dimūqrāṭiyya, Ḥurriyya, Jumhūriyya:* The Modernization of the Arabic Political Vocabulary." *Asian and African Studies* 23:23–42.

Ayittey, George B. N. 1990. "La démocratie en Afrique précoloniale." *Afrique 2000* 2:39–75.

Azan, H. 1864. "Notice sur le Oualo." *Revue Maritime et Coloniale* 10:327–60; 466–98.

Barber, Benjamin R. 1993. "Reductionist Political Science and Democracy." In *Reconsidering the Democratic Public,* ed. George E. Marcus and Russell L. Hanson. University Park: Pennsylvania State University Press.

Barkan, Joel D. 1976. "Comment: Further Reassessment of 'Conventional Wisdom': Political Knowledge and Voting Behavior in Rural Kenya." *American Political Science Review* 70, no. 2: 452–55.

——. 1979. "Bringing Home the Pork: Legislator Behavior, Rural Development and Political Change in East Africa." In *Legislatures in Development: Dynamics of Change in Old and New States,* ed. Joel Smith and Lloyd D. Musolf. Durham, N.C.: Duke University Press.

Barker, Jonathan S. 1973. "Political Factionalism in Senegal." *Canadian Journal of African Studies* 7, no. 2: 287–303.

Bates, Robert H. 1981. *Markets and States in Tropical Africa.* Berkeley: University of California Press.

Behrman, Lucy C. 1970. *Muslim Brotherhoods and Politics in Senegal.* Cambridge: Harvard University Press.

Bel Cadi, Miloud. 1986. "Le mot démocratie dans le discours électoral de 1977 au Maroc. Analyse des réseaux sémantiques." Thèse de troisième cycle, Paris III–Sorbonne Nouvelle.

Bérenger-Féraud, L. J. B. 1879. *Les peuplades de la Sénégambie.* Paris: Leroux.

Berg, Elliot. 1990. *Adjustment Postponed: Economic Policy Reform in Senegal in the 1980s.* Report prepared for USAID/Dakar. Alexandria, Va.: Elliot Berg Associates.

Bergen, Geoffrey Hansen. 1994. "Unions in Senegal: A Perspective on National Development in Africa." Ph.D. dissertation, University of California at Los Angeles.

Bernard, H. Russell. 1988. *Research Methods in Cultural Anthropology.* Newbury Park, Calif.: Sage.

Bernard-Duquenet, Nicole. 1977. "Lamine Guèye: De l'ancienne Afrique au Sénégal nouveau." In *Les Africains,* ed. Charles-André Julien, vol. 3. Paris: Jeune Afrique.

Bienen, Henry. 1971. "Political Parties and Political Machines in Africa." In *The State of the Nations: Constraints on Development in Independent Africa,* ed. Michael F. Lofchie. Berkeley: University of California Press.

Blanchet, Gilles. 1983. *Elites et changements en Afrique et au Sénégal.* Paris: ORSTOM.

Boilat, Abbé David. 1853. *Esquisses sénégalaises.* Paris: Bertrand.

——. 1858. *Grammaire de la langue woloffe.* Paris: Imprimerie Royale.

Boulay, Harvey, and Alan DiGaetano. 1985. "Why Did Political Machines Disappear?" *Journal of Urban History* 12, no. 1: 25–49.

Bratton, Michael. 1994. "Peasant-State Relations in Postcolonial Africa: Patterns of Engagement and Disengagement." In *State Power and Social Forces: Domination and Transformation in the Third World,* ed. Joel S. Migdal, Atul Kohli, and Vivienne Shue. Cambridge: Cambridge University Press.

Calvet, Louis-Jean. 1987. *La guerre des langues et les politiques linguistiques.* Paris: Payot.

"Campagne électorale 1983: Discours en Wolof." 1991. Dakar: IFAN, Cheikh Anta Diop. Mimeographed.

Cashdan, Elizabeth A. 1985. "Coping with Risk: Reciprocity among the Basarwa of Northern Botswana." *Man* 20:454–74.

Casswell, N. 1984. "Autopsie de l'ONCAD: La politique arachidière au Sénégal, 1966–1980." *Politique Africaine* 14:39–73.

Cavell, Stanley. 1976. *Must We Mean What We Say?* Cambridge: Cambridge University Press.

Charlton, Roger. 1993. "The Politics of Elections in Botswana." *Africa* 63, no. 3: 330–70.

Cohen, Denis L. 1983. "Elections and Electoral Studies in Africa." In *Political Science in Africa: A Critical Review,* ed. Yolamu Barongo. London: Zed.

Copans, J., et al. 1972. *Maintenance sociale et changement économique au Sénégal; I. Doctrine économique et pratique du travail chez les Mourides.* Travaux et Documents de l'ORSTOM. Paris: ORSTOM.

Coppedge, Michael, and Wolfgang H. Reinicke. 1990. "Measuring Polyarchy." *Studies in Comparative International Development* 25, no. 1: 51–72.

Cottingham, Clement. 1970. "Political Consolidation and Centre-Local Relations in Senegal." *Canadian Journal of African Studies* 4, no. 1: 101–20.

——. 1973. "Traditional Society, Change, and Organizational Development." *Journal of Modern African Studies,* 11, no. 4: 675–81.

Coulon, Christian. 1970. "Political Elites in Senegal." *Mawazo* 2, no. 3: 9–22.

——. 1981. *Le marabout et le prince: Islam et pouvoir au Sénégal.* Paris: Pedone.

——. 1995. "Senegal: The Development and Fragility of Semidemocracy." In *Politics in Developing Countries: Comparing Experiences with Democracy,* ed. Larry Diamond, Juan Linz, and Seymour Martin Lipset. Boulder, Colo.: Lynne Rienner.

Cox, Gary W. 1987. *The Efficient Secret: The Cabinet and the Development of Political Parties in Victorian England.* Cambridge: Cambridge University Press.

Creevey, Lucy, Richard Vengroff, and Ibrahima Gaye. 1995. "Devaluation of the CFA Franc in Senegal: The Reaction of Small Businesses." *Journal of Modern African Studies* 33, no. 4: 669–83.

Crowder, Michael. 1962. *Senegal: A Case Study in French Assimilation Policy.* London: Oxford University Press.

Cruise O'Brien, Donal B. 1971. *The Mourides of Senegal: The Political and Economic Organization of an Islamic Brotherhood.* Oxford: Clarendon.

——. 1975. *Saints and Politicians: Essays in the Organization of a Senegalese Peasant Society.* Cambridge: Cambridge University Press.

——. 1976. "Clan, Community, Nation: Dimensions of Political Loyalty in Senegal." In *The Search for National Integration in Africa,* ed. David R. Smock and Kwamena Bentsi-Enchill. New York: Free Press.

——. 1979. "Ruling Class and Peasantry in Senegal, 1960–1976: The Politics of a Monocrop Economy." In *The Political Economy of Underdevelopment: Dependence in Senegal,* ed. Rita Cruise O'Brien. Beverly Hills, Calif.: Sage.

——. 1988. "Charisma Comes to Town: Mouride Urbanization, 1946–1986." In *Charisma and Brotherhood in African Islam,* ed. Donal B. Cruise O'Brien and Christian Coulon. Oxford: Clarendon.

Dahl, Robert A. 1956. *A Preface to Democratic Theory.* Chicago: University of Chicago Press.

——. 1971. *Polyarchy: Participation and Opposition.* New Haven: Yale University Press.

——. 1979. "Procedural Democracy." In *Philosophy, Politics and Society,* 5th ser., ed. Peter Laslett and James Fishkin. New Haven: Yale University Press.

——. 1984. *Dilemmas of Pluralist Democracy: Autonomy vs. Control.* New Haven: Yale University Press.

——. 1992. "The Problem of Civic Competence." *Journal of Democracy* 3, no. 4: 45–59.

Dard, Jean. 1825. *Dictionnaire français-wolof et français-bambara, suivi du dictionnaire wolof-français.* Paris: Imprimerie Royale.

——. 1826. *Grammaire wolofe.* Paris: Imprimerie Royale.

Das Gupta, Monica. 1987. "Informal Security Mechanisms and Population Retention in Rural India." *Economic Development and Cultural Change* 36, no. 1: 101–20.

Descemet, L. 1864. *Recueil d'environ 1,200 phrases françaises usuelles avec leurs traduction en regard en Ouolof de Saint-Louis.* St-Louis, Senegal: Imprimerie du Gouvernement.

Desouches, Christine. 1983. *Le Parti Démocratique Sénégalais.* Paris: Berger- Levrault.

Diagne, Pathé. 1976. "De la démocratie traditionelle." *Présence Africaine* 97:18–42.

——. 1981. "Le pouvoir en Afrique." In *Le concept de pouvoir en Afrique.* Paris: UNESCO.

Diamond, Larry. 1987. "Sub-Saharan Africa." In *Democracy: A Worldwide Survey,* ed. Robert Wesson. New York: Praeger.

Diom, Babacar W. 1986. "Tendances et clans: Politiser et dépersonnaliser." *Perspectives Socialistes* 1:12–16.

Diop, Abdoulaye-Bara. 1981. *La société wolof: Tradition et changement.* Paris: Karthala.

——. 1985. *La famille wolof: Tradition et changement.* Paris: Karthala.

——. 1992. "Les paysans du bassin arachidier: Conditions de vie et comportements de survie." *Politique Africaine* 45:39–61.

Diop, Madame Aram, et al. 1968–72. *Le wolof fondamental.* 4 vols. Dakar: Centre de Linguistique Appliquée de Dakar.

Diop, Cheikh Anta. 1987. *L'Afrique noire précoloniale.* 2d ed. Paris: Présence Africaine.

Diop, Momar Coumba. 1982. "Le phénomène associatif Mouride en ville: Expression du dynamisme confrérique." *Psychopathologie Africaine* 18, no. 3: 293–318.

Diop, Momar Coumba, and Mamadou Diouf. 1990. *Le Sénégal sous Abdou Diouf: Etat et société.* Paris: Karthala.

Diop, Thierno. 1988. "Autour et alentours du code électoral." *Perspectives Socialistes* 4, no. 1: 27–32.

Diouf, Bara. 1987. "Le soleil et son destin?" *Mondes et Cultures* 47, no. 3/4: 521–30.

Diouf, Makhtar. 1992. "La crise de l'ajustement." *Politique Africaine* 45:62–85.

Diouf, Mamadou. 1990. *Le Kajoor au XIX^e siècle.* Paris: Karthala.

Di Palma, Giuseppe. 1990. *To Craft Democracies: An Essay on Democratic Transitions.* Berkeley: University of California Press.

Dorès, M., and M. Mbodj. 1972. "Bilinguisme et psychopathologie." *Psychopathologie Africaine* 8, no. 3: 425–41.

Downs, Anthony. 1957. *An Economic Theory of Democracy.* New York: Harper & Row.

Dreyfus, Martine. 1987. "Enfants et pluralinguisme." *Réalités Africaines et Langue Française* 21:23–40.

Dumont, Pierre. 1973. *Les emprunts du wolof au français.* Dakar: Centre de Linguistique Appliquée de Dakar.

——. 1983. *Le français et les langues africaines au Sénégal.* Paris: Karthala.

Dunleavy, Patrick. 1992. *Democracy, Bureaucracy and Public Choice: Economic Explanations in Political Science.* Englewood Cliffs, N.J.: Prentice Hall.

Dunn, John. 1975. "Politics in Asunafo." In *Politicians and Soldiers in Ghana, 1966–1972,* ed. Dennis Austin and Robin Luckham. London: Frank Cass.

Eckstein, Harry. 1966. *Division and Cohesion in Democracy: A Study of Norway.* Princeton: Princeton University Press.

Eliot, T. S. 1940. *The Idea of a Christian Society.* New York: Harcourt, Brace & World.

Enda. 1991. *Set setal: Des murs qui parlent, nouvelle culture urbaine à Dakar.* Dakar: Enda.

Equipe IFA. 1983. *Inventaire des particularités lexicales du français en Afrique noire.* Paris: EDICEF.

Esherik, Joseph W., and Jeffrey N. Wasserstrom. 1994. "Acting Out Democracy: Political Theater in Modern China." In *Popular Protest and Political Culture in Modern China,* ed. Jeffrey N. Wasserstrom and Elizabeth J. Perry, 2d ed. Boulder, Colo.: Westview.

Evans-Pritchard, E. E. 1940. *The Nuer: A Description of the Modes of Livelihood and Political Institutions of a Nilotic People.* New York: Oxford University Press.

Fafchamps, Marcel. 1992. "Solidarity Networks in Preindustrial Societies: Rational Peasants with a Moral Economy." *Economic Development and Cultural Change* 41, no. 4: 147–74.

Fal, Arame. 1990. *Alphabétisation en wolof: Guide orthographique.* Dakar.

Fal, Arame, Rosine Santos, and Jean Léonce Doneux. 1990. *Dictionnaire wolof-français suivi d'un index français-wolof.* Paris: Karthala.

Fall, Abdou Salam. 1994. "Et si l'insertion urbaine passait par l'investissement dans des réseaux sociaux? Réseaux formels et informels de solidarité et de dépendence dans les quartiers de Dakar." In *Les associations paysannes en Afrique: Organisation et dynamiques,* ed. Jean-Pierre Jacob and Philippe Lavigne Delville. Paris: Karthala.

Fatton, Robert, Jr. 1987. *The Making of a Liberal Democracy: Senegal's Passive Revolution, 1975–1985.* Boulder, Colo.: Lynne Rienner.

——. 1992. *Predatory Rule: State and Civil Society in Africa.* Boulder, Colo.: Lynne Rienner.

——. 1995. "Africa in the Age of Democratization: The Civic Limitations of Civil Society." *African Studies Review* 38, no. 2: 67–99.

Fishman, Joshua A. 1979. Review of *Politics, Language, and Thought,* by David D. Laitin. *Language* 55, no. 2: 471–72.

Foltz, William J. 1977. "Social Structure and Political Behavior of the Senegalese Elites." In *Friends, Followers, and Factions: A Reader in Political Clientelism,* ed. Steffan W. Schmidt et al. Berkeley: University of California Press.

Fox, Jonathan. 1994. "The Difficult Transition from Clientelism to Citizenship: Lessons from Mexico." *World Politics* 46, no. 2: 151–84.

Frankenberger, Timothy R., and Mark B. Lynham. 1993. "Household Food Security and Coping Strategies along the Senegal River Valley." In *Risk and Tenure in Arid Lands: The Political Ecology of Development in the Senegal River Basin,* ed. Thomas K. Park. Tucson: University of Arizona Press.

Gaden, Henri. 1912. *Légendes et coutumes sénégalaises: Cahiers de Yoro Dyao.* Paris: Leroux.

Gallie, W. B. 1955–56. "Essentially Contested Concepts." *Proceedings of the Aristotelian Society* 56:167–98.

Gérard, Jérôme. 1993. "Election présidentielle au Sénégal (février 1993): «SOPI» pour la jeunesse urbaine." *Politique Africaine* 50:108–15.

Gersovitz, Mark, and John Waterbury. 1987. "Introduction." In *The Political Economy of Risk and Choice in Senegal,* ed. Mark Gersovitz and John Waterbury. London: Frank Cass.

Gilligan, Carol. 1982. *In a Different Voice: Psychological Theory and Women's Development.* Cambridge: Harvard University Press.

Girault, Arthur. 1895. *Principes de colonisation et de législation coloniale.* Paris: Larose.

Goetz, Stephan J. 1992. "Economies of Scope and the Cash Crop–Food Crop Debate in Senegal." *World Development* 20, no. 5: 727–34.

Golan, Elise H. 1994. "Land Tenure Reform in the Peanut Basin of Senegal." In *Searching for Land Tenure Security in Africa,* ed. John W. Bruce and Shem E. Migot-Adholla. Dubuque, Iowa: Kendall/Hunt.

Gontier, Dominique. 1981. "La presse écrite de langue française et la francophonie au Sénégal." Pt. 1. *Réalités Africaines et Langue Française* 14:61–73.

Goodell, Grace, and John P. Powelson. 1982. "The Democratic Prerequisites of Development." In *Freedom and the World: Political and Civil Liberties, 1982,* ed. Raymond D. Gastill. Westport, Conn.: Greenwood.

Goodman, David S. G. 1981. *Beijing Street Voices: The Poetry and Politics of China's Democracy Movement.* Boston: Marion Boyars.

Goody, Jack. 1982. *Cooking, Cuisine and Class: A Study of Comparative Sociology.* Cambridge: Cambridge University Press.

Gosnell, Harold F. 1968. *Machine Politics: Chicago Model.* 2d ed. Chicago: University of Chicago Press.

Graham, Carol. 1994. *Safety Nets, Politics, and the Poor: Transitions to Market Economies.* Washington, D.C.: Brookings.

Gramsci, Antonio. 1985. *Selections from the Cultural Writings.* Ed. David Forgacs and Geoffrey Nowell-Smith. Trans. William Boelhower. Cambridge: Harvard University Press.

Greenstein, Fred I. 1964. "The Changing Pattern of Urban Party Politics." *Annals of the American Academy of Political and Social Science* 353:1–13.

Griffiths, Ieuan Ll. 1994. *The Atlas of African Affairs.* 2d ed. New York: Routledge.

Guèye, Lamine. 1966. *Itinéraire africain.* Paris: Présence Africaine.

Gumperz, John J. 1982. *Discourse Strategies.* Cambridge: Cambridge University Press.

Guy-Grand, R. V. J. 1890. *Dictionnaire français-volof.* 3d ed. Saint Joseph de Ngazobil: Imprimerie de la Mission.

——. 1923. *Dictionnaire français-volof. Précédé d'un abrégé de la grammaire volofe.* Rev. ed. Ed. R. P. O. Abiven. Dakar: Mission Catholique.

Haggis, Jane, et al. 1986. "By the Teeth: A Critical Examination of James Scott's *The Moral Economy of the Peasant.*" *World Development* 14, no. 12: 1435–55.

Hall, Anthony. 1977. "Patron-Client Relations: Concepts and Terms." In *Friends, Followers, and Factions: A Reader in Political Clientelism,* ed. Steffen W. Schmidt et al. Berkeley: University of California Press.

Halperin, Rhoda. 1977. "Redistribution in Chan Kom: A Case for Mexican Political Economy." In *Peasant Livelihood: Studies in Economic Anthropology and Cultural Ecology,* ed. Rhoda Halperin and James Dow. New York: St. Martin's Press.

Hammersley, Martyn, and Paul Atkinson. 1983. *Ethnography: Principles in Practice.* London and New York: Tavistock.

Hanham, H. J., ed. 1969. *The Nineteenth-Century Constitution, 1815-1914: Documents and Commentary.* Cambridge: Cambridge University Press.

Hayward, Fred M. 1976. "A Reassessment of Conventional Wisdom about the Informed Public: National Political Information in Ghana." *American Political Science Review* 70, no. 2: 433–51.

Healey, John, Richard Ketley, and Mark Robinson. 1993. "Will Political Reform Bring About Improved Economic Management in Sub-Saharan Africa?" *IDS Bulletin* 24, no. 1: 31–38.

Healey, John, and Mark Robinson. 1992. *Democracy, Governance and Economic Policy: Sub-Saharan Africa in Comparative Perspective.* London: Overseas Development Institute.

Heath, Deborah. 1990. "Spatial Politics and Verbal Performance in Urban Senegal." *Ethnology* 29, no. 3: 209–23.

Held, David. 1987. *Models of Democracy.* Stanford: Stanford University Press.

Heredia-Deprez, Christine de. 1987. "Des enfants et des langues dans les villes." *Réalités Africaines et Langue Française* 21:41–59.

Holm, John D. 1987. "Elections in Botswana: Institutionalization of a New System of Legitimacy." In *Elections in Independent Africa,* ed. Fred M. Hayward. Boulder, Colo.: Westview.

Honigmann, John J. 1970. "Sampling in Ethnographic Field Work." In *A Handbook of Method in Cultural Anthropology,* ed. Raoul Naroll and Ronald Cohen. New York: Columbia University Press.

Huntington, Samuel P. 1991. *The Third Wave: Democratization in the Late Twentieth Century.* Norman: University of Oklahoma Press.

Hyden, Goran. 1970. "Language and Administration." In *Development Administration: The Kenyan Experience,* ed. Goran Hyden, Robert Jackson, and John Okumu. Nairobi: Oxford University Press.

Irvine, Judith T. 1993. "Mastering African Languages: The Politics of Linguistics in Nineteenth-Century Senegal." *Social Analysis* 33:27–46.

Jackson, Robert H., and Carl G. Rosberg. 1985. "Democracy in Tropical Africa: Democracy versus Autocracy in African Politics." *Journal of International Affairs* 38, no. 2: 293–305.

Johnson, G. Wesley, Jr. 1971. *The Emergence of Black Politics in Senegal.* Stanford: Stanford University Press.

July, Robert W. 1968. *The Origins of Modern African Thought: Its Development in West Africa during the Nineteenth and Twentieth Centuries.* London: Faber & Faber.

Ka, Moustapha. 1986. "Parti Socialiste: La logique des tendances." *Perspectives Socialistes* 1:10–11.

Ka, Omar. 1981. *La dérivation et la composition en wolof.* Dakar: Centre de Linguistique Appliquée de Dakar.

Kanté, Babacar. 1994. "Senegal's Empty Elections." *Journal of Democracy* 5, no. 1: 96–108.

Karatnycky, Adrian, et al. 1995. *Freedom in the World: The Annual Survey of Political Rights and Civil Liberties, 1994–1995.* New York: Freedom House.

Karl, Terry Lynn. 1986. "Imposing Consent? Electoralism vs. Democratization in El Salvador." In *Elections and Democratization in Latin America, 1980–85,* ed. Paul W. Drake and Eduardo Silva. San Diego: Center for Iberian and Latin American Studies, University of California, San Diego.

Karlström, Mikael. 1996. "Imagining Democracy: Political Culture and Democratisation in Buganda." *Africa* 66, no. 4: 485–505.

Kay, Paul, and Willett Kempton. 1984. "What Is the Sapir-Whorf Hypothesis?" *American Anthropologist* 86, no. 1: 65–79.

Kesteloot, Lilyan, and Cherif Mbodj. 1983. *Contes et mythes wolof.* Dakar: Nouvelles Editions Africaines.

Key, V. O., Jr. 1961. *Public Opinion and American Democracy.* New York: Knopf.

Kim, Kyung-won. 1993. "Marx, Schumpeter, and the East Asian Experience." In *Capitalism, Socialism, and Democracy Revisited,* ed. Larry Diamond and Marc F. Plattner. Baltimore: Johns Hopkins University Press.

King, Dwight Y. 1981. "Regime Type and Performance: Authoritarian Rule, Semi-Capitalist Development, and Rural Inequality in Asia." *Comparative Political Studies* 13, no. 4: 477–504.

Kirkpatrick, Jeane. 1981. "Democratic Elections, Democratic Government, and Democratic Theory." In *Democracy at the Polls: A Comparative Study of Competitive National Elections,* ed. David Butler and Austin Ranney. Washington, D.C.: Institute for Public Policy Research.

Knack, Stephen. 1992. "Civic Norms, Social Sanctions, and Voter Turnout." *Rationality and Society* 4, no. 2: 133–56.

Kobès, Mgr. A. 1869. *Grammaire de la langue volofe.* Saint Joseph de Ngazobil: Imprimerie de la Mission.

——. 1923. *Dictionnaire volof-français.* Rev. ed. Ed. R. P. O. Abiven. Dakar: Mission Catholique.

Kpundeh, Sahr John, ed. 1992. *Democratization in Africa: African Views, African Voices.* Washington, D.C.: National Academy Press.

Kuhn, Sherman M., ed. 1968. *Middle English Dictionary.* Ann Arbor: University of Michigan Press.

Labov, William. 1966. *The Social Stratification of English in New York City.* Washington, D.C.: Center for Applied Linguistics.

——. 1969. "The Logic of Nonstandard English." *Georgetown Monographs on Language and Linguistics* 22:1–22, 26–31.

Lachenmann, Gudrun. 1993. "Civil Society and Social Movements in Africa: The Case of the Peasant Movement in Senegal." *European Journal of Development Research* 5, no. 2: 68–100.

Lacroix, Jean-Bernard, and Saliou Mbaye. 1976. "La vote des femmes au Sénégal." *Ethiopiques* 6:26–43.

Laitin, David D. 1977. *Politics, Language, and Thought: The Somali Experience.* Chicago: University of Chicago Press.

——. 1992. *Language Repertoires and State Construction in Africa.* Cambridge: Cambridge University Press.

Lakoff, Robin Tolmach. 1976. *Language and Woman's Place.* New York: Octagon.

Lancaster, Carol. 1993. "Governance and Development: The Views from Washington." *IDS Bulletin* 24, no. 1: 9–15.

Landell-Mills, Pierre, and Ismaïl Serageldin. 1992. "Governance and the External Factor." *Proceedings of the World Bank Annual Conference on Development Economics, 1991.* Washington, D.C.

Lasswell, Harold. 1951. "Democratic Character." In *The Political Writings of Harold Lasswell.* Glencoe, Ill.: Free Press.

Lecomte, Bernard. 1992. "Senegal: The Young Farmers of Walo and the New Agricultural Policy." *Review of African Political Economy* 55:87–95.

Lemarchand, René. 1964. *Political Awakening in the Congo.* Berkeley: University of California Press.

——. 1989. "African Peasantries, Reciprocity and the Market." *Cahiers d'Etudes Africaines* 29, no. 3: 33–67.

Lewis, Bernard. 1988. *The Political Language of Islam*. Chicago: University of Chicago Press.

Lewis, Martin Deming. 1962. "One Hundred Million Frenchmen: The 'Assimilation' Theory in French Colonial Policy." *Comparative Studies in Society and History* 4, no. 2: 129–53.

Lijphart, Arend. 1977. *Democracy in Plural Societies: A Comparative Exploration*. New Haven: Yale University Press.

——. 1984. *Democracies: Patterns of Majoritarian and Consensus Government in Twenty-one Countries*. New Haven: Yale University Press.

——. 1985. *Power-Sharing in South Africa*. Berkeley: Institute of International Studies, University of California.

Linz, Juan J. 1978. "Crisis, Breakdown, and Reequilibrium." In *The Breakdown of Democratic Regimes*, ed. Juan J. Linz and Alfred Stepan. Baltimore: Johns Hopkins University Press.

Lipset, Seymour Martin. 1983. *Political Man: The Social Bases of Politics*. Exp. ed. London: Heinemann.

Lively, Jack. 1975. *Democracy*. Oxford: Basil Blackwell.

Lofchie, Michael F. 1985. "Africa's Agrarian Malaise." In *African Independence: The First Twenty-five Years*, ed. Gwendolen M. Carter and Patrick O'Meara. Bloomington: Indiana University Press.

Lotchin, Roger W. 1981. "Power and Policy: American City Politics between the Two World Wars." In *Ethnics, Machines, and the American Urban Future*, ed. Scott Greer. Cambridge, Mass.: Schenkman.

Ly, Boubakar. 1967. "L'honneur et les valeurs morales dans les societés oulouf et toucouleur du Sénégal." Thèse de doctorat du troisième cycle, Université de Paris.

Macpherson, C. B. 1966. *The Real World of Democracy*. Oxford: Clarendon.

Mansbridge, Jane J. 1980. *Beyond Adversary Democracy*. New York: Basic.

Margoliouth, D. S. 1922. "The Sense of the Title *Khalifah*." In *A Volume of Oriental Studies Presented to Edward G. Browne*, ed. T. W. Arnold and Reynold A. Nicholson. Cambridge: Cambridge University Press.

Markovitz, Irving Leonard. 1969a. *Léopold Sédar Senghor and the Politics of Negritude*. New York: Atheneum.

——. 1969b. "The Political Thought of Blaise Diagne and Lamine Gueye: Some Aspects of Social Structure and Ideology in Senegal." *Présence Africaine* 72:21–38.

——. 1970. "Traditional Social Structure, the Islamic Brotherhoods, and Political Development in Senegal." *Journal of Modern African Studies*, 8, no. 1: 73–96.

Martin, Victor, and Charles Becker. 1976. "Les Teen du Baol: Essai de chronologie." *Bulletin de l'IFAN*, ser. B, 38, no. 3: 449–505.

Mauny, R. 1952. *Glossaire des expressions et termes locaux employés dans l'ouest africain*. Dakar: Institut Français d'Afrique Noire.

McWilliams, Wilson Cary. 1973. *The Idea of Fraternity in America*. Berkeley: University of California Press.

Miles, William. 1988. *Elections in Nigeria: A Grassroots Perspective*. Boulder, Colo.: Lynne Rienner.

Mill, John Stuart. 1975. "Considerations on Representative Government." In *Three Essays*. New York: Oxford University Press.

Milroy, Lesley. 1987. *Observing and Analysing Natural Language: A Critical Account of Sociolinguistic Method*. New York: Basil Blackwell.

Moe, Terry. 1980. "A Calculus of Group Membership." *American Journal of Political Science* 24, no. 4: 593–632.

Monteil, Vincent. 1962. "Une confrérie musulmane: Les Mourides du Sénégal." *Archives de Sociologie des Religions* 14:77–101.

Morgenthau, Ruth Schacter. 1964. *Political Parties in French-Speaking West Africa.* Oxford: Clarendon.

Mottin-Sylla, Marie-Hélène. 1987. "L'argent et l'intérêt: Tontines et autres pratiques féminines de mobilisation de moyens à Dakar." *Enda-Graf-Argent* 11:1–23.

Mouradian, Jacques. 1963. "Notes sur quelques emprunts de la langue wolof à l'Arabe." In *Wolof et Sérèr: Etudes de phonétique et de grammaire descriptive,* ed. Gabriel Manessy and Serge Sauvageot. Dakar: Université de Dakar, Faculté des Lettres et Sciences Humaines, Publications de la Section de Langues et Littératures.

Moyo, Jonathan N. 1992. *Voting for Democracy: Electoral Politics in Zimbabwe.* Harare: University of Zimbabwe Publications.

Murphy, William P. 1990. "Creating the Appearance of Consensus in Mende Political Discourse." *American Anthropologist* 92, no. 1: 24–41.

Nathan, Andrew J. 1985. *Chinese Democracy.* Berkeley: University of California Press.

National Democratic Institute for International Affairs. 1990. "Evaluation du code électoral sénégalais: Rapport de la délégation internationale." Dakar, September 28–October 3.

Ndione, Emmanuel Seyni. 1987. *Dynamique urbaine d'une société en grappe: Un cas, Dakar.* Dakar: Enda.

——. 1992. *Le don et le recours: Ressorts de l'économie urbaine.* Dakar: Enda.

Needham, Rodney. 1972. *Belief, Language, and Experience.* Oxford: Basil Blackwell.

Ngom, Benoît Saaliu. 1989. *L'arbitrage d'une démocratie en Afrique: La Cour Suprême au Sénégal.* Dakar: Présence Africaine.

Niane, Idy Carras, Vieux Savané, and Boubacar Boris Diop. 1991. *Set setal: La seconde génération des barricades.* Dakar: Sud.

Nida, Eugene A. 1959. "Principles of Translation as Exemplified in Bible Translating." In *On Translation,* ed. Reuben Brower. Cambridge: Harvard University Press.

Nida, Eugene, and William D. Reyburn. 1981. *Meaning across Culture.* Maryknoll, N.Y.: Orbis.

Nyong'o, Peter Anyang. 1988. "Political Instability and the Prospects for Democracy in Africa." *Africa Development* 13, no. 1: 71–86.

Nzouankeu, Jacques Mariel. 1984. *Les partis politiques sénégalais.* Dakar: Clairafrique.

——, ed. n.d. *Abdou Diouf, allocutions et discours.* Dakar: Revue des Institutions Politiques et Administratives du Sénégal.

O'Barr, William M. 1978. Review of *Politics, Language, and Thought,* by David D. Laitin. *American Ethnologist* 5, no. 4: 797–99.

Odeyé-Finzi, Michèle. 1985. *Les associations en villes africaines: Dakar-Brazzaville.* Paris: Harmattan.

Omar, Ariffin. 1993. *Bangsa Melayu: Malay Concepts of Democracy and Community, 1945–1950.* Kuala Lumpur: Oxford University Press.

Oppenheim, Felix E. 1981. *Political Concepts: A Reconstruction.* Chicago: University of Chicago Press.

Ortiz, Sutti. 1967. "The Structure of Decision-making among Indians of Colombia." In *Themes in Economic Anthropology,* ed. Raymond Firth. London: Tavistock.

Ottaway, Marina. 1993. "Should Elections Be the Criterion of Democratization in Africa?" *CSIS Africa Notes* 145:1–5.

Pagès, Monique. 1991. "L'explosion de la presse en Afrique francophone au sud du Sahara." *Afrique Contemporaine* 159:77–82.

Parlett, David. 1990. *The Oxford Guide to Card Games.* New York: Oxford University Press.

Parti Démocratique Sénégalais. 1986a. *Propositions pour un code électoral démocratique.* Dakar, March 31.

———. 1986b. *Sénégal: La fraude électorale institutionalisée.* Dakar, March 31.

———. 1988. "Résolution de politique générale." Troisième Congrés Ordinaire, Dakar, January 2–3. Mimeographed.

Parti Socialiste du Sénégal, Ecole du Parti. 1987. *Le code électoral sénégalais: Une oeuvre pour la démocratie.* Dakar.

Pateman, Carole. 1970. *Participation and Democratic Theory.* Cambridge: Cambridge University Press.

Patterson, Amy S. 1996. "Participation and Democracy at the Grassroots: A Study of Development Associations in Rural Senegal." Ph.D. dissertation, Indiana University.

Pellegrin, M. Louis. 1914. Profession de foi de M. Louis Pellegrin, commerçant à Louga. April 26, 1914, legislative elections. Archives du Sénégal, folder 20G-21.

"Petit vocabulaire français, yolof, et serere, 18ᵉ siècle." N.d. Bibliothèque Sainte-Geneviève. Microfilm, Archives du Sénégal.

Pitkin, Hanna Fenichel. 1972. *Wittgenstein and Justice: On the Significance of Ludwig Wittgenstein for Social and Political Thought.* Berkeley: University of California Press.

Pitkin, Hanna Fenichel, and Sara M. Shumer. 1982. "On Participation." *Democracy* 2, no. 4: 43–54.

Platteau, Jean-Phillipe. 1991. "Traditional Systems of Social Security and Hunger Insurance: Past Achievements and Modern Challenges." In *Social Security in Developing Countries,* ed. Ehtisham Ahmad et al. Oxford: Clarendon.

Popkin, Samuel L. 1979. *The Rational Peasant: The Political Economy of Rural Society in Vietnam.* Berkeley: University of California Press.

Posner, Richard A. 1980. "A Theory of Primitive Society, with Special Reference to Law." *Journal of Law and Economics* 23, no. 1: 1–53.

Post, K. W. J. 1963. *The Nigerian Federal Election of 1959: Politics and Administration in a Developing Political System.* London: Oxford University Press.

Powell, G. Bingham, Jr. 1982. *Contemporary Democracies: Participation, Stability, and Violence.* Cambridge: Harvard University Press.

Prewitt, Kenneth, and Goran Hyden. 1967. "Voters Look at the Elections." In *One-Party Democracy: The 1965 Tanzania General Elections,* ed. Lionel Cliffe. Nairobi: East Africa Publishing House.

Price, Robert M. 1975. *Society and Bureaucracy in Contemporary Ghana.* Berkeley: University of California Press.

Przeworski, Adam. 1991. *Democracy and the Market: Political and Economic Reforms in Eastern Europe and Latin America.* Cambridge: Cambridge University Press.

Putnam, Robert D., with Robert Leonardi and Raffaella Y. Nanetti. 1993. *Making Democracy Work: Civic Traditions in Modern Italy.* Princeton: Princeton University Press.

République du Sénégal, Ministère de l'Economie et des Finances, Direction de la Statistique, Bureau Informatique. 1990. *Recensement général de la population et de l'habitat, mai–juin 1988: Résultats définitifs.* Dakar.

République du Sénégal, Ministère de l'Education Nationale, Direction de la Planification et de la Réforme de l'Education. 1990. *Tableau de bord: Année scolaire, 1988/1989.* Dakar.

République du Sénégal, Ministère de l'Intérieur. 1992. *Synthèse de la carte électorale des élections de 1993.* Dakar.

République du Sénégal, Présidence de la République, Secrétariat Général, Délégation au Plan et aux Politiques Economiques, Direction de la Prévision et de la Statistique. 1989. *Les principaux résultats provisoires du recensement de la population de l'habitat du Sénégal.* Dakar.

Rieder, Jonathan. 1994. "Doing Political Culture: Interpretive Practice and the Earnest Heuristic." *Research on Democracy and Society* 2:117–151.

Roger, Baron. 1829. *Recherches philosophiques sur la langue ouolofe, suivi d'un vocabulaire abrégé français-ouolof.* Paris: Librarie Orientale de Dondey-Dupré.

Rosanvallon, Pierre. 1995. "The History of the Word 'Democracy' in France." *Journal of Democracy* 6, no. 4: 140–54.

RR.PP. Missionaires de la Congrégation du Saint-Esprit et du Sacré-Coeur de Marie. 1855. *Dictionnaire français-wolof.* Rev. ed. Dakar: Imprimerie de la Mission.

Rustow, Dankwart A. 1970. "Transitions to Democracy: Toward a Dynamic Model." *Comparative Politics* 2, no. 3: 337–63.

Sabato, Larry J., and Glenn R. Simpson. 1996. *Dirty Little Secrets: The Persistence of Corruption in American Politics.* New York: Times Books.

Sahlins, Marshall. 1972. *Stone Age Economics.* Chicago: Aldine-Atherton.

Salem, Gérard. 1992. "Crise urbaine et contrôle social à Pikine: Bornes fontaines et clientèlisme." *Politique Africaine* 45:21–38.

Samarin, William J. 1967. *Field Linguistics: A Guide to Linguistic Field Work.* New York: Holt, Rinehart & Winston.

Samb, Babacar. 1989. "Le rôle des associations islamiques dans la régulation politique et sociale en milieu urbain au Sénégal." *Annales de la Faculté des Lettres et Sciences Humaines* 19:95–105.

Sandbrook, Richard. 1986. "The State and Economic Stagnation in Africa." *World Development* 14, no. 3: 319–32.

——. 1988. "Liberal Democracy in Africa: A Socialist-Revisionist Perspective." *Canadian Journal of African Studies* 22, no. 2: 240–67.

Sankoff, Gillian. 1980. *The Social Life of Language.* Philadelphia: University of Pennsylvania Press.

Sartori, Giovanni. 1970. "Concept Misformation in Comparative Politics." *American Political Science Review* 64, no. 4: 1033–46.

——. 1987. *The Theory of Democracy Revisited.* Chatham, N.J.: Chatham House.

Schaffer, Frederic C. 1994. "*Demokaraasi* in Africa: What Wolof Political Concepts Teach Us about How to Study Democracy." Ph.D. dissertation, University of California at Berkeley.

Schatzberg, Michael G. 1986. "The Metaphors of Father and Family." In *The Political Economy of Cameroon,* ed. Michael G. Schatzberg and I. William Zartman. New York: Praeger.

Schmitter, Philippe C., and Terry Lynn Karl. 1991. "What Democracy Is . . . and Is Not." *Journal of Democracy* 2, no. 3: 75–88.

Schumacher, Edward J. 1975. *Politics, Bureaucracy, and Rural Development in Senegal.* Berkeley: University of California Press.

Schumpeter, Joseph A. 1962. *Capitalism, Socialism, and Democracy.* 3d ed. New York: Harper & Row.

Scott, James C. 1976. *The Moral Economy of the Peasant: Rebellion and Subsistence in Southeast Asia.* New Haven: Yale University Press.

———. 1985. *Weapons of the Weak: Everyday Forms of Peasant Resistance.* New Haven: Yale University Press.

Scotton, Carol Myers. 1983. "The Negotiation of Identities in Conversation: A Theory of Markedness and Code Choice." *International Journal of the Sociology of Language* 44:115–36.

———. 1988. "Code Switching and Types of Multilingual Communities." In *Language Spread and Language Policy,* ed. Peter H. Lowenberg. Washington, D.C.: Georgetown University Press.

———. 1990. "Elite Closure and Boundary Maintenance: The Case of Africa." In *Language Policy and Political Development,* ed. Brian Weinstein. Norwood, N.J.: Ablex.

———. 1993. *Social Motivations for Codeswitching: Evidence from Africa.* Oxford: Clarendon.

Searle, John R. 1969. *Speech Acts: An Essay in the Philosophy of Language.* Cambridge: Cambridge University Press.

Senghor, Léopold Sédar. 1964a. "Democracy and Socialism: Lecture Delivered at the University of Ibaden." April. Mimeographed.

———. 1964b. *On African Socialism.* Trans. Mercer Cook. New York: Praeger.

———. 1971. *Liberté II: Nation et voie africaine du socialisme.* Paris: Seuil.

———. 1980. *Léopold Sédar Senghor: La poésie de l'action. Conversations avec Mohamed Aziza.* Paris: Stock.

———. 1983. *Liberté IV: Socialisme et planification.* Paris: Seuil.

Shefter, Martin. 1983. "Regional Receptivity to Reform: The Legacy of the Progressive Era." *Political Science Quarterly* 98, no 3: 459–83.

Siga, Niang Fatou Niang. 1990. *Reflets de modes et traditions saint-louisiennes.* Dakar: Centre Africain d'Animation et d'Echanges Culturels, Editions Khoudia.

Simuyu, V. G. 1988. "The Democratic Myth in the African Traditional Societies." In *Democratic Theory and Practice in Africa,* ed. Walter O. Oyugi et al. Portsmouth, N.H.: Heinemann.

Sklar, Richard. 1983. "Democracy in Africa." *African Studies Review* 26, no. 3–4: 11–24.

———. 1987. "Developmental Democracy." *Comparative Studies in Society and History* 29, no. 4: 686–714.

Smith, Thomas C. 1959. *The Agrarian Origins of Modern Japan.* Stanford: Stanford University Press.

SODEVA-CETAD. 1991. *Sàrtu Réewum Senegaal.* Dakar.

Somerville, Carolyn M. 1991. "The Impact of the Reforms on the Urban Population: How the Dakarois View the Crisis." In *The Political Economy of Senegal Under Structural Adjustment,* ed. Christopher L. Delgado and Sidi Jammeh. New York: Praeger.

Somolekae, Gloriah. 1989. "Do Batswana Think and Act Like Democrats?" In *Democracy in Botswana,* ed. John Holm and Patrick Molutsi. Athens: Ohio University Press.

Sourdel, D., et al. 1978. "Khalifa." In *The Encyclopaedia of Islam.* New ed. Leiden: E. J. Brill.

Stave, Bruce M. 1970. *The New Deal and the Last Hurrah: Pittsburgh Machine Politics.* Pittsburgh: University of Pittsburgh Press.

Swigart, Leigh. 1992. "Practice and Perception: Language Use and Attitudes in Dakar." Ph.D. dissertation, University of Washington.

———. 1994. "Cultural Creolisation and Language Use in Post-Colonial Africa: The Case of Senegal." *Africa* 64, no. 2: 175–89.

Sylla, Assane. 1978. *La philosophie morale des wolof.* Dakar: Sankoré.

Taylor, Charles. 1977. "Interpretation and the Sciences of Man." In *Understanding and Social Inquiry,* ed. Fred R. Dallmayr and Thomas A. McCarthy. Notre Dame: University of Notre Dame Press.

Thiam, Iba Der, Eliane Pflieger, and Ibou Faye. 1980. *L'education civique: Classe de 4ᵉ*. Dakar: Nouvelles Editions Africaines.

Trimingham, J. Spencer. 1962. *A History of Islam in West Africa*. Oxford: Oxford University Press.

Uhlaner, Carole Jean. 1989. "'Relational Good' and Participation: Incorporating Sociability into a Theory of Rational Action." *Public Choice* 62:253–85.

UNESCO. 1991. Sixth Conference of Ministers of Education and Those Responsible for Economic Planning in African Member States Held at Dakar, 9–11 July 1991. *Development of Education in Africa: A Statistical Review*. Paris.

UNESCO-UNICEF. 1990. *Special Breda-Stat: Towards Education for All in Africa, Starting Point*. Dakar.

USAID. 1990. "The Democracy Initiative." December. Mimeographed.

USAID Africa Bureau. 1991. "Africa Democracy and Human Rights Fund Project Paper." April 25. Mimeographed.

Venema, L. B. 1978. *The Wolof of Saloum: Social Structure and Rural Development in Senegal*. Wageningen, Netherlands: Centre for Agricultural Publishing and Documentation.

Villalón, Leonardo A. 1993. "Charisma and Ethnicity in Political Context: A Case Study in the Establishment of a Senegalese Religious Clientele." *Africa* 63, no. 1: 80–101.

———. 1994. "Democratizing a (Quasi) Democracy: The Senegalese Elections of 1993." *African Affairs* 93:163–93.

———. 1995. *Islamic Society and State Power in Senegal: Disciples and Citizens in Fatick*. Cambridge: Cambridge University Press.

"Vocabulaires guiolof, mandingue, foule, saricole, séraire, bagnon et floupe, recueillis à la côte d'Afrique pour le service de l'ancienne Compagnie Royale du Sénégal et publiés pour la première fois d'après un manuscrit de la Bibliothèque Royale." 1845. *Mémoires de la Société Ethnologique* 2:205–67.

Wade, Abdoulaye. 1987. "Quel avenir pour le Sénégal? La réponse du PDS." Discours d'ouverture, Convention Nationale. Dakar, January 15–17. Mimeographed.

Waterbury, John. 1987. "The Senegalese Peasant: How Good Is our Conventional Wisdom?" In *The Political Economy of Risk and Choice in Senegal,* ed. Mark Gersovitz and John Waterbury. London: Frank Cass.

Watts, Michael J. 1984. "The Demise of the Moral Economy: Food and Famine in a Sudano-Sahelian Region in Historical Perspective." In *Life before the Drought,* ed. Earl Scott. Boston: Allen & Unwin.

Waylen, Georgina. 1994. "Women and Democratization: Conceptualizing Gender Relations in Transition Politics." *World Politics* 46, no. 3: 327–54.

Weiner, Myron. 1987. "Empirical Democratic Theory." In *Competitive Elections in Developing Countries,* ed. Myron Weiner and Ergun Özbudun. Durham, N.C.: Duke University Press.

Widner, Jennifer A. 1994. "Single Party States and Agricultural Policies: The Cases of Ivory Coast and Kenya." *Comparative Politics* 26, no. 2: 127–47.

Wieger, L. 1965. *Chinese Characters*. Trans. L. Davrout. 2d ed. New York: Dover.

Wittgenstein, Ludwig. 1972. *Philosophical Investigations*. Trans. G. E. M. Anscombe. 3d ed. New York: Macmillan.

Wolfinger, Raymond E. 1972. "Why Political Machines Have Not Withered Away and Other Revisionist Thoughts." *Journal of Politics* 34, no. 2: 365–98.

World Bank. 1989. *Sub-Saharan Africa: From Crisis to Sustainable Growth*. Washington, D.C.

———. 1995a. *Senegal: An Assessment of Living Conditions*. Vol. 1. Report no. 12517-SE. Washington, D.C.

———. 1995b. *Social Indicators of Development, 1995*. Baltimore: Johns Hopkins University Press.

———. 1995c. *Trends in Developing Economies, 1995*. Washington, D.C.

Wynne, Edward A. 1980. *Social Security: A Reciprocity System under Pressure*. Boulder, Colo.: Westview.

Young, Tom. 1993. "Elections and Electoral Politics in Africa." *Africa* 63, no. 3: 299–312.

Zuccarelli, François. 1987. *La vie politique sénégalaise, 1789-1940*. Paris: CHEAM.

# Index

## The Wilder House Series in Politics, History, and Culture

A series edited by

David D. Laitin
George Steinmetz